Images of Voting/Visions of Democracy

IMAGES OF VOTING

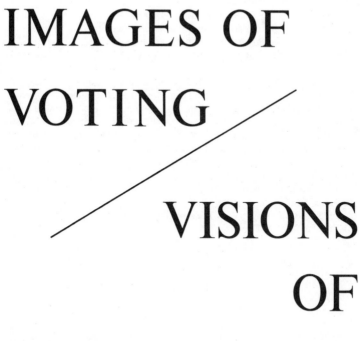

VISIONS OF DEMOCRACY

PETER B. NATCHEZ

With an Introduction by John C. Blydenburgh

Basic Books, Inc., Publishers   New York

The following publishers have generously given permission to use extended quotations from copyrighted works: From *The Authoritarian Personality,* by T. W. Adorno et al. Copyright 1950 by The American Jewish Committee. Reprinted by permission of Harper & Row, Publishers, Inc. From *The People's Choice: How the Voter Makes Up His Mind in a Presidential Campaign* (2nd ed.), by Paul F. Lazarsfeld, Bernard Berelson, and Hazel Gaudet. Copyright 1948 by Columbia University Press. Reprinted by permission. From *Voting,* by Bernard Berelson, Paul F. Lazarsfeld, and William McPhee. Copyright 1954 by The University of Chicago Press. Reprinted by permission. From "Continuity and Change in American Politics: Parties and Issues in the 1968 Election," by Philip E. Converse et al. Paper presented to the American Political Science Association, New York, September 1969, and subsequently published in the *American Political Science Review* (December 1969):1095–1101, with minor revision. Reprinted by permission of Philip E. Converse and the American Political Science Assocation. From "Images of Voting: The Social Psychologist," by Peter B. Natchez, in *Public Policy* 18(4):553–88. Copyright 1970 by Harvard University Press. Reprinted by permission of John Wiley & Sons, Inc.

Library of Congress Cataloging in Publication Data

Natchez, Peter B., 1941–1981.
   Images of voting/visions of democracy.

   Bibliographic references: p. 243
   Includes index.
     1. Voting—United States. 2. Voting research—
United States. 3. Democracy. 4. Political science.
I. Title.
JK1967.N28   1984   324.973   83–46087
ISBN 0–465–03203–6

To my son, Jonathan, and to my daughter, Sarah

In the hope that you each

will trust, and love, and create

יִשְׂרָאֵל בְּטַח בַּיהוָה

I love that the Lord should hear
My voice and my supplications.
Because He hath inclined His ear unto me,
Therefore will I call upon Him all my days.

The cords of death compassed me,
And the straits of the nether-world
   got hold upon me;
I found trouble and sorrow.
But I called upon the name of the Lord:
"I beseech Thee, O Lord, deliver my soul."
Gracious is the Lord, and righteous;
Yea, our God is compassionate.
The Lord preserveth the simple;
I was brought low, and He saved me.

Return, O my soul, unto thy rest;
For the Lord hath dealt bountifully with thee.
For Thou hast delivered my soul from death,
Mine eyes from tears,
And my feet from stumbling.
I shall walk before the Lord
In the lands of the living.
I trusted even when I spoke:
"I am greatly afflicted."
I said in my haste:
"All men are liars."

How can I repay unto the Lord
All His bountiful dealings toward me?
I will lift up the cup of salvation,
And call upon the name of the Lord.
My vows will I pay unto the Lord,
Yea, in the presence of all His people.

—Psalm 116

CONTENTS

ix

Contents

ACKNOWLEDGMENTS

Peter Natchez loved life, he loved ideas, and he loved politics. Although his death from cancer in August 1981 robbed him of the opportunity to complete his manuscript in the way he wished, his spirit and passion, his concern and insight, are reflected in these pages.

The ideas that are elaborated in this book were outlined, in the main, more than a decade ago. As Peter once wrote, these ideas "would have gone unwritten indefinitely were it not for the encouragement, criticism, and outright impatience of friends, colleagues, and institutions." In the many drafts of the manuscript that he worked on in his last years, he never finalized a list of acknowledgments, although he commented often on the help he wanted to recognize. I take the liberty, therefore, of expressing publically what I know to have been his deeply-felt gratitude to those friends and colleagues who he felt enriched both his scholarship and his life.

Peter's acknowledgments surely would have begun with his gifted teacher and steadfast friend, Michael O. Sawyer. As an undergraduate at Syracuse University, Peter felt fortunate to have been able to take courses from Michael O. Sawyer, and his fascination with the political process and democracy was born. His good fortune in working with gifted scholars who generously contributed their time continued at Harvard with Seymour Martin Lipset and H. Douglas Price, both of whom acted as his thesis advisors. Their supervision of his dissertation project encouraged the germination of many of the ideas presented in this volume. Peter commented often on how much he benefitted from working with these two men, before whose prodigious knowledge of American history and politics he stood in awe. V. O. Key, Jr., was another scholar to whom Peter felt deeply indebted. Although never actually his student, Peter felt that Key had been very much his teacher.

Many special friends and colleagues in graduate school and at his teaching institutions also contributed to Peter's intellectual enrichment and scholarly growth. Chip Bupp, Gary Orren, and Bill Schneider were a very special group of friends. The years of Socratic dialogue amongst them over issues of voting behavior and the electoral process were among Peter's fondest memories. With Bill Schneider, in particular, whose love of politics he shared, Peter felt a special bond of creative inspiration and deep friendship. From his colleagues at Brandeis—Marty Levin, Ruth Morgen-thau, and, most especially, George Armstrong Kelly—Peter received the triple gift of intellectual stimulation, personal kindness, and warm support. But it was at Clark University that Peter felt truly at home. His colleagues in the Department of Government and International Relations, his students, and the institution itself all provided him with an environment of intellectual vitality, friendship, and ease within which he could thrive. The warm and spirited colleagueship of John Blydenburgh, Cynthia Enloe, Sharon Krefetz, Charlie Coleman, and Morris Cohen meant more to Peter than perhaps they will ever know. Clark was for Peter a very special place.

There are many others towards whom Peter felt a great deal of gratitude. Sid Verba was particularly gracious in responding to questions about the intellectual origins of his own work, material which Peter intended to use primarily in his next project. And to the authors of the voting studies, whose work Peter places under scrutiny here, Peter felt he owed a large debt. These studies were, for him, very important works, and if he felt that there was much about which to be critical, he felt, at the same time, that these studies represented substantial scholarship. He certainly wanted to express clearly that his criticisms are less of individual scholars than of a period of scholarship. If there are others to whom an acknowledgment is due, I hope that they will understand that, in this case, it is my oversight and not Peter's ingratitude that prompts their omission.

But there are two very special thanks that I know Peter would have wanted to acknowledge. The first goes to John Blydenburgh. Peter did not expect to die, even with full knowledge of the severity of his cancer. With characteristic spirit, he decided to simply "outgrow" the cancer, as he put it. He had worked on the ideas of this book for many years, often resisting the gentle prodding of friends to get the draft at hand published. The book was not ready, he felt, and he continued to polish, to rewrite, and to rethink its contents. Near the end of his life he came to realize, he said, that he really had two books—one, an intellectual history of the study and understanding of voting; the other, his own exposition and analysis of voting, political participation, and democracy. When it was certain that he was in fact dying, he asked both John and me to see if we could get the manuscript out in publishable form. Virtually the entire burden of this effort fell to John.

It became clear immediately that both of the "books" Peter had envisioned from his manuscript could not be published. Peter's original table of contents listed thirteen chapters, including separate chapters on participation and elections. Yet too much of Peter's own reanalysis and interpretation in "the second book" was left undone. He had planned to do extensive data analysis of his own and this was incomplete. And although he had written much of these later chapters, or had extensive outlines of his arguments, it is this latter part that had to be deleted from this volume.

Chapters 1 through 7, then, are intact from Peter's draft. Many of these chapters Peter did consider to be final book drafts, while in some cases, such as chapter 7, he had intended some final rewriting and reworking of ideas. Yet the arguments were presented so clearly and cogently that they are published as Peter left them. To John fell the laborious task of reconstructing, in many cases, full footnote citations from Peter's own shorthand references to himself. This was, in some chapters, such as chapter 3, an enormous job.

It is in chapter 8 that significant editing of Peter's text was required, for several reasons. First, the length of the original manuscript required that what Peter had left as two separate chapters (8 and 9) be condensed into this one final chapter. Second, it was these later chapters that Peter was working on at the time of his death. Peter's original chapter 8 was not in final form, so that chapter and sections from other drafted chapters were reorganized into a conclusion. This means that some material that Peter felt was very significant had to be omitted from this volume. Peter believed, for example, that Stanley Milgram's experiments with authority were crucial material for students of politics. People's capacity to suspend their value systems and their sense of responsibility in order to accept the commands of "legitimate authority" was, he thought, of enormous importance for theories of democracy. Although Peter had completed extensive writing on Milgram's experiments, only a small portion of that material is included here in chapter 8. It should be noted, however, that even in this final chapter 8, despite substantial editing, all of the ideas and arguments are Peter's. All of the words are Peter's as well, with the exception of some four pages of text, which John did have to rewrite in order to link together Peter's argument and to provide for smooth transitions between ideas. Certainly, given the nature of the enterprise, we hope that any author whose work, by error, we slight, understands the complexity of the process by which this volume was produced. We apologize in advance for any errors in scholarship that might be contained herein.

The enormity of John's efforts in bringing this book to publication cannot be adequately expressed by merely describing the content and organization of this book. It was an arduous and time-consuming project. Nor can Peter's and my appreciation of John's efforts adequately be conveyed by acknowledging here his great contribution on Peter's behalf. John once said to me, as I thanked him for the long hours he was putting into this project, that he felt it was an act of love for Peter to ask him to prepare the manuscript for publication. It was an extraordinary act of friendship, and love, for John to do so.

For our children, Jonathan and Sarah, I know that Peter would have reserved his final, most special thank you. For the joy and the love they brought into his world, for the warmth and the hugs, for the laughter and the tickles which were always, in that last year, "the best medicine"—for all of this and much, much more, it is to Jonathan and to Sarah that this book is lovingly dedicated. If these pages help to give them, and others who read this book, another glimpse of who Peter Natchez was—his extraordinary vitality, his boundless curiosity, his deep, deep concern for his world—then perhaps his journey was more complete than his death would allow us to believe.

Finally, it would be disingenuous of me to suggest that Peter did not make an acknowledgment of my participation in the evolution of his book. Suffice it to say, as in all our endeavors, that his loving response made any support or help a joyous enterprise.

LOIS WASSERSPRING NATCHEZ

Images of Voting/Visions of Democracy

Introduction

by John C. Blydenburgh

When the new technology of social science—survey research, statistics, and electronic data processing—was introduced, it "held out great promise that a new level of political knowledge would be created."[1] Applied to the study of voting behavior, survey research promised an instant understanding of the factors determining the outcome of an election, that political history could be based on rich and current data, and that we could begin to understand the role of elections in constitutional democracy. But the tragic truth is that despite the enormous opportunity provided by this technological revolution, the voting "studies have failed to make significant contributions to both democratic theory and political history."[2]

Images of Voting/Visions of Democracy by the late Peter Natchez laments the failure of political science to make this revolution into an opportunity. The book is a lament because there is an element of tragedy in the causes of the failure: historical events confronted the discipline's basic questions in such a way that it lost self-confidence. Before the evil of Nazism confronted the democratic ideal, political science was a science of the possible, an optimistic discipline. Optimism, which is validated by belief in

3

revealed truth, was replaced by empirical methodology, which takes no a priori position on its product. The truth of optimism involves values; thus disappointment can lead to disillusionment. But the truth of empiricism does not involve values, so it avoids disillusionment. Disillusionment after Nazism led to a decline in the importance of values and normative political theory in political science, a decline that was more than matched by the rise of empirical research bolstered by revolutionary developments in statistics, survey research, and electronic data processing. On the question of the possibilities of the human condition, the discipline shifted from optimism to rigid neutrality.

The findings of the voting studies have, through their forty years of success, spread from the universities into the political system with a rather grim message. In its simplest form the message is this: The electorate does not measure up to the task thrust upon it by democracy. The studies conclude that voters choose candidates for reasons having little relevance to the success of the political system, little relevance even to politics. Thus political science, in shifting from an optimistic focus on theory to a strong emphasis on empiricism, became a source of pessimism. The effect on the political system has been to nurture cynicism about politics and government.

Among academics, the effect of this shift from values to empiricism was fundamental: a generation of political theorists did not talk to empirical researchers; the political science department in one university had nearly no contact with that of another; empirical research ignored theory and theory denied empirical research. In the conflict, the discipline lost its identity and its soul. The field of political science resembled two warring camps more than a group of scholars pursuing a set of common concerns. On one side were the political theorists who sought to reestablish values and normative theory in the center of the discipline. On the other were the empiricists, known as behavioralists, who sought truth through empirical method.

In chapter 1 Natchez describes and explains this shift with constructive criticism of these last four decades of election research.

He traces the evolution of the application of survey research to election studies from Paul Lazarsfeld on, by tracing the development of the conception of the role of elections in democracy from one research orientation to another. The strategy of his argument is not to deny the results of this research, but to point out that false theory and inappropriate concepts have led to a failure to use this research in a constructive way. A central argument in this book is that the new technology was not successfully applied because those who sought to apply it "never have had a clear understanding of the guiding principles involved in the creation of the modern democratic state."[3]

That is a very serious indictment, but Natchez makes a very powerful argument. His first point, clearly made in chapter 1, is on the order of politely noting that the emperor has no clothes. The findings of the voting studies have been interpreted by those who produced them in terms of the requirements placed on voters by "classical democratic theory" (see especially chapter 2 on Lazarsfeld). Such theory is purported to hold that voters should be "rational," they should cast a ballot by considering the impact of their choice on the future state of the collectivity. This requires of the voter a certain level of information, sophistication, and consciousness about the electoral process, the candidates, and the consequences of choice. But there is no classical democratic theory that identifies such requirements. It simply does not exist. The theoretical meaning assigned to the findings of the voting studies is not based on a theory of the type identified because such a theory does not exist. The findings of the voting studies simply do not mean what they have been said to mean.

The misidentification of democratic theory, and its narrow concept of voter rationality, led to further confusion about the role of elections in democracy. Paradoxically, the electorate was criticized for being nonpolitical on the basis of research findings that attempt to explain voting behavior with nonpolitical categories. Natchez identifies the early application of psychological theory to politics in his critical review of *The Authoritarian Personality* (chapter 4), and he traces its development and impact to its culmination in *The*

American Voter. The findings from these efforts are nonpolitical, he argues, because the research is not organized around political categories, and not necessarily because the object of the research is nonpolitical. The essence of politics is values, but the bulk of this research explains voter behavior with "value neutral" psychological concepts, such as attitudes and perceptions.

The problem is well illustrated by Natchez in his critical analysis of concepts developed at the University of Michigan's Survey Research Center (SRC, and now called the Center for Political Studies). Chapter 6 reviews and analyzes this research and the comprehensive and sophisticated national sample surveys on which it is based. The major contribution of the SRC's work is to explain voter behavior in terms of party identification: the great majority of the American electorate vote for a candidate of the party with which the voter identifies.

The implication of this explanation is on the one hand gloomy. It explains party identification by a voter's attitudes and perceptions, personal history, parents' political party preference, social and economic background, level of education, and so forth. Thus psychological and nonpolitical background variables, and not a rational assessment of the body politic, cause voting via party identification.

An electorate motivated by party identification is highly stable. The SRC found that Republican and Democratic party identification has been fairly stable over time. This led to the concept of the "normal vote,"[4] the idea that, other things being equal, one party, because of its advantage in party identification, was the majority party and, other things equal, would win all elections. Throughout the period of the SRC's research, the Democrats have had a majority party identification in the electorate.

Of course, "other things" are rarely equal. The conception of a stable electorate based on stable party identification is not a very satisfying one in the face of recent history. For example, since 1948 the Republican party has won the presidency six times, while the Democrats have won four times. And in elections for the House of Representatives and the Senate, research shows that the most powerful variable (statistically) explaining outcome is incumbency. The candidate who holds the office at election time has a great advantage over a challenger, regardless of the party of either.*

These facts, however, are anything but comforting because the theory holds that outcome is the consequence of irrationality in the electorate working through party identification. There is a "Catch-22" element in the theory: no matter what happens it is ominous for democracy. If the Democrat wins, it is due to party identification and the long-term irrational factors that cause it; if the Republican wins, it is due to short-term irrational factors. The psychological basis of the concept makes it a poor one in terms of contributing to our understanding of American politics. One cannot give a politically meaningful interpretation to a nonpolitical explanation.

On the face of it, then, party identification does not provide very satisfying political explanations. The point to which Natchez returns throughout *Images of Voting* is that the basis of this weakness is a failure to address the questions of normative political theory, a failure to come to terms with politics as "a science of values." The voting studies illustrate this failure, and Natchez makes the case well in terms of both intellectual history and assessing how political scientists have gone about voter research. Consistent with Natchez's argument is my own point of view, that the root of the problems with this literature can be traced to a persistent misunderstanding of the scientific method, a misunderstanding that was widely shared among social scientists.

Many behavioralists made two interlocking assumptions, neither of which is necessary to the pursuit of science but which jointly were at the heart of their problems. First is the assumption of the existence of an objective, ordered reality in which order is discoverable by scientific method. This assumption enabled behavioralists to identify as their goal the discovery of the true order of objective reality. This approach can be characterized as "naive realism," the

---

*My own analysis of aggregate data, designed to predict individual congressional election outcomes efficiently, shows incumbency to be the most powerful variable in the model.

belief that a true picture of reality emerges from objectively gathered data. Second is the assumption that the order is, to one degree or another, determined. This enabled behavioralists to ignore, to the degree of the strength of the assumption, value questions. A fruitful scientific method should be agnostic on both points.

The problem with attempting to discover reality by observing the facts is that the facts cannot speak for themselves, for there are no facts qua facts. All facts exist in the context of generalizations, and these in turn rest on assumptions, which are the stuff of theory. Thus facts are the product of theory. Facts cannot speak for themselves because they speak for the assumptions and the theory that make them believable as facts. Therefore, naive realism as an approach to scientific method begs the question in attempting to avoid a priori theory by denying it. The theory is there, in the facts the researchers choose to accumulate.[5] Assuming an ordered, discoverable reality is inconsistent with the concurrent assumption of objectivity because one must begin to collect facts somewhere. The choice of where to begin, and whatever subset of all experience is accumulated, is informed by the current beliefs about what is reality, and that is a theory.

When one assumes an objective ordered reality, one concedes that there is only one true way to perceive the present. Add to that a belief in a method for discovering the order, and speculation about which possible present ought to exist is meaningless. There is only this possible present, thus questioning it is a fruitless task; one accepts the present as it appears. Given that a task of theory is to justify some normative position, naive realism leaves theory only to speculate about alternative perceptions or arrangements of the present. Therefore, the assumption of a discoverable objective order renders normative theory a largely useless enterprise.

The second assumption, that of a determined order, has serious consequences too. It renders speculation about the future futile because the determinist is not concerned about how the future ought to be; rather the determinist seeks to predict how the future will be. In a strictly determined world one can expect to play a role in the future, but one cannot choose alternative futures. Thus the determinist social scientist has little use for normative theories that consider how the world ought to be: it is going to be one way or it is going to be another.

The essential imperative of scientific method is replicability, and the imperative takes the form of specifying an operational rule for all phases of inquiry, including the evaluation of the findings from research. But naive realism holds that objectivity, and not replicability, is the essential imperative of science. Thus it holds that the scientist only has to get it right once to discover the order in reality, and objectivity is the route to getting it right. Evaluation of research is unnecessary if the method is objective. This approach does not provide the basis for an external standard to evaluate research, and thus it denies a major element of the scientific method, the role of theory in establishing an external operational rule for evaluating findings.

An empiricist's answer to this charge might be that an external standard for evaluating research exists in that current findings should be consistent with previous ones. But this admits other problems: Where does one begin research? Is any one hypothesis better than any other? The problem with this standard is that the focus of research could be anywhere if the subject were new, and anywhere previous research had gone if it were not.

In the voting studies, this meant that research could be built on Lazarsfeld's findings, even though the reasons they were purported to be important are, as Natchez makes abundantly clear, entirely wrong. Lazarsfeld invented the "classical democratic theory" which he uses to explain the importance of his work. A generation of students of voting behavior took Lazarsfeld's conclusions seriously in the sense that they identified the importance of his findings in terms of a theory that does not exist.

How could political scientists not know that Lazarsfeld's position was incorrect? There are two reasons, I believe, both of which grow out of the faulty assumptions just outlined. First, at the operational level this approach holds that theory is meaningless, so it simply does not matter that Lazarsfeld's representation of theory was wrong. There was no reason to question his position. The findings, the facts, are the thing, and they were thought to be their own justification, so a misrepresentation of something that is essentially meaningless is no loss.

The second reason resides in the intellectual historical factors Natchez identifies in the struggle between theorists and empiricists: Lazarsfeld did not merely ignore theory, he said it was wrong! He made an important contribution to the cause of empiricists in the competition for preeminence in political science. Lazarsfeld dedicated *The Language of Social Research* with a quote from Plato's *Phaedrus* in which Socrates proposes to give Phaedrus examples of art. Phaedrus replies: "Nothing could be better; and indeed I think that our previous argument has been too abstract and wanting in illustration." The language of social research was not to include theory.

The problem, the reason why such an error could have occurred, can be understood in yet another way, in the very sense of identity of political science: What are we doing this for, anyway? What is our justification for activities as scholars? A naive realist does not have to answer the question. Since he or she is trying to discover the order in reality, research is its own justification; a normative position is not required to justify proceeding. One who accepts this approach might well fail to see that this is itself a normative position and, ironically, a very conservative one. The status quo does not require normative questioning.

In some particularly poignant passages in chapter 5, Natchez reminds us that the best of political scientists did not resist McCarthyism: "The striking aspect of writing in the fifties and sixties is the absence of any critical quality . . . Certainly no one can question the diligence and integrity of the people involved in the voting studies . . . Yet they all yielded, however unconsciously, to the prevailing anticommunist prejudice of their times." The absence of criticism is, I believe, synonomous with the absence of normative theory.

Natchez, a committed democrat and patriot in the best sense of the word, elaborates in chapter 5 his own position on this question in his admiration of the approach of *The Civic Culture* and in chapter 8 in outlining his own conceptualization of voter behavior. He proposes to develop democratic political theory and use it especially to understand the workings of the political system of the United States. The end of all research, he argues—and now most would agree—is the development of theory (although we would still disagree on a definition of theory). However, the theory he proposes is a theory to address a set of value problems in which he is particularly interested: those surrounding the success or failure of the political system of the United States.

Natchez's conception of theory is very important; he does not argue here for the development of descriptive theory only, he argues for the development of normative theory. (He might argue that the two are inseparable; good normative theory provides the categories for accurate description and an accurate description is based on concepts useful in normative theory.) For Natchez it is insufficient to conclude research with a series of correlation coefficients. The bottom line is this: What do the results tell us about how the system in fact works with regard to the ends of democratic theory and therefore democracy? The ends of democracy, he reminds us, are freedom and tolerance. What do the results of research tell us about how to achieve freedom and tolerance, and what do they tell us about what reforms might be made in the system to produce more freedom and more tolerance? To answer these questions, we need an explanatory theory of the actual operation of the system in producing these values, and we need a normative theory that favorably links institutional arrangements to their production.

Some might argue that Natchez is unscientific. In fact, however, nothing is further from the truth. Science is not identified by its ends but by its means; science is a way of proceeding, an operational code, it is not a way to select ends. It is a way to solve problems, and all problems become problems because they involve value judgments.

Natchez's point of view is well represented in his chapter 8 discussion and criticism of the hydraulic model of voting that today permeates our understanding of the findings of voting research. In many ways these are the most important pages in the book. The hydraulic model holds that the connection between voter behavior and public policy output is one where voters' preferences, attitudes, perceptions, and opinions lead automatically to policy outputs. The word "automatically" is the focus of Natchez's criticism. Assuming an automatic connection of voter and policy means that the researcher need only identify voters' views to understand the policy process; there is no need to give attention to the question of how voters' views are taken into account in policy making. The hydraulic model implies a model of how the political system (by implication, the political system of the United States) works. Most important, the model is not clearly stated in the literature (similar to the way that classical democratic theory was never identified); it assumes that voters' policy views are the basis of public policy. The nature of the hydraulic process is unaccounted for, it is not addressed, because the model is thought to be reality; it needs no attention, because that is the way the world is.

But of course the hydraulic model does have normative implications. Ironically, there is good reason to believe that the very theory that the early empiricists falsely identified as classical democratic theory is what led to the hydraulic conception of American politics. Classical democratic theory, as it was thought to exist, placed sovereignty with the individual; power and policy preference rose through the system from the electorate to policy makers. The model leaves little independence for political leadership, or for an elite to have flexibility to make policy on its own. Yet while the findings from the voting studies were becoming widely known, an active independent elite was clearly evident in control of the political process. The model left no place to lay blame for this failure of the system to be democratic but at the doorstep of a failed electorate. Political science told the electorate that if they did not like public policy, it was their own fault, and the situation is very nearly unrectifiable. A reasonable reading of these results is that a meaningful role for the individual citizen in public policy making is hopeless. No wonder that cynicism has been the product of this research.

And here is Natchez's point: research cannot avoid normative implications by ignoring theory or defining it away. In the study of voter behavior and elsewhere in political science, normative questions must be confronted directly and consciously through normative political theory. They have not been addressed in the study of voter behavior, and the political system has suffered the consequences of this failure.

It is valid, I believe, to understand that one of Natchez's aims is to get political scientists to reread the works of V. O. Key, Jr., especially on these issues. Natchez went to Harvard in 1963 to study with Key, only to be thwarted by the great scholar's untimely death. Nevertheless, he pursued Key's work throughout graduate school, and he even makes use of Key's correspondence here and in his Ph.D. thesis. The inspiration for some of Natchez's arguments here can be teased out of Key's presidential address to the American Political Science Association in 1958[6] and in Key's review of *The American Voter.*[7] Natchez makes the point that Key was not the clearest of writers, and though the two works cited illustrate this, the bases of the arguments are there, I believe.

V. O. Key had been a critic of the voting studies from the start, and his review of *The American Voter* is an excellent representation of his position. He was, on the one hand, strongly supportive of empirical research, but, on the other, strongly critical of the apolitical nature of the approach of the book. His attempt at reconciling political theory and empiricism is *The Responsible Electorate,* but it was read in the context of the dominant interpretation of voter research. The debate over theory versus empiricism did not occur. Instead, the debate focused on whether issue-based (or rational) voting existed in any meaningful measure.

Natchez gives us two original views of Key in chapter 7. First is his reinterpretation of Key's theory of voter behavior and the emphasis on retrospective voting. Neither Natchez nor Morris Fiorina[8] had knowledge of the other's work, but their interpretations are quite similar. Their intellectual contexts are dissimilar, however. Fiorina uses retrospective voting to address the rationality debate, distinguishing between prospective and retrospective substantive choice. Natchez uses Key to send us off in a new direction, arguing that the very conflict should be abandoned. Fiorina takes a short sure step in the direction Natchez would have us go. Natchez gives us a reinterpretation in the context of the intellectual history of the voting studies. He enables us to see that Key's work was a missed opportunity; in the context of the imperialism of methodology, Key's theoretical position could not be recognized.

Natchez's second original view of Key is his recognition of the timidity with which Key expressed his reservations about the direction the voting studies took. Key expressed his concern about Lazarsfeld's interpretation of "classical democratic theory" in the Elmira study; and he stated fairly strongly to Campbell, in private correspondence, his reservations about the political substance of *The American Voter*. But in neither case were his views well received among the community of scholars, and in neither case was Key persistent. Perhaps his concern for the development of empirical political science outweighed his concern for theory.

The value of this insight into Key's role in the history of the voting studies should not reflect on him personally; our task is the production and dissemination of knowledge about voting. But the latter incidents and the clear theoretical alternative Key presented to deaf ears highlight the power of the dominant epistemology at the time. Even V. O. Key could express his doubts about the foundation of the work and not be heard. There truly existed methodological imperialism.

The message that comes through forcefully in *Images of Voting* is the necessity for a normative commitment in research. One cannot study democracy or the democratic process without a point of view on democracy. The scientific method *requires* a point of view: science is not a method for discovering reality, but a method for addressing well-structured questions. The failure of the voting studies is a failure to recognize the importance of theory in developing, on the one hand, those well-structured questions and providing, on the other, a yardstick for evaluating results. The point I wish to emphasize here is that theory and only theory provides meaning to questions addressed with scientific method and to the results of scientific inquiry.

The goals Natchez identifies for democracy, freedom and tolerance, entail consciousness in decision making (both as an end and as a precondition). To be free is to be able to choose with an awareness of the consequences of choice; tolerance is the conscious recognition of the legitimacy of the views of others. To maintain this position one must assume a benevolent nature of human beings, that freedom implies tolerance and vice versa. Natchez's position is that of a humanist, one with great faith in humanity, and his faith is a product of his consciousness. Freedom implies tolerance for those who have this faith.

It is not his view, it seems to me, that one must be a democrat or a humanist to be a scientist, only that one must be *something*. A scientist must be able to recognize the value implications of her or his work. Thus Natchez's aims for science and for scientists are the same: consciousness. The aim of political science for him is democracy because democracy promotes and entails consciousness, and the aim of science is to pursue normative theory because theory consciously deals with values. My understanding of Natchez's message, which I hope is effective and enduring, is to admit and respect the role of values in research, to reconcile normative theory and empirical research in political science.

CHAPTER 1

Democracy, Elections, and the Voting Studies

The Promise of the Voting Studies

Democracy is at once a powerful and alluring concept—a form of politics that is valued both for its individual freedoms and for its principles of public action. This is an unusual combination in many respects; for these ideas, both having their basis in the individual, lead in several different, often contradictory, directions. There is, at the very least, the strong sense of personal rights, of vast areas of human activity placed beyond political interference. In these domains, the motivating forces are individual freedom and initiative. But at the same time, there is in democratic theory a strong sense of the public good, the expectation of an active government producing authoritative public policies. This notion of the public good is all the more interesting because it is forged in the process of electoral competition and involves the participation and preferences of all who wish to vote. This is a marvelous, if not altogether stable, combination of the public and the private. Little wonder that the democratic idea is so highly valued, at least in the rhetoric of government.

Unfortunately, less is known about maintaining the good working order of electoral democracies than is commonly supposed. It is widely believed that the fundamental principles of democratic politics are written out somewhere, that if only these were practiced, that if only every citizen participated in the electoral process, then the political system would function smoothly, almost flawlessly. It would be very convenient indeed if the essential problems with democratic governments were matters merely of more library work and technical expertise, and more participation in politics.

The difficulties in the theory and the practice of democratic politics are substantially greater than this, of course. Indeed, one of the greatest problems is that the theory and the practice of democratic politics have never formed a coherent whole. Rather, each developed separately, from different traditions and in response to different concerns. Democratic government has its theoretical origins in constitutionalism, a rich and original strand of political thought that brought the idea of the individual into the organization of government. In developing this idea, constitutionalists worked out the major assumptions of politics and government—assumptions that continue in contemporary constitutional structures. But to the constitutionalists, the individual was a highly abstract concept. It was never intended that this abstraction should participate in government or that it could control political power through a system of elections.

Mass participation and electoral politics, the bases of modern democratic government, were acquired by constitutional regimes during the nineteenth century, while the development of constitutionalism as a theory came to an abrupt halt at the end of the eighteenth century. Unlike the development of other constitutional devices, precious little thought was given to the *theory* of either mass participation or electoral competition. Rather additions to the political system were created in the fires of group conflict. The electoral process emerged as different groups contended for power. No time was taken to assess the meaning of these changes or to develop a set of expectations about how the electoral system should function. Such considerations were quite beside the point at the time.

But the fact that the electoral process was appended to the constitutional design in the push and pull of political history should not be taken to mean that questions of theory are pointless. Far from being idle or abstract concerns, electoral theory is of vital importance, and its absence—the unexplored and incomplete nature of electoral theory—has contributed to our present political malaise. There exist no theoretical standards against which to judge the performance of electoral systems. By not having in mind the functions that voting and elections are expected to perform, the quality of every effort at political evaluation and criticism suffers. The work of political analysts is deprived of substance and meaning; and, in turn, the political system is deprived of a stream of sound advice and disciplined criticism.

To many, this may not seem like such a great loss, but political analysis is currently usually undervalued. Over time, the lack of quality in political criticism takes its toll. It amounts to a loss of critical intelligence, which is an element essential to the success of democratic regimes. Political theory is hardly a luxury item, then. Rather it is an indispensable way of establishing common understandings and locating value systems; at its best, political theory amounts to a description of the aspirations of the system as a whole.

But modern political theory, for a variety of reasons we will consider later, has stopped short of the electoral process. Changes of enormous magnitude have been made in the constitutional idea. Yet their meaning and functions remain unassessed. There is no theory of the electoral process, or rather such theory as there is has been worked out by those with little appreciation and training in the rigors of political thought. This, in turn, has added to the confusion, as we shall see. While the electoral process has become the central feature of modern democratic politics, our knowledge of its meaning and the functions it serves remains slight and woefully incomplete.

It is here, in the understanding of the electoral process, that the voting studies should have produced huge gains. For, in truth, a great part of the problem with the electoral process was technological in nature. No person, no matter how gifted a political analyst, can understand the inner workings of the electoral process by relying upon intellect alone. The mass public is too vast; people in electoral politics operate at too many different levels; the electoral process is itself too complicated, with too many variables at play. No single human mind is strong enough to take the measure of an electorate without introducing a series of biases and outright mistakes.

Consider A. Lawrence Lowell and Walter Lippmann: both were brilliant political analysts, both had profound insight into the nature of public opinion, both had a seemingly endless fund of original ideas. Yet neither could fully comprehend the mass public; each was forced to make unrealistic assumptions about the electorate, assumptions that tend to shift and sway from work to work. Consequently, much of the power and perceptiveness in their analyses has been lost.[1]

Political surveys resolve the problem of the mass public's vastness and complexity by producing representative samples of the electorate. Rather than making assumptions about the mass public, political analysts are afforded the opportunity to examine how people actually behave in politics. Sample surveys make electorates visible in a sense that they were not previously. Different sources of political motivation can be discovered; the level of political information that people maintain can be evaluated; the effects of different political issues can be studied; the attitudes and actions of different demographic groups in the electorate can be compared. In short, political surveys remove much of the mystery of electoral politics and provide, instead, valid estimates of what people are doing in politics and why.

Clearly, the introduction of the technology of survey research into political analysis marks a major watershed, for with these techniques, political analysts can peer into the innermost workings of the electoral process. The very heartland of democratic politics becomes accessible. To be sure, like any technology, survey research has its less desirable attributes. Electoral surveys themselves are no better than the questions that compose them, and it turns out that asking the right questions within the limited confines of a questionnaire poses difficult problems indeed. Then too, survey research requires new skills and the mastery of new techniques. There is always the tendency for techniques to overwhelm substance. Also, it should be said that surveys are limited devices, providing information only at the time they are taken. Like a photograph, they provide a picture of the electorate that is frozen in time. Of course, a series of surveys taken at appropriate points in time can produce a fairly reliable history. Thus the static quality of political surveys can be removed. But the availability of such data puts even greater stress on the quality of questions that were asked and on the analyst's skill and insight. The real work of political analysis remains. Insight is not acquired through mindless analysis of survey data.

But these caveats do nothing to diminish the importance of survey research. The early voting studies, the first systematic application of survey research techniques to studies of the electorate, held out great promise that a new level of political knowledge would be created. Through them democratic politics would be understood in ways that previously were not possible.

As a category of analysis, "the voting studies" can mean different things to different people. I use the term to refer to a broad range of political surveys conducted by scholars at various universities in the United States. Thus I mean to include all of the leading studies of electoral behavior and not restrict my analysis to the work of the Survey Research Center (later the Center for Political Studies) and the Bureau of Applied Social Research, however much these two institutions have dominated the field. Also, commercial pollsters have made important contributions from time to time, particularly during the early years of survey research. These will be included, of course, where appropriate.

More specifically, two promises were contained in the introduction of the voting studies. The first involved the expansion of democratic theory to include the mass public. With the emergence of the technology of survey research, it would be possible to develop a much more complete understanding of how the democratic ideal operates in practice. Democratic theory would enjoy a new level of sophistication, meaning, and accuracy. Substantial developments in the quality of democratic theory were to be forthcoming. But no less important was a second promise made by the voting studies. Political history would now be understood as it was being made. No longer need we wait decades to discover what really had happened. Now there would be a complete record of popular motivations, of the impact of events on the mass public, of the relative importance of different issues and the emergence of new ideas. The level of political understanding—the critical intelligence of democracy—would increase greatly.

I want to stress that at the time the studies were introduced, both these promises were quite realistic. Voting studies should have made significant contributions in both of these areas. But the studies have been going on for more than forty years now, and the simple truth is that they have not realized their original potential. Rather than becoming an integral part of democratic theory and monitoring the flow of political history, the study of electoral behavior has become its own area of specialization, separating itself from the larger, more enduring concerns of other political analysts.

As with any of the separate approaches in political science, there is a substantial amount of validity for the emergence of electoral behavior as an independent field of specialization. The technical barriers alone mitigate in favor of differentiation. Then too, surveys of the electorate have unearthed an enormous quantity of information. There is a full literature about American voters and nonvoters, not to mention cross-national studies. Just keeping track of current research involves a major effort.

There is no need, then, for students of electoral behavior to be apologetic about the nature of their enterprise. Yet, at the same time, there has been a marked failure of the voting studies to grow, to address more fundamental and challenging questions, and to make the sorts of significant contributions that were once expected of them. If anything, the voting studies have retreated altogether from these concerns. The truly demanding questions about democratic governments, the political process, and the meaning of elections, which were originally central to the voting studies, increasingly have been abandoned, ignored, or reduced to an impossibly narrow, technical level.

Aspirations and Intentions

In this book, I have three objectives. First, I want to explore what went wrong with the voting studies. That the studies have failed to make significant contributions to both democratic theory and political history has not been an intellectual accident, the luck of the draw, as it were. Rather it has been the result of a pattern of confusion and misunderstanding over the fundamentals of modern politics. The designers of the voting studies never have had a clear understanding of the guiding principles involved in the creation of the modern democratic state, particularly the development of political parties. Nor have they ever possessed an appreciation of the fundamental principles of modern political theory. It was bad enough that the errors resulting from these areas of ignorance were incorporated into the voting studies from the outset. But worse, other scholars permitted these misunderstandings to remain and to prosper. The voting studies form an altogether remarkable episode in the history of ideas. Much can be learned, I believe, by examining how they failed to fulfill their considerable potential.

At the same time, the voting studies have produced a steady stream of new data and valid relationships. An immense literature on electoral behavior has developed over the last forty years. It is absolutely essential to recognize that the empirical underpinnings of these findings (although often not the inferences drawn from them) are quite reliable. This is especially true with regard to the discoveries concerning political participation and the sources of voter motivation.

The second aspiration of this book is to present the major findings of the voting studies in a clear and systematic fashion. The studies may have failed to make the contributions that were (and should have been) expected of them, but they are hardly futile exercises. Indeed, a major part of their fascination for me results from this paradox—that the designers of these electoral surveys could have been confused and misguided about the fundamentals of politics, while at the same time being so precise and original in their findings.

Finally, I want in these pages to give special attention to the question of voter rationality. For reasons that will become clear as I examine the development of the voting studies, this question became the leading controversy in the field, occupying more than twenty years of discussion and criticism and dominating completely the attention of the designers of the voting studies themselves. Much of the old fire has gone out of this dispute as it has become increasingly clear that, in recent elections, voters are capable of voting their issue interests. But there is little pleasure in such issue-oriented behavior. For one thing, the proportion of the electorate capable of making issue-motivated choices, even when such choices are desperately clear, remains relatively small,[2] but, more important, such behavior has become apparent just at the time when most electoral democracies are experiencing severe political problems.

Without pretending to consider (much less resolve) the political problems confronting contemporary democratic governments, I want to reconsider the meaning of political issues and to reexamine the functions that those issues serve in electoral politics. There can be no doubt that political issues occupy a central position in the electoral process. But for a variety of reasons, their nature and the functions that they serve have remained unconsidered—both in principle and in practice. It is my hope to make a contribution in this regard, not only by raising the problem, but also by examining it in a systematic fashion.

This book is composed of oddly matched pieces, then. In part it is written as intellectual history, and in part it is intended to be a working summary of the major findings of the voting studies. Also it focuses on a particular aspect of the studies, the controversy over issue voting, and attempts to resolve this problem first by expanding the way we think about political issues and second by sharpening our understanding of the functions that these issues serve in the electoral process. If these concerns sound disparate as they are introduced, they are joined in the voting studies themselves in such a way that one cannot be examined without touching upon the others. Actually I feel that these themes represent a fairly narrow selection from among the possibilities presented by the voting studies. Years of electoral surveys provide a multitude of fascinating information and a wide variety of different questions. I hope that I have chosen the most important among them.

Some additional words of explanation about the organization of this book are in order. I have tried to intermix theory and data in a manner that, while frequently recommended, is uncommon in the voting studies. This approach has been maintained at several different levels of analysis. Most important, it is political theory in its traditional meaning. This is linked to the voting studies both in the errors and dreadful misunderstandings that occurred as well as by the sheer force of the data via the implications of the relationships that have been discovered.

But another level of theory also demands attention. This type of theory is what Robert Merton has called "research orientation."[3] I have found that empiricists, because they so often strive so hard to be "value free," are frequently prisoners of the unspoken assumptions of particular research traditions.[4] Needless to say, these assumptions become caught up in the data and hence in the inferences that are made from their analysis. The work of the Survey Research Center suffers especially in this regard. Thus, in the pages that follow, I have attempted to be attentive to both political theory in its traditional meaning and to "research theory" in the sense that different traditions of empirical research impose critical assumptions on unsuspecting practitioners.

The view of theory taken here—both as political thought and empirical research—is that it is an incomplete and unfinished set of principles. This is what makes the intermixing of political theory and data analysis extremely difficult—and, I suspect, why, despite all the laudatory words promoting this combination, it is so rarely done. It is common among data analysts to think of democratic theory as a settled affair, that theory exists as a set of coherent principles found in a collection of master works that locate a tradition of thought and describe its development. But it is a tradition that stops short of the electoral process, even as it establishes a series of assumptions and expectations for the conduct of government. From my perspective, democratic theory is very much an unsettled proposition. This point is difficult for political analysts to acknowledge, because it demands their having not only a working knowledge of a tradition of thought and how it developed, but also it requires them to extend that tradition themselves, in the expectations and functions that they attribute to the mass public and to the electoral process. Every analysis of electoral politics presupposes an original effort in political theory.

Similarly, each statistical technique, and every tradition of research, contains assumptions of its own. Contrary to the feeling of many nonempiricists, the methods of data analysis are not self-evident. Rather every analysis involves a careful choice among techniques and great care in the interpretation of results. Questions of method involve choices among different models, choices among different theories. In matching method and problem, analysts are very much on their own. Just as democratic theory requires analysts to take chances, to make assumptions, so too the analysis of data is always an uncertain and original enterprise.

In exploring the development of the voting studies, I have tried to be sensitive to both these aspects of analysis. Passages from the original publications are cited as often as possible, as are pieces of data analysis. However, I have not hesitated to rerun relationships myself where I believed such changes in form would be more useful, just as I have not hesitated to summarize to escape the excessive burden of citations.

The American electorate is the basis of a disproportionate amount of the discussion. This reflects the development of the voting studies, wherein the application of survey technology to other national electorates came more slowly. It must be observed also that the United States is a particularly interesting case, both because American politics has some extremely unusual features and because the nation occupies a unique position in political history. The United States was both last and first in the development of the constitutional idea. It caught the last breath of the Enlightenment, a singular moment in time, when constitutionalism achieved something approaching a consensus in theory and at the same time was a theory aching to be practiced. But constitutionalism in the United States was modified by the electoral process much sooner and much more dramatically than were the institutional designs of other regimes. These features combine to make electoral politics in the United States particularly interesting, something of a "critical case," to borrow Harry Eckstein's phrase.[5] Still, however remarkable, the United States is only one case. While it is overemphasized in the data, I have tried to be careful to make comparisons to other nations and point out where findings about the American electorate are generalizable and where they are unique.

Finally, by way of introduction, I want to present some notes on the development of democratic theory and on the emergence of the electoral process. The following are, at best, sketches of ideas and principles. They are intended as orientational material, certainly not as complete accounts. Since keeping one's bearing in the voting studies has proven to be an exceptionally difficult matter, I thought some brief introductory material would be appropriate. Should these aspects of political history and political theory seem entirely unfamiliar, the accompanying notes suggest sources that trace their development far more carefully, fully, and thoughtfully than is possible or appropriate here.

Aspects of Constitutional Theory

To understand the theoretical significance of voting and elections, one has to appreciate how far democratic theory has had to come to accept these ideas. Modern democratic theory has its origins in the idea of the individual, of course. But individualism in theory was not meant to extend into the political arena. Not only was the principle of political equality not embraced, it was, by most theorists, positively abhorred. The development of the individual—of people with personal, political, and social rights—has been curious and contradictory, wherein theory and history have worked in something less than perfect harmony. The flow of concepts and events has been rough, the directions of development often circuitous.

The idea of the individual emerged in response to the industrial revolution and the rise of the nation-state. Beginning with Machiavelli—some would say beginning with Marsilius of Padua—the entire structure of government and the political theory that described it were overhauled. So too was the organization of the marketplace. In both cases—in government and in economics—it was the feudal order that lost ground and eventually crumbled.[6]

European feudalism had at its core a system of mutual economic and social obligations.[7] These were fixed within a fairly tight range at birth and, of course, were hierarchical in nature. There was no hint of equality in this system, not in any of its manifestations—personal, economic, political, or social. Individualism was neither a habit of mind nor a principle of society.

The feudal system, however, did provide a modicum of security for all persons, particularly economic security. This was especially true in the agricultural sector where traditions of tenancy and common lands made poverty extremely rare. Such trade and commerce as existed were controlled by a strong system of regulation and by a series of monopolies. The "guild system" simultaneously limited recruitment, established conditions of employment, and regulated the terms of trade. Prices, both for labor and for finished goods, were not determined by the marketplace. Rather they were set within the community and did not vary with market conditions. It was altogether a stable and secure system.

The industrial revolution attacked this system at its very core. The revolution was a system predicated on the free movement of labor and capital, a system where prices and products varied. Emphasis was given to "individual choice," unfettered by traditional obligations. The notion of individual consent and of free will, particularly in market situations, appeared. A new economic and social order emerged.

It is wrong, of course, to speak of the industrial revolution as if it were an articulate doctrine. Rather it was a slow, and often violent, shift from a system of mutual obligations to a market system—both in agriculture and in industry. By and large, differences in status remained, lingering on into the twentieth century, but the tradition of tenancy and the custom of common lands vanished altogether, as did the guild system of regulation. Industry and commercial agriculture were premised on the idea of the individual and on the idea of wage labor. Correspondingly, the concepts of contract and consent emerged as accepted doctrine.

It is easy to see why such powerful forces as these give rise to divergent interpretations. Surely it was the strength of the industrial revolution much more than the pens of political theorists that established the predominance of these ideas. But in the hands of political theorists, the idea of the individual became the basis for new assertions and for original concepts.[8] Contract and consent became the bases not only of the industrial order, but also for the idea of citizenship, the inherent rights of persons, and of limited government. If the industrial revolution placed people on their own, giving them a new definition, it also created a series of political paradoxes that in the end resulted in the creation of the modern state. In this view, when Rousseau wrote "man is born free, but is everywhere in chains," he penned an epigram that both described the era during which he lived and that spoke for the philosophical problem he wished to resolve.[9] For indeed, people were free in a sense that they had not been previously. The oppressive hierarchy of the feudal order was in disarray, and so too its restrictive covenants. The concept of law was expanding, and with it the notion that people were fundamentally equal, with everyone being entitled to the protection of fundamental liberties and to due process, a guarantee enforced by the authority of the state. However ennobling this new status, the concept of the individual was fueled by the rigors of economic necessity. Industrialism depended on a system of wage labor, and this in turn depended on the idea of individual consent. People could now "choose" to live in a degree of poverty and economic uncertainty that was unknown under the feudal system.

Was the individual born free or were people more deeply enslaved? "It is here that it is most difficult to draw a balance," E. P. Thompson wrote, speaking of the changes in the status of women in particular.

On the one hand, the claim that the Industrial Revolution raised the status of women would seem to have little meaning when set beside the record of excessive hours of labour, cramped housing, excessive childbearing and terrifying rates of child mortality. On the other hand, the abundant opportunities for female employment in the textile districts gave to women the status of independent wage-earners. The spinster or the widow was freed from dependence upon relatives or upon parish relief. Even the unmarried mother might be able, through the laxness of "moral discipline" in many mills, to achieve an independence unknown before. . . .
The period reveals many such paradoxes.[10]

Rousseau arrived at his own ingenious solution to this paradox, one outside the general drift of political theory in his time. The problem was a general one, however. Indeed, much of Rousseau's originality lies in his ability to generalize the idea of individual equality in politics and society. Most philosophers concentrated on the other side of the paradox. Their concern was to secure inequalities among people in the marketplace and in the political arena. But how could these manifest inequalities among persons—inequalities of property and in political power—be justified in the face of the rights and privileges that people acquired at birth? Political inequalities were particularly troublesome in this regard, for if people were born equal and all had inalienable rights, how could systems of government be maintained wherein the representation of individuals was manifestly unequal?

For many thinkers, a great part of the solution to this problem lay in emphasizing the idea of the personal rights of citizens—and, correspondingly, emphasizing the limits of a new and powerful concept: the state. This was the theory of constitutionalism, of course, along with its companion doctrine of citizenship. Succinctly and with remarkable acuity, T. H. Marshall has observed that the formative period for civil rights occurred during the eighteenth century, just as the nineteenth century saw the concept of citizenship expanded to include political rights.[11]

The civil element [of citizenship] is composed of the rights necessary for individual freedom—liberty of the person, freedom of speech, thought and faith, the right to own property and to conclude valid contracts, and the right to justice. The last is of a different order from the others, because it is the right to defend and assert all one's rights on terms of equality with others and by due process of law.[12]

Inequality among persons was justified because people possessed the same inalienable liberties and because all could insist on their rights through the courts. As countless critics of this line of thought have argued, this is an unfair definition of the individual, for status, power, and property all affect the capacity of people to exercise these liberties. Formulating individualism in these terms justifies these inequities among persons without providing any compensating remedies. The emergence of the citizen, of the concept of inalienable rights, had the remarkable consequence of justifying the status quo.

Although few would argue that personal liberties complete the definition of the individual, still, it is important to observe that this aspect of citizenship marks a tremendous advance in democratic theory. By means of this concept, people obtained rights and privileges independent of the political order. These were "natural rights," "the Rights of Man." They belonged to people by virtue of their individuality; they were not granted by political authority; they could not be modified by government. These were rights that God had ordained; they were a fixed part of the human universe. The individual now preceded the state. In principle, the individual even was thought to precede society.

If it can be said that the industrial revolution forged the outlines of the nation-state, it can be said equally that political theorists created the doctrine that national government was intrinsically limited. The concept of limited government, a government "deriving its just powers from the consent of the governed," was entirely original. Again, the bedrock of the idea is in the individual—the individual as a person independent of the state. In principle, then, politics is a restricted sphere—restricted not only by the civil rights of persons but equally by the notion that the individual is intrinsically a private person. This notion includes the belief that only certain activities fall into the public domain. Those powers and areas of activity not granted to the state, a grant to which people presumably have "consented," are retained by the individual.

But the concept of limited government was not intended to imply that governments were to be inherently weak and inactive. To the contrary, although governments are limited in scope, constitutional theorists tended to grant them a broad range of powers in economic matters, social affairs, and international relations. Given the emergence of the modern nation-state, it would have been difficult for theorists to avoid the reality of powerful central governments. But the theory of governmental power was not prompted by necessity alone. It originated by design also, as a integral part of constitutional theory.

Strong and active governments were essential to preserve and promote the public good. Although never defined with precision, "the public good" was not an idle or abstract category. Rather it constituted the entire justification for political power. Policies were indivisible in their benefits. It did not matter that some might gain more, or more immediately, from governmental action. What mattered was the quality of the policy itself. To borrow from our current vocabulary, governmental policy involved the production of public goods.

It is worth mentioning in passing that there was no general agreement on the content of public policy, not even in the economic realm.[13] But to look for a substantive consensus on the public good in constitutional theory is to miss the point. Agreement was less on particular policies than it was on the method of policy making. Reason was to control the formulation of public policy. Early in constitutional theory the voice of reason was identified with the will of God. Later, in the hands of the deists, it was identified with the natural order of the universe, while free thinkers made reason an essentially human attribute. Whatever the religious variation, the meaning was the same. People were to reason to the public good, and, in so doing, the tremendous powers granted to government would always be well used.

Surely reason was the active ingredient in public policy, but it was not left to work in isolation. Constitutional theorists universely supposed that the political elite would maintain a strong set of public values. Political leaders were assumed to be very principled people. Again, there was a tendency to be vague about the precise composition of these value systems. Montesquieu subsumed everything under the heading of "honor"; Locke tended to rely on "character"; Whig and American theorists, on the other hand, used the unlimited category of "public virtue." Whatever the variation, there is little doubt about what was intended on this score. Constitutional theorists had in mind a highly idealized concept of aristocratic virtue.

It would be interesting to attempt to identify what values, beyond that of reason, were presupposed by this fantasy. As a method of government, constitutionalism is anything but value free. Yet its fundamental values have not been nearly so well identified as one might believe.[14] But again, emphasis should not be on the lack of specificity, but on the general consensus surrounding these elements of the theory. Reason and an aristocratic code of personal conduct were the mechanisms by which power was to be exercised.

These aspects of constitutional theory also provided the logical justification for political inequality, thus resolving the great paradox of the constitutional design for government. Clearly reason and the other public virtues were not distributed widely across the population. Equality of persons in the political process was not plausible. The only way to ensure that political power simultaneously served the public good and protected the rights of the individual was to organize government so that particular types of motivations ruled. Representation was not of the people, then, but of values in the majority, as Locke indicated.[15]

This led constitutional theorists to concentrate on the structure of government—on the separation of powers, checks and balances, multiple constituencies—in short, on the familiar features of constitutional design. Governmental power was always derived from the individual, but there was never any intention to count individual preferences equally in the formulation of policy. Rather the architecture of the theory was intended to protect government from the mass public.

From the perspective of the voting studies, constitutionalism is rich with possibilities, for the electoral process did emerge triumphant. One person, one vote, became the methodology of political power, despite the best efforts of constitutional theory. The voting studies could examine the political behavior of the mass public, comparing it to the assumptions of constitutionalism. Or the fundamental values themselves of the electorate could have been investigated. Or, if the studies were truly imaginative, they could have explored the additions to constitutional theory that are presumed by the electoral process.

Unfortunately, the voting studies seized none of these possibilities. Rather, a distorted vision of "classical democratic theory" guided them. The image was of a participant citizen, of a theory designed for participation, and of a system of representation intended to translate the will of the people into public policy. These confusions in theory were to exact a heavy toll from the studies.

Notes on the Development of the Electoral Process

If constitutionalism constituted a revolution in thinking at the top, among the political elite—a revolution in ideas and in the organization of government—then the electoral process is best conceived of as a political revolution that took place at the bottom, among the people. Here the motivating forces were the exigencies of practical politics and the seemingly inexhaustible conflicts among groups. It was considerations of power and political advantage that gave nurture to the electoral process. Voting and elections were thrust into the constitutional design without any attempt to probe the theoretical ramifications of these changes.

The impetus to enlarge the franchise originated in the same nexus of historical forces that had sustained the flowering of political theory in the seventeenth and eighteenth centuries. Industrialism, nationalism, and the emergence of the nation-state established major cleavages between population groups and set in motion a series of conflicts between them. These group conflicts often were expressed in terms of "the right to vote," this "right" being altogether a part of the struggle between groups as they tried either to maintain or to alter the distribution of influence within the political system.

Political parties were the cutting edge of this process. Parties began to emerge first as elite factions and gradually extended themselves into the mass public.[16] The factors that shaped political parties and party competition varied from nation to nation and do not seem to form a simple, one-dimensional pattern. Although all began as elite factions, the conflicts that caused the disputes were quite different. So too there were differences from nation to nation in the internal structure of political parties and in the nature of their appeals.

E. E. Schattschneider has described the inherent tendency of conflicts among political elites to generalize so that eventually they include substantial segments of the population. The logic behind his proposition is rooted in the advantage that each minority faction gains by drawing additional groups of people into its coalition, a logic that is repeated by the contending political parties until everyone is included in the conflict.[17] Schattschneider was writing from the perspective of a political system where the franchise was already extended and the remaining questions concerned the basis of party competition. However, his analysis is even more appropriate for the extension of the franchise itself, for it emphasizes the bitterly contested nature of the process and its focus on which groups are to control the political power of the state.

The various group interests set in motion by the gathering forces of industrialism and nationalism, each group with distinct grievances, sought to redress (or maintain) the distribution of power through the political process. The extension of the franchise became a focal point of these struggles as unrepresented groups sought the right to compete on an equal footing with those already "represented." Usually the addition of new groups to the political process meant altering the balance of power. This is why the right to vote has such an explosive history in the nineteenth century. The conflict was simultaneously over pressing group interests and a fundamental restructuring of the political process. Schattschneider is correct in observing that the cutting edge of this process was the effort of one or another political party to obtain (or enlarge) its competitive advantage.

Struggles to extend the franchise were universally couched in the rhetoric of democracy and equality, of course. But these were much more in the nature of campaign slogans than they were in the tradition of political theory. Certainly the idea of the equality of votes—of voters rationally considering alternative party programs, of people coolly considering the public good—does not describe the political realities whereby the vote was extended. These were highly partisan affairs.

For example, the enfranchisement of blacks in American politics was prompted less by considerations of political equality (amendments to this effect had been defeated in half a dozen northern states following the Civil War) than by the desire of the Republican party to maintain its predominant position in the electorate. There was never any question about which way blacks would vote. Little thought was given to the notion of the public good. Rather it was power politics straight down the line.[18] Such is the political history of the expansion of the electorate. No thought was given to the meaning of the electoral process within the constitutional design; there was little consideration of principle. Rather the question was whose interests would benefit and whose would be ignored. The divisions were clear and intense. Indeed, the intensity of group conflict in European politics was such that groups often forced their way into the electoral arena under their own party banner.[19]

The staying power of group cleavages is one of the most arresting features of modern politics. The logic by which mass participation was achieved seems to have combined with the logic of party competition to produce very stable political divisions. If the substance of these conflicts varies from nation to nation, the relative stability of divisions born long ago seems curiously permanent— the more so when measured against the great changes and tumultuous events of the twentieth century.

With remarkable prescience, Lipset and Rokkan have observed that the various groups struggling for representation in "western" political systems originate from four fundamental social cleavages: subject versus dominant culture (the conflict between "central nation-building culture" and distinct characteristics of local groups), church(es) versus government, secondary versus primary economies, and workers versus employers and owners.[20] These cleavages were born of the industrial and national revolutions in their broadest outlines. But they were incorporated into politics in terms of the struggle for participation.

The point to be stressed is that group conflicts "generally tended to manifest themselves *before* any lowering of the threshold of representation."[21] Moreover, the question of representation tended to provide severe tests for emerging political organizations; in most cases the "decisive moves" to extend the franchise came from established parties rather than from "pressures to establish new mass movements."[22]

The process whereby these cleavages, and the group interests that sprang from them, were incorporated into political systems gave the idea of political equality shape and definition. It was an argument that took place not in theory but in the competition for power. If, as T. H. Marshall has noted, the nineteenth century added to the concept of citizenship the essential elements of political rights,[23] then it must be observed also that government was twice transformed. In the first instance, the status of the individual was altered: the abstractions implicit in the notion of "the rights of man" were realized, for good and for ill, as people acquired political power. And second, the architecture of the state was recast: the constitutional ideal and particularly the doctrine of separation of powers acquired a vastly different meaning as parties competed for power.

The intensity of the conflicts that generated these transformations still forms the basis of contemporary political competition. Wrote Lipset and Rokkan in 1967:

[T]he party systems of the 1960's reflect, with few but significant exceptions, the cleavage structures of the 1920's. This is a crucial characteristic of Western competitive politics in the age of "high mass consumption": The party alternatives, and in remarkably many cases the party organizations, are older than the majorities of the national electorates. To most of the citizens of the West the currently active parties have been part of the political landscape since their childhood or at least since they were first faced with the choice between alternative "packages" on election day.

This continuity is often taken as a matter of course; in fact it poses an intriguing set of problems for comparative sociological research. An amazing number of the parties which had established themselves by the end of World War I survived not only the onslaughts of Fascism and National Socialism but also another world war and a series of profound changes in the social and cultural structure of the polities they were part of. How was this possible? How were these parties able to survive so many changes in the political, social, and economic conditions of their operations? How could they keep such large bodies of citizens identifying with them over such long periods of time, and how could they renew their core clienteles from generation to generation?[24]

Fifteen years later, despite a sea of survey data and analysis, these questions remain valid. Of course, from my perspective, the remarkable quality of our ignorance is that the voting studies have contributed so little. The questions of how political parties build and maintain followings in the mass public are preeminently questions for survey analysis. Yet, despite the massive historical stability of political parties, the voting studies were confounded by the great strength of the relationships among social characteristics, party identification, and voting. To say that survey analysts have not possessed an acute sense of political history is to make a very understated observation, indeed.

The Voting Studies—Past and Present

The voting studies have had a difficult time with fundamentals. From the first, survey analysts were out of touch with the history of democratic theory. By failing to take the development of constitutionalism as their point of departure, a broad range of misleading expectations for the democratic citizen was established. It was expected that people would be active in politics, that they would enjoy political conflict and understand the rules by which it took place, and that they would be efficacious about their own participation in it. Furthermore, people were expected to be informed about electoral choices; voting decisions were to be made on the basis of the issues in the campaign. Rationality, above all, was the standard for political behavior.

This, as we have seen, is simply awful political theory, and it is equally bad as political history. As theory, it missed completely constitutionalists' deep and abiding distrust of people in general and of the "common man" in particular. Of course, it can be (and probably should be) argued that constitutionalism's fears of these matters are wrong, or at least inappropriate. But this still leaves unsettled the crucial problem of what values are presupposed for the mass public by constitutional theory. This problem alone could have occupied the voting studies during the last forty years to the great profit of all. As it was, the entire problem was garbled, so much so that forty years later the voting studies are still confused about the theory of the democratic citizen.

As political history, the expectations rooted in the voting studies proved equally misleading. Rather than attempting *to explain* the stability of political behavior, survey analysts kept rediscovering it. The political dynamics of the process whereby parties renew the loyalties of groups over the years, through generations, remains a mystery. Of course, it is of some comfort to know that the evidence from the surveys confirms in individual detail what appears in the large throughout the history of the period. But one still longs to understand how this process works, how parties rooted in old, distant, and frequently irrelevant conflicts are able to continue their appeals when the substance of politics is so markedly different.

The original voting studies, then, were weakest precisely where they needed to be strong. After all, political theory and political history form the heartland of the problems they wanted to address. Much of the vitality of those political surveys was lost because of inattention to basics. But, by contrast, the voting studies are most interesting for the raw empiricism of their work, for the multitude of relationships that were uncovered. While this literature makes difficult reading, largely because of its weakness on fundamentals, it is nevertheless vital and original, literature that is essential to an understanding of the electoral process. Much of the effort in the pages that follow is devoted to untangling the findings made by the voting studies.

I do not want to make it seem, however, that answers about the nature of the electoral process, and the functions that it serves in democratic theory, will come easily. Even from the limited discussion in the preceding two sections, it should be readily apparent that the theory of the democratic ideal and the history of democratic politics are poorly matched. Political power in democratic theory is predicated on the concept of the public good. While it is relatively easy to make constitutional theory democratic by opening the formulation of the public good to everyone, it is much more difficult to square the concept of the public good with the political history of the electoral process.

Intransigent group loyalties, the capacity of political elites to manipulate the relevance of these ties well beyond their historical validity, and the oppressively low level of political information in the electorate, among other things, do nothing to inspire confidence in the public good as it is formulated through the electoral process. If democratic theory is somewhat unclear about what is expected from electoral politics, it is evident that more is expected than this.

The imbalance between democratic theory and democratic politics creates splendid opportunities for the voting studies. It permits political analysts to work both sides of the street, as it were—to assist in clarifying the democratic ideal insofar as it involves questions of fundamental values and the links between the belief systems in the mass public and among the political elite, but equally to explore the dynamics of contemporary politics to discover how the public good is formulated and reformulated in our own time. If the voting studies have failed in the past to address these questions, there is no reason that they must continue to do so. As much as it attempts to understand what has been discovered (and left undiscovered) by the voting studies, this book contains a hope that we retain a sense of excitement that political surveys once possessed and a hope that we can promote further political exploration.

PART I

THE VOTER AND

THE VOTING STUDIES

Despite all these developments, it is too early to conclude that governments can ignore public opinion or that democratic government amounts only to a hoax, a ritual whose performance serves only to delude the people and thereby to convert them into willing subjects of the powers that be. . . . Unless mass views have some place in the shaping of policy, all the talk about democracy is nonsense. As Lasswell has said, the "open interplay of opinion and policy is the distinguishing mark of popular rule." Yet the sharp definition of the role of public opinion as it affects different kinds of policies under different types of situations presents an analytical problem of extraordinary difficulty.

V. O. KEY, JR.
Public Opinion and American Democracy

CHAPTER 2

Social Politics

The first efforts at systematic inquiry into voting behavior were prompted neither by a concern with the status of the democratic citizen nor by any curiosity about the electoral process. In fact, the first voting studies were virtually unrelated to politics in any of its formal manifestations. The idea of studying political behavior by means of survey research came initially from the disciplines of sociology and social psychology.

From the outset, then, there was a good deal of distance between the questions that political scientists were accustomed to asking about elections and democratic theory and those that were first asked in the voting studies. These were not trivial differences in interest and perspective, but rather they amounted to investigating substantially different problems. It is not that one approach is more valid or perceptive than the other, but rather that each concentrates upon fundamentally different concerns. However, in the voting studies, these intellectual differences became entangled in such a way that the relationship between the electoral process and democratic theory was all but lost, while the meaning of voting and elections was obscured even as individual political behavior was being understood for the first time.

Much of the responsibility for this confusion is appropriately attributed to political science as a profession. Neither political theorists nor American political scientists adjusted easily to the quantitative aspects of survey research or to the wealth of material contained in the early voting studies. Political theorists, for their part, are involved with the voting studies primarily in their absence. Both by inclination and by training, they were entirely unprepared for the quantitative revolution with its emphasis on causal analysis and hypothesis testing. They thought quantitative research intrinsically shallow—a view that undoubtedly was reinforced by the simplistic rendering of democratic theory that appeared in the voting studies. The relevance of survey research to studying the moral dimensions of democratic regimes—to questions of values in the mass public and among the political elite—apparently was never seen. Indeed, today political theorists and the voting studies remain as isolated from each other as they were almost forty years ago.

Students of American politics, on the other hand, chose a different fate. They became so enthralled with electoral studies and with the methodology of survey research that they seemingly forgot everything that they had learned previously about politics in the United States. By the late 1930s, when the voting studies were beginning, American political scientists had developed a fairly sophisticated understanding of the electoral process. It was understood, most importantly, that elections were part of a larger political process, that public policy was not simply a response to voting decisions, that the effects of parties and pressure groups had to be taken into account, and also that there were the considerable effects of election laws, direct primaries, patronage, and political machines. To be sure, voting occupied an important place in the system, but at the tutoring of Charles Merriam, Harold Gosnell, Peter Odegard, Edward Sait, and a young scholar named V. O. Key, Jr., it was clear that the electoral process was not a flat, barren expanse in which the will of the people alone directed government and policy.[1]

This understanding of the electoral process began to crumble in the late 1940s before the onrush of the voting studies. Soon every question was stated in terms of political surveys. Methodology quickly became its own subfield, inexorably linked to studies of

American politics. Parties, pressure groups, and political institutions were reduced to individual behaviors and attitudes. The generalizations of the preceding twenty years suddenly disappeared.

The net result of the voting studies, then, was to separate the electoral process from other aspects of government—from the logic of political parties and party competition, from political institutions, and from democratic theory. Voting would be explained, but the cost of that explanation was to diminish the relationship to an embarrassingly low level. However, it truly can be said that none of these concerns were on Paul Lazarsfeld's mind in 1939 when he and his associates began to plan their study of voting in Erie County, Ohio, during the forthcoming presidential election.

Voting and the Marketplace

Paul Lazarsfeld's interest in voting grew out of his pioneering studies in the field of consumer behavior and market research. Scholars in these areas had become involved in the methodology of survey research for the same reasons that had motivated commercial pollsters. The unifying theme for both groups was the potential of radio and the printed page to influence individual behavior in mass markets—the effects of advertising on consumer decisions, to be more precise.[2]

It was altogether a curious combination of enterpreneurs and professors that bore down upon potential consumers. Commercial pollsters such as George Gallup, Mervin Field, Elmo Roper, and Archibald Crossley were busy in the 1940s and early 1950s perfecting the technical aspects of the enterprise (sample design, questionnaire validity, interviewing, and related field problems) while at the same time they were attempting to attract customers for this new technology.[3] The academics, on the other hand, were more sensitive to the questions of methodology and analysis. In particular they were concerned with the general problem of why certain types of advertising campaigns were more successful than others.[4]

But the heart of survey research, whether in the university or in commerce, was the consumer. It was a focus that was frankly manipulative in character. Wrote Arthur Kornhauser and Lazarsfeld in 1935:

> The need for a psychological view grows out of the very nature of market research. For that research is aimed predominantly at knowledge *by means of which to forecast and control consumer behavior.* It is a matter of ascertaining sales opportunities in order that these opportunities may be utilized and developed on the facts. Sales opportunities exist—or fail to exist—in people's minds.[5]

A simple, intelligently constructed survey can provide advertisers with two enormously powerful pieces of information essential to merchandising consumer goods. First, a survey can reveal the reasons why people find a product appealing (or unappealing). Second, an otherwise undifferentiated population can be divided into relevant subgroups, thus enabling sellers to select the advertising strategy that will appeal to the greatest number of potential buyers.

Take, for example, the problem of marketing laundry detergents. By asking the appropriate question, it was discovered that most people buy laundry soap for the wizardry of its cleaning power, the magic of its chemistry. In the late thirties and forties it was also true that the people who were most likely to buy laundry detergents were nonworking, middle-aged housewives with families. So it was that the "soap opera" emerged as an art form, for these programs attracted the audience most likely to purchase laundry detergent. It was clear, too, that appeals to these consumers should be couched in a family setting but should also emphasize the product's "new and improved" chemistry.

Thus identifying the psychological motivations of consumers and breaking down the population of potential consumers by subgroups presented advertisers with all the information they needed (or wanted) to know. Neither manufacturers nor advertising agencies were interested in the more sophisticated questions of consumer buying: How did the mass media actually motivate people, and why were some people affected and not others? Why were certain advertising campaigns more successful than others? How did people manage the conflicting claims of competing products? These questions were left for scholarly attention, and it was precisely these questions that Paul Lazarsfeld wanted to answer.

Consumer decisions, however, are particularly resistant to systematic study, for a number of reasons. The world of commerce is so cluttered with advertising stimuli that focusing on the effects of any one campaign becomes extremely difficult. Even more difficult, from a methodological point of view, is isolating the actual decision to buy. People continuously come and go in the marketplace, but surveys of consumers are restricted to discrete periods of time and thus can fail to capture whole classes of consumer motivations. From a researching perspective, there are also problems with advertising campaigns themselves. The campaigns usually do not run promotions in every possible medium. Thus analysts often cannot make the appropriate comparisons between the effects of different techniques.

It was with these considerations in mind that Paul Lazarsfeld thought of the electoral process. To Lazarsfeld, the idea of voting seemed the perfect analogy to consumer behavior in the marketplace. It was a striking metaphor. After all, political campaigns are essentially highly organized efforts to influence voter decisions, just as advertising campaigns are highly organized efforts to influence consumer decisions. But as opposed to studying advertising campaigns in the marketplace, the political arena held out enormous methodological advantages. Indeed, Lazarsfeld saw in studying voting decisions a solution to all the nagging problems that had plagued earlier consumer studies.

In the first place, voters in the electoral process all cast their ballots on the same day, which is an extremely attractive attribute from a methodological perspective. Furthermore, political campaigns involve the communications process and organized efforts to influence individual opinions on a grand scale. Every form of advertising is used—the mass media, newspapers, magazines, leaflets, and so forth. There are also partisan activities in the form of rallies, meetings, individual initiatives, campaign work—formal and informal efforts at persuasion.

In Lazarsfeld's eyes elections provided very nearly a perfect laboratory for studying how people respond to the flow of information and to the pressures of making (and remaking) decisions. Thus the plan of the Erie County study was to "follow the individual voter along the path to his vote [in order] to discover the relative effects various influential factors had upon his final vote."[6]

It should be stressed that the image of politics that Lazarsfeld had in mind did not include the electoral process as a whole but concentrated instead on the specific act of voting. Voting, in turn, was conceived of as a process in which huge stores of information were consumed and where the voter constantly vacillated "between one and another candidate as propaganda from both sides filters down to him. Finally, he comes to a decision, perhaps at the last moment before he enters the polling booth."[7]

In order to capture the vicissitudes of public opinion, Lazarsfeld invented the panel survey, a technique whereby the same sample of voters would be interviewed at regular intervals during the campaign. As it finally emerged, there were seven panels in the Erie County study. From an initial survey of three thousand respondents, six hundred were selected to be part of the continuing panel, while four groups of six hundred were selected as "control" groups so that the effects of repeated interviewing on opinions might itself be assessed. The panel survey was an entirely original piece of methodology in its own right, but it was as a technique to gauge opinion flows during an extended campaign that this method held exciting possibilities.

Interviewing the same panel of people on different occasions made it possible to collect an enormous amount of information about each person. Interviewers probed respondents' backgrounds, inquired about their political philosophy, and recorded their personal political history. Notes were also taken on respondents' issue concerns, the degree to which they cared about the election, their group and peer group identifications. Every effort was made to monitor the ways in which the campaign reached people, including, of course, personal contacts by either party, discussions among friends or with family or at work, reading about the campaign in newspapers or in magazines, listening to radio programs and news reports.

These efforts did not stop with the interview process. Attention was also paid to objective factors. Researchers kept a running account of the important events in the campaign in order to see if events themselves constituted an important influence on voting behavior. Additionally, an elaborate effort was made to assess the character and content of news about the election. Before the political campaign had gotten underway, a team of researchers from the Bureau of Applied Social Research arrived in Erie County so that the flow of news and the various efforts at political mobilization might be recorded from the first. Did the county's newspapers give more space to Wilkie than to Roosevelt? What was the gist of editorial opinion, and did those opinions drift over to the reporting of the campaign? Were the appeals of both candidates presented equally and fairly on the radio? Did stories about one or the other constantly appear at the top of the news? What about the character of party activity? Were both parties about equally well organized? Did they both engage in the same types of activities?

These aspects of the research were done in monthly summaries to coincide with each panel of the survey. Thus it would be possible to analyze not only the effects of political advertising, but the influence of the manner in which the news was reported.

Each strand of the problem had been carefully elaborated and plans were meticulously drawn so that each would be measured accurately. Methodological problems had been anticipated in advance; objective factors had been enumerated; individual predispositions had been recorded; and the flow of the campaign in all its manifestations had been carefully monitored throughout. It was altogether a stunning piece of research in both its design and execution.

However, the guiding assumption of the research—the association between consumer behavior and voting decisions—proved to be erroneous. In a way, this could have been a very substantial finding. It would have been of great importance to know how, in 1940, voting decisions in electoral politics were dissimilar to consumer decisions in the marketplace. Such an approach would have been doubly valuable in subsequent studies, because American politics became more fluid later. The similarities and differences between consumer and voting behavior still have to be stated systematically. But these were not the questions that the Erie County study had been designated to answer, and hence the comparison between the voter and the consumer was never made.

Actually, it was not at all clear to Lazarsfeld how the data from the Erie County study should be reorganized, given the failure of its principal assumption. The data in all of the seven panels made it painfully clear that most voters had made their decisions well before the campaign had gotten underway. Of the six hundred people in the continuing panel, only fifty-four were observed to have changed their minds during the course of the campaign. A few others started out without any inkling of a choice, and a much larger number of people had their underlying political predispositions activated as the campaign rolled along. But, all in all, the survey simply did not report the type of information that it had been designed to collect.

The thrust of the research had been to study votes "in the making." Instead, wave after wave of the panel reported that voting decisions had already been made. All the elaborate indices that had been so thoughtfully implanted in the questionnaires, the great care that had been taken to monitor the quality of the reporting and the nature of the political campaign—indeed, the panel design itself —were all for naught. It is understandable that the Erie County study was abandoned for a time. And when Lazarsfeld, Bernard Berelson, and Hazel Gaudet finally wrote *The People's Choice,* which described their study, it was with anything but a sense of excitement and discovery.

The People's Choice is a slight volume that was rather in the nature of a research report. Almost entirely descriptive in character, it went about summarizing the data without much attention to either nuance or theory. The authors say nothing about their original expectations, and they say surprisingly little about the research design. Yet despite the authors' obvious disappointment, the Erie County study contains a very nearly complete description of voting decisions.

A few years later Lazarsfeld and Berelson returned to the study of voting decisions, knowing this time what to expect. They designed a study of the 1948 presidential election, reducing the number of panels from seven to four and selecting Elmira County, New York, as the research site. Very little original insight was provided by this study.[8] However, the authors were much more thorough in the presentation of its results. A multitude of relationships are specified in exacting detail, and the implications of these findings for democratic theory are clearly specified.

In many ways, this was the Bureau of Applied Social Research's summary volume. Although several other political studies were to be conducted under its auspices, and although many formidable scholars received their training at the Bureau, the future of the electoral survey belonged to other institutions—the Survey Research Center of Ann Arbor, Michigan, in particular.[9] The Bureau of Applied Social Research withdrew from the field because of bad institutional luck in the struggle for funding. The impact of its work, however, should not be underestimated. From a technical standpoint, the relationships that its studies postulated were absolutely correct, as subsequent research showed time and again. But more important, the questions that Lazarsfeld and his associates formulated—or, more accurately, misformulated—gave direction to the field, if only in the disputes they created. The voting studies —a powerful technology and a multitude of newly formulated empirical relationships—were fully launched in a sea of ill-conceived inferences and a confusion of ideas.

Individual Voting Decisions

Voting decisions, Lazarsfeld and his associates discovered, were not made during the course of the presidential campaign. Rather, most people had determined their preferences before the political campaigns had begun, even before the candidates were chosen. "What the political campaign did, so to speak, was not to form new opinions but to raise old opinions over thresholds of awareness and decision. Political campaigns are important primarily because they activate latent predispositions."[10] Unlike opinions in the marketplace, Lazarsfeld was discovering that political preferences were highly differentiated, at least in 1940. The campaign functioned not to produce change but to refocus already established predispositions in the appropriate partisan terms.

The origins of individual political predispositions lay in the social process—in primary group associations (family, friends, and co-workers), in group loyalties (union memberships, regional identifications), and more generally in the system of social stratification (occupation, religion, ethnicity). "Repeatedly in this study," the authors concluded, "we found indications that people vote 'in groups.'"[11] This is most easily seen in the primary group associates that surround most voters. To begin with, the notion that voters are isolated decision makers is incorrect. "By and large, the voter is tied into a network of personal associations that is both homogeneous and congenial."[12]

How may we explain the fact that social groups are politically homogeneous and that the campaign increases this homogeneity still more? There is, first, the fact that people who live together under similar external conditions are likely to develop similar needs and interests. They tend to see the world through the same colored glasses; they tend to apply to common experiences common interpretations. . . .

But this is only part of the picture. There may be group members who are not really aware of the goals of their own group. And there may be many who, even if they were aware of those goals, would not be sufficiently interested in current events to tie the two together consciously. They acquiesce to the political temper of the group under the steady, personal influence of their more politically active fellow citizens. Here again, we find the process of activation by which the predisposed attitudes of some are brought out by the influence of others.[13]

Social groups did not affect everyone the same way, of course. Their influence tended to be related to a person's age and position in the community. For people who had just moved into the community, the significance of group influence was less noticeable, as it was for the young; although in both cases the group effects were still strong. But as people became older, and remained longer in the same community, "political homogeneity" was more likely to characterize the "environment" in which they lived.[14] (See figure 2.1.)

Political information, then, tended to be viewed by most people in a highly selective way. Not only did people approach politics with predispositions that were already firmly established, but the social milieu in which people lived and worked tended to reinforce those predispositions and acted as an additional barrier to dissonant information. Among family and friends, for example, Lazarsfeld and his associates found "almost perfect agreement" on political matters.[15]

The barrage of political news and campaign propaganda did nothing to diminish the selective perceptions with which people viewed politics. The power of these perceptual screens tended to *increase,* in fact, the more people cared about the campaign and the more interest they had in it.[16] People with little interest in politics and with chronically low levels of information were likely to be the most sensitive to new information, if, that is, that information was able to make it over the barriers of inertia and inattentiveness. In most cases, this was unlikely, the lack of information and low levels of political involvement being most strongly associated with nonvoting. But when such people do vote, their lack of involvement and lack of information make them the most susceptible to political influence.

This was an alarming finding, for it leads inescapably to the inference that those who are least informed are making the most

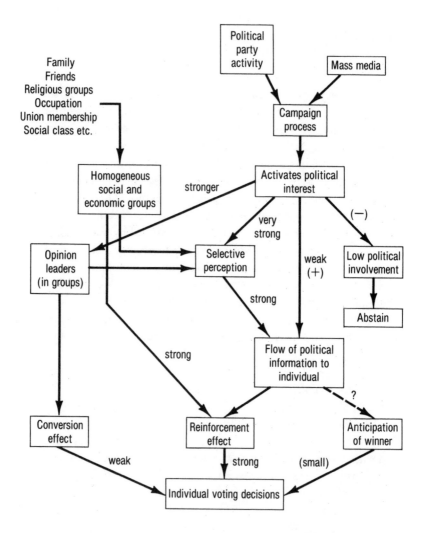

FIGURE 2.1 *The Process of a Campaign Reinforces Political Attitudes Derived from the Social Process*

SOURCE: Natchez, Peter B. "The Reasonable Voter." Ph.D. diss., Harvard University, 1969, p. 37.

important political decisions, that the segment of the electorate that cares least about the outcome of the election is determining, to a disproportionate degree, who wins and who loses. It appeared that victory in the electoral process is bestowed by those uniquely unprepared to act with thoughtfulness and vision. Wrote Lazarsfeld, Berelson, and Gaudet:

> That tells the story of the two party changers. . . . These people, who in a sense were the only ones of the entire electorate to make a complete change during the campaign, were: the least interested in the election; the least concerned about its outcome; the least attentive to political material in the formal media of communication; the last to settle upon a vote decision; and the most likely to be persuaded, finally, by a personal contact, not an "issue" of the election.
>
> In short, the party changers . . . the people who could swing an election during those last days—were, so to speak, available to the person who saw them last before Election Day. The notion that the people who switch parties during the campaign are mainly the reasoned, thoughtful, conscientious people who were convinced by the issues of an election is just plain wrong. Actually, they were mainly just the opposite.[17]

A less imaginative analyst would have had some difficulty with these data. For if most voting decisions could have been explained by reference to the social characteristics that surrounded them, then what could account for political change, particularly when such change was essentially nonpolitical in character? But Lazarsfeld argued that the social process accounted for these votes too. In the first place, he argued that the social process was not always consistent in its impact on voters, that some people are caught in a web of inconsistent social forces. Those caught in between conflicting social forces, "cross-pressured voters," tend to resolve the conflict by losing interest in politics.[18] This explained the low levels of involvement and the lack of interest so prevalent among this group of voters as well as the substantial amount of nonvoting that tended to characterize this group.

It did not explain, however, what finally determined the voting decisions of those who actually did participate. There was no discernible pattern of action in the data. People seemed to resolve these conflicts "subjectively," each person deciding on a different basis how to vote. But Lazarsfeld was not content to leave this as the conclusion of the analysis.

A close examination of the original interview schedules suggested a second line of interpretation to explain the behavior of cross-pressured voters, and voters generally, as it turned out. The conflicts implicit in these voters tended to be resolved by the personal influence of family or friends. It was the personal nature of this influence that Lazarsfeld found remarkable, not its partisan nature. The direction of the influence was irrelevant, in fact—a quality that showed up in the absence of distinct relationships in the data. Rather it was the casual and personal nature of the appeal that moved people one way or the other.

These personal contacts are what one might call *amateur machines* which spring up during elections—individuals who became quite enthusiastic or special groups that try to activate people within their reach. One might say that the most successful propaganda—especially last-minute propaganda—is to "surround" the people whose vote is still dubious so that the only path left to them is the way to the polling booth.[19]

This character of political influence—its personal, casual, and associative properties—was believed to be valid generally, not merely as an explanation for the behavior of cross-pressured voters.

The weight of personal contacts upon opinion lies, paradoxically, in their greater casualness and non-purposiveness in political matters. . . . Personal influence is more pervasive and less self-selective than the formal media. In short, politics gets through . . . because it comes up unexpectedly as a sideline or marginal topic in casual conversation.

Such passive participation in conversation is paralleled in the case of the formal media by accidental exposure, e.g., when a political speech is heard because it follows a favorite program. In both conversation and the formal media, such chance communication is particularly effective. And the testimony to such influence is much more frequent in the case of personal contacts.[20]

The "two-step model" of personal influence, as this model came to be called, was "discovered almost accidentally" as Lazarsfeld struggled to find an explanation for the decisions of cross-pressured and otherwise uninformed voters.[21] This discovery turned out to be applicable to communication flows generally. In a subsequent study (this time in Decatur, Illinois), Elihu Katz and Paul Lazarsfeld tested the idea of personal influence in four distinct areas— politics, fashion, movie-going, and marketing (food and household goods). In general, the idea of the two-step flow of communications worked out quite nicely. The mechanics by which personal influence was exercised followed very closely the pattern Lazarsfeld had observed in his reading of the interview schedules from the Erie County study. Almost always there was a shared set of norms that bound leaders and followers, norms that were embedded in primary group structures. "Person-to-person" contacts were an essential part of the process. And finally, personal influence tended to be most effective when it was exerted casually, in the context of informal gatherings and chance meetings, when some other matter was manifestly the focus of attention. "Shared interest, in short, appears to be a channel through which communications flow."[22]

If the process of leadership was similar among the four different areas, the characteristics of opinion leaders themselves varied considerably. Perhaps the most intriguing finding in this regard was that leadership tended to not be cumulative. "By and large, the hypothesis of a generalized leader receives very little support in this study. There is no overlap in any of the pairs of activities. Each arena, it seems, has a corps of leaders of its own."[23] In turn, two characteristics seemed to be disproportionately significant for opinion leaders in politics. First, political leaders were "gregarious" in a way that other leaders were not. They enjoyed the ebb and flow of human contacts and the swirl of social affairs—a disposition that seemingly originated deep within the structure of personality. For the political leader the press of human contacts was not a burden but a pleasure. Political leadership was also distinctive in its strong association with social class. Indeed, politics was the only one of the four areas investigated by Katz and Lazarsfeld where class was a significant factor. In part, the reason for this relationship was that higher status people have more political information than do others. Yet this was only a partial explanation, for the relationship remained strong even when controlling for the effects of information.

The typical public affairs leader, then, is quite different from opinion leaders [in other arenas]. . . . Life-cycle type, which was so important in both those [other] areas, makes only a little difference here in the incidence of opinion leadership except on the low status level. On the other hand, social status—which was only remotely related to marketing leadership and somewhat deviously to leadership in fashions—plays a very much more important role in public affairs leadership. . . . the effect of status can still be seen even when gregariousness is held constant.[24]

The two-step flow of communications completed the Bureau of Applied Social Research's argument that the analysis of voting decisions had to be conducted in social terms. Not only were most votes formed from the social environment in which voters resided, but social forces also acted to explain political change and opinion leadership. (See figure 2.2.) If the partisan content of political change could not be predicted with any certainty, the underlying process could be specified. Politics and political change were a manifestation of the larger social process, not in abstract and ideological categories, but in the voting decisions that were made by individuals.

Voting—Causes and Consequences

The model of voting that emerged from the work of the Bureau of Applied Social Research was remarkably comprehensive. It followed votes from the beginning of the campaign to election day, accomplishing in fact exactly what it set out to do. (See figure 2.3.) The role that campaigning had in heightening political awareness and in reawakening dormant political disposition was fully docu-

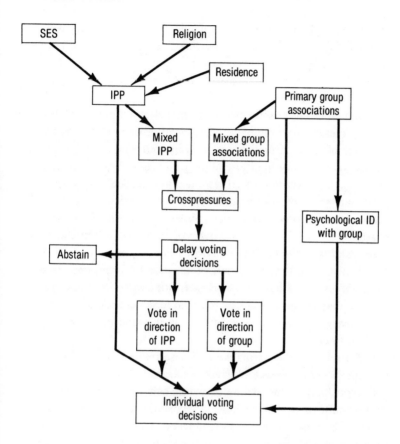

FIGURE 2.2 *The Social and Economic Bases of Voting*

SOURCE: Natchez, Peter B. "The Reasonable Voter." Ph.D. diss., Harvard University, 1969, p. 51.

mented. Similarly, the way screens of selective perception regulated the flow of information to the individual was completely specified. The model of voting identified the causes of political involvement as well as the causes of uninvolvement; it considered the consequences of homogeneous social signals as well as the effects of social conflict, and the effects of primary group loyalties as well as identifications with secondary groups.[25] It examined leaders as well as followers. Lazarsfeld and his associates were nothing if not systematic. In reporting the results of the Elmira study, they identified 209 separate relationships that their work either identified or verified, clearly identifying each in the exposition of the evidence.[26]

Throughout this examination of voting, electoral politics is seen as a manifestation of the underlying social process. However, the influence of social structure was used in both its descriptive and normative senses, without any effort to distinguish the two. It is one thing to observe that social identifications account for a disproportionate share of voting (and nonvoting) decisions. It is quite another matter to conclude that politics is determined by social relationships. The descriptive power of that observation can be quite valid without implying anything about causes. For social determinism to be the appropriate explanation for voting decisions, social forces would have to be self-activating in politics. Alternatively, it may be that the matrix of social forces establishes a range of influences which can have different weight and meaning from election to election.

Unfortunately, the normative and descriptive aspects of social structure were hopelessly blurred in Lazarsfeld's own mind and, not surprisingly, in his writing on voting behavior. This confusion appears quite early, and in a most inopportune way, in *The People's Choice*. The evidence that group influences controlled voting decisions was overwhelming. One way of presenting these data was to form a simple ranking index incorporating the three most powerful social forces. In the case of Erie County, the appropriate social characteristics were socioeconomic status (SES level), religion (Catholic or Protestant), and residence (urban or rural). This index, rough as it was, predicted voting decisions more accurately than any other attribute of voters in Erie County. (See table 2.1.)

It was not important, Lazarsfeld later insisted, which three social characteristics formed the index, or indeed that the index be limited to three characteristics.[27] It was entirely an empirical proposition. In other communities different factors might be relevant. In this sense, Lazarsfeld was using the explanatory power of social

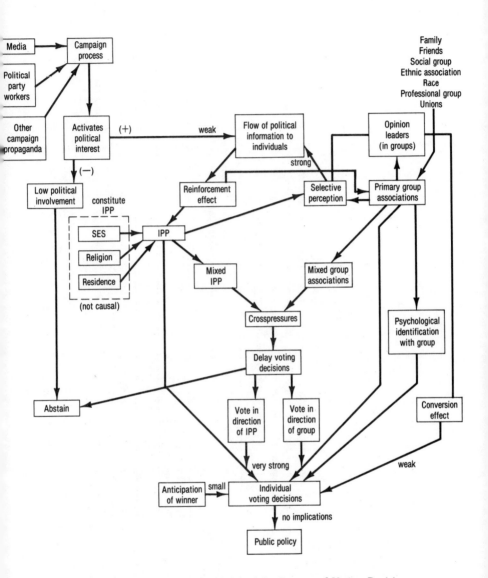

FIGURE 2.3 *The Lazarsfeld Model of the Sources of Voting Decisions*

SOURCE: Natchez, Peter B. "The Reasonable Voter." Ph.D. diss., Harvard University, 1969, p. 61.

TABLE 2.1

Index of Political Predisposition

High SES level, affiliation with the Protestant religion, and rural residence predispose a voter for the Republican party; the opposite of these factors make for Democratic predisposition. Summarized in an index of political predisposition (IPP), their effect is illustrated by the high correlation with vote intention.

Voted	Strongly Republican 1	Moderately Republican 2	Slightly Republican 3	Slightly Democratic 4	Moderately Democratic 5	Strongly Democratic 6,7
Republican	74%	73%	39%	44%	30%	17%
Democratic	26%	27%	61%	56%	70%	83%
N	(148)	(239)	(467)	(319)	(283)	(144)

SOURCE: Paul F. Lazarsfeld, Bernard Berelson, and Hazel Gaudet, *The People's Choice: How the Voter Makes Up His Mind in a Presidential Campaign*, 2d ed. (New York: Columbia University Press, 1948), 26. Copyright © Columbia University Press, 1948. Reprinted by permission. These data have been reorganized in tabular form.

characteristics in a descriptive sense. That different factors might come into play leaves open the question of causality. Why some social factors are relevant and not others becomes an intriguing problem rather than an exercise in dialectics. However, Lazarsfeld, Berelson, and Gaudet stated the relationship of the index of political predisposition (IPP) to voting in the most unfavorable way possible.

> There is a familiar adage in American folklore to the effect that a person is only what he thinks he is, an adage which reflects the typically American notion of unlimited opportunity, the tendency toward self-betterment, etc. Now we find that the reverse of the adage is true: a person thinks, politically, as he is, socially. Social characteristics determine political preference.[28]

This last sentence could not possibly have been more poorly phrased. It seemed designed to bridle students of American politics, as in fact it did. Rather than debate forming around the broader themes that Lazarsfeld and his colleagues had presented, the more narrow question of social determinism quickly became the center of controversy. However, the confusion between the normative and descriptive dimensions of social determinism was quite apparent in Lazarsfeld's own thinking about politics.

Paul Lazarsfeld's personal and intellectual roots were in Austria —in the tradition of empirical social psychology that he studied as a graduate student and in the political turmoil that swept through Austria following the First World War.[29] Through the ill-fated years of the Austrian Republic, Lazarsfeld considered himself a democratic socialist and thought of politics in terms of groups struggling for power, in terms of social conflict.[30] Politics was a representation of social and cultural divisions in which group cleavages were clear, deep, abiding, and highly articulate. Everyone knew who was on which side. Each group was highly mobilized. The Socialist party in Austria, Lazarsfeld recalled, repeatedly captured more than 40 percent of the vote. A slight increase in this percentage would have given the Socialists an opportunity to form a government. Politically the problem was how to mobilize their supporters more effectively, rather than how to shift the political identifications that people already possessed. Given the context of Austrian politics, there were simply very few "floating voters."

Amid the debris of his original research design for the Erie County study, Lazarsfeld began combining the data in search of those factors that seemed to explain individual voting behavior. Upon finding that votes were most associated with "social characteristics," it seemed to him that, contrary to the conventional wisdom, American politics did not differ significantly from the politics he had studied and experienced as a student in Vienna. The normative implications of social determinism in *The People's Choice* were altogether intentional, then.

Regarding those implications, students of American politics, for a variety of unrelated motivations, were spoiling for a fight. For them, social determinism represented an easy mark. A great deal of additional argumentation could be poured out while laying social determinism to rest. But in restricting criticisms of the first voting studies to this level, two important themes were lost.

First, the inference that voting decisions were related to election outcomes except in a most mechanical fashion went largely unnoticed. Electoral politics derives its meaning and significance insofar as it is a contest for power. Winning and losing are not trivial matters or isolated events in the personal careers of the candidates. Election outcomes must have important consequences in terms of governmental power if they are to have value at all. Yet the voting studies conducted under Lazarsfeld's direction failed to discern any meaning in this regard. Individual voting decisions were made, but the very complete explanation of these votes that Lazarsfeld and his associates developed rendered the outcome of the election meaningless.

Similarly, voting decisions, in Lazarsfeld's model, were unrelated to public policy. The election carried with it no implications for government, just as the policies of the incumbent administration had very little bearing on the formulation of voting decisions. There was only the steady push and pull of social characteristics.

The distinctiveness of the electoral process as a method of government had been lost—or, more accurately, the linkages between
electoral politics and public policy had yet to be discovered.

By and large, Paul Lazarsfeld and Bernard Berelson were insensitive to these questions. Nothing in their training or in their previous work had prepared them for research on these concerns. To
them, electoral politics seemed obvious and rudimentary. The unknown domain lay in the world of voting decisions, in how individual voters actually thought and behaved. This was, at bottom, an
empirical problem. That the charting of voters and voting decisions
depends crucially on the questions being asked never entered into
the first voting studies, either in the design of the research or in the
analysis of the data.

Thus the two organizing concerns about the electoral process—
how voters combine in order to produce election outcomes and
what implication the outcome of the election has for public policy
—were never asked. The studies' principal authors were unaware
that these were the essential questions. It was clear to Lazarsfeld
and Berelson, however, that the findings that emerged from their
surveys were novel and unexpected. The appropriate perspective
from which to assess the meaning of these results was theoretical,
they believed. Nothing less than a complete reformulation of the
place of the voter in democratic theory was required.

Adventures in Democratic Theory

There was not the slightest doubt in the minds of Berelson and
Lazarsfeld that the results from the first voting studies had under-
mined the foundations of "classical democratic theory." Evidence
had confronted theory, and theory had been found wanting. Striking a tone that borders on condescending, these authors wrote of
the political theorists who do not engage directly in politics:

They might explore the relevance, the implications, and the meaning of such empirical facts as are contained in this and similar studies. Political theory written with reference to practice has the advantage that its categories are the categories in which political life really occurs.[31]

The content of what was intended by the category "classical democratic theory" was by no means clear. Nor was it obvious which classical writers they had in mind. What is certain is the standard of evaluation against which voters were being measured. The electoral components of classical democratic theory, in Berelson's and Lazarsfeld's hands, boiled down to the requirements of high levels of citizen participation and political activism, a keen interest in politics along with concomitant discussions and debates among all segments of the community, a large store of political information and a variety of articulate positions on various and important issues, and, most of all, voting decisions made on the basis of rational calculation.[32] This is the image of citizens as active, participant, and rational.

These strands of democratic thought were quite current during the 1940s and the early 1950s. They represented a popular understanding of the meaning of democratic government—the sort of well-meaning, good-citizen, textbookish approach that characterizes groups that set out to reform the system in the public interest. It is the music of reformers and citizen activists.

This is not to argue that there is no foundation in political thought for these ideas. In the history of ideas, they originate first with the utilitarians and later, in a more familiar form, with the American Progressives. These strands of thought have enjoyed an influence far beyond their value in democratic theory, Progressives in particular holding an enduring attraction for American scholars.

But this is history and culture, not democratic theory.[33] Both utilitarianism and progressivism can be viewed as unsuccessful attempts to integrate voting and elections into democratic theory. What is of interest is less the sources of the failure of each of these strands of theory, than that they should be mistaken for the heart of classical democratic theory. This was an error of stunning proportion. It indicates first that neither Lazarsfeld nor Berelson—nor any of their associates—was at all familiar with the development of constitutional thought, that in the realm of political theory they were groping for a standard of comparison, and that they lacked any familiarity with the development of the democratic idea. In choosing the standards that they did, they were relying less on political theory than on intellectual stereotypes—adulterated ideas that were no less ingenuous because they held wide currency among academics. To say that Lazarsfeld and Berelson lacked a feel for political theory is to put the matter very gently.

The image of democratic theory maintained by the voting studies did irreparable damage at both the theoretic and empiric levels. Actually, voting and elections remain intriguing and unresolved problems at the theoretical level. Constitutionalism developed in explicit opposition to the electoral process as a primary method for conferring power.[34] Where the machinery of voting and elections was used, as for example in the Constitution of the United States, it was always in a very limited capacity wherein great care was taken to limit the popular aspects of government.

The utilitarians and American Progressives aside, most constitutional theorists have been pessimistic about the ability of most people to reason to the public good; they have thought most people stupid and uninformed, and they have judged the mass public deficient in character and lacking in moral fiber. In short, the expectations of "classical" democratic theory come painfully close to the report on the mass public that was contained in the first voting studies. From an empirical perspective it would have been a challenging problem indeed to discover why electoral systems do not fold altogether.

Lazarsfeld and Berelson were unaware that these problems existed. Rather they set about revising classical democratic theory as they understood it. The heart of their effort in reconstruction is the argument that the shortcomings of voters were the characteristics of *individuals* only and that the electorate as a whole contains a *distribution of characteristics* that compensates for the inadequacies of individual voters.

That is the paradox. *Individual* voters today seem unable to satisfy the requirements of a democratic system of government outlined by political theorists. But the *system of democracy* does meet certain requirements for a going political organization. The individual members may not meet all the standards, but the whole nevertheless survives and grows. This suggests that where the classic [sic] theory is defective is in its concentration on the *individual citizen*. What are undervalued are certain collective properties that reside in the electorate as a whole and in the political and social system in which it functions.

The political philosophy we have inherited, then, has given more consideration to the virtues of the typical citizen of the democracy than to the working of the *system* as a whole. Moreover, when it dealt with the system, it mainly considered the single constitutive institutions of the system, not those general features necessary if the institutions are to work as required.[35]

Thus where theory requires rational calculation in voting decisions but where the evidence indicates people are voting the unperceived influence of various social characteristics, the collective nature of the electoral process remedies the problem, for in the aggregate, groups express the political needs and aspirations of the past and the present. Thus the "total information and knowledge possessed in a group's past and present generations can be made available for the group's choice," and in this way become embodied in each vote.[36]

In this way, the strength of the electoral process compensates for the weaknesses of the individuals within it. The characteristics of the electoral process itself ensure the stability of democratic outcomes. If politics is the expression of social groups, it is also true that the social groups represented in these voting studies were diverse in composition and disparate in their political interests. Thus diversity and balance are built into the system, diversity maintained ironically by the pressure of homogeneous social pressures.

The distribution of specific attitudes and behaviors in the electorate as a whole stabilizes and blends these diverse and contradictory elements into a coherent whole. Berelson, Lazarsfeld, and McPhee note that political traditions, particularly the "obvious agreements on the 'rules of the game,'" have become norms of the political system, norms that individuals and groups assimilate into their own value structure as the basis for political competition.[37] They concluded with:

> [It] seems to us that modern political theory of democracy stands in need of revision and not replacement by empirical sociology. The classical political philosophers were right in the direction of their assessment of the virtues of the citizen. But they demanded those virtues in too extreme or doctrinal a form. The voter does have some principles, he does have information and rationality, he does have interest—but he does not have them in the extreme, elaborate, comprehensive, or detailed form in which they were uniformly recommended by political philosophers. . . . Happily for the system, voters distribute themselves along a continuum:

SOCIABLE MAN	POLITICAL MAN	IDEOLOGICAL MAN
(Indifferent to public affairs, non-partisan, flexible . . .)		(Absorbed in public affairs, highly partisan, rigid . . .)

> And it turns out that this distribution itself, with its internal checks and balances, can perform the functions and incorporate the same values ascribed by some theorists to each individual in the system as well as to the constitutive political institutions![38]

This is not an example of crisp theoretical insight where data and theory have brought new meaning to old problems. The entire effort would be well worth forgetting were it not for the fact that subsequent voting studies, and the criticism that developed around them, compounded the errors that originated here. Matters would get worse, as a matter of fact. As to the central premise by which the first voting studies attempted to resolve questions of theory— the idea that the distribution of attitudes and behaviors in the electorate as a whole could compensate for the shortcomings of individual voters—it would demonstrate remarkable resiliency.

The idea appears repeatedly as other analysts struggle with the implications of different surveys, each analyst apparently formulating this explanation independently of previous work. By the time it reached *The Civic Culture*, the idea had acquired more sophistication and meaning, as we shall see. Still, as theory the concept is dreadfully incomplete no matter how clever the variations of the theme.[39]

Lower Criticism

That the voting studies possessed very little talent in the realm of political theory is not hard to see. It is more difficult to understand why theorizing that was so patently inadequate was permitted to stand. The critical process, after all, is an essential part of intellectual life, even if it has its painful and petty aspects. No idea, no matter how original or imaginative, ever arrives fully developed and completely specified. Not even Einstein's theorems emerged in a single breath; and, by comparison, democratic theory comprises a universe that poses much more irregular and intractable problems. If the authors of the voting studies lacked familiarity with the development of constitutional thought, with the emergence of individualism and the "liberal democratic tradition," and with the progression of ideas in modern political thought, why were students of political thought not quick to straighten them out?

But higher criticism was not forthcoming. An exposition of ideas never occurred, in part because political theorists themselves were divided on the current status of modern democratic theory, and in part because they found the quantitative revolution very threatening. Political theorists are not neutral referees in the history of ideas, of course. The results of the voting studies proved difficult for one segment of that community because it desired to extend the participatory bases of politics as a philosophical matter. Constitutional theory was restrictive and prejudicial in its view of the mass public and in its organization of political power. In these terms the central problem in contemporary democratic theory was a more equitable distribution of power, a more participatory democracy.[40]

One criticism of the voting studies, then, was that they choose a "conservative" set of political values, that they were overly sympathetic to the established political system and all the inequities it contained, and that they gave far too much significance to political stability. All these judgments were essentially correct, it should be noted, and they are hardly irrelevant considerations. But the nub of the problem was in the approach that the voting studies took to democratic theory in the first place. Here these theorists said nothing. There was simply no percentage for them in an exposition of the limitations of constitutionalism, for it was precisely this strand of democratic thought that these theorists were attempting to remedy. Their goal was to empower the citizen and to broaden participation. Although a formal discussion of constitutional theory was never consciously avoided, the opportunity for such a review passed without a word being spoken.[41]

Other political theorists were so furious at the violence that the voting studies did to democratic theory in general, and to their own appreciation of political thought in particular, that they spit out invective without clarifying the source of their criticism. Fumed Leo Strauss,

> The very complex pros and cons of liberal democracy have thus become entirely obliterated by the poorest formalism. The crisis of liberal democracy has become concealed by a ritual which calls itself methodology or logic. The almost willfull blindness to the crisis of liberal democracy is part of that crisis.[42]

Walter Berns was more specific in his remarks, but no less hostile:

> There is a shocking contrast between the importance, and today, the urgency of political problems and the modern social scientists' interest in voting behavior. What in these studies could possibly justify the time, energy, and enormous sums of money consumed in their making? Even

assuming their findings to be accurate, of what political interest are they? Are we told that because of these studies we now have knowledge of the gap between older democratic theory and practice? As we have seen, *Voting* does not present an adequate description of practice—it does not demonstrate, for example, that there was an absence of "true discussion." But assuming that we do have some knowledge of the gap between theory and practice that was formerly hidden, what follows from this discovery? Do we, following Berelson, Lazarsfeld, and McPhee, revise our goals downward by ignoring requirements of a safe and sound political order? Or are we not still required to try to discover the goals and requirements of political life and then to recommend those measures that can be said reasonably to conduce these goals and fulfill these requirements?[43]

Whether the substance of these remarks is correct or incorrect is quite irrelevant. The tone is not one of intelligent criticism but of ruthless conflict. Unfortunately, matters did not improve with the passage of time. The quality of discussion as it appeared in the various publications of the profession was almost uniformly poor. The most perceptive and penetrating observations on the questionable usage of democratic theory by the voting studies appear in a letter to Bernard Berelson from V. O. Key, Jr., reviewing "Democratic Theory and Public Opinion" while it was still in manuscript form. "Your treatment of political theorists, in some ways at least, seems to me to miss the mark," Key wrote with characteristic understatement.

> . . . Most of your references are to those theorists who have vented some normative observations about how the citizen ought to act. Now, these fellows don't receive much attention among political theorists generally, and I suspect that most political scientists would regard them as of lesser importance for your purposes than others. Other political scientists would point out that much of the theory you mention had not been uttered with any serious belief, that such behaviors were demonstrably essential for certain ends or even necessarily produced for such ends. This sort of theory was often used to batter down privileged orders and at times in utopian construction which serves a propagandistic purpose.[44]

But Key was unwilling to utter these criticisms publicly. This is symptomatic, in a way, of the relationship that developed between political theory and the voting studies. The avenues of criticism were there, and the voting studies, lacking an instinct for theory, were much in need of criticism, but somehow the two never met in public.

There was another reason why political theorists and the voting studies have never enjoyed a productive relationship. This has to do more broadly with the quantitative revolution and the position of political theory as a field of specialization at the time that quantitative methods entered the discipline. When quantitative methods were entering political science—an entrance made with a flourish, full of confidence, the wave of the future—political theory was experiencing a period of self-doubt and uncertainty.

Wasn't political theory old stuff, a tired progression of the same history of ideas? Of course, students of politics should have some knowledge of this tradition, just as they ought to know some modern political history and something of comparative government. But suddenly political theory did not seem alive; it was a specialization that did not seem to relate to the present, much less to be the wave of the future. "The query put with suspicious frequency in English speaking countries," lamented Isaiah Berlin, "questions the very credentials of the subject: It suggests that political philosophy, whatever it may have been in the past, is dead or dying."[45]

Berlin spoke the thoughts, it seemed, of many. The other fields in political science were enjoying a period of rapid expansion. There was new money and a new level of concern. But political theory did not seem to be going anywhere. To observe in retrospect that political theorists need not have worried so, that soon their area would sparkle with new interpretations and ideas, was quite beside the point. Equally it could be said that political theorists were missing a splendid opportunity by failing to use the methodology of survey research for their own purposes—the opportunity to actually estimate the public's philosophy and to evaluate it by an appropriate normative standard. Such a judgment too enjoys the benefit of retrospective analysis.

What seemed pressing at the time was the sense of increasing isolation. This expressed itself in very personal terms. Political theorists began to think of jobs and promotion, departmental organization and requirements for graduate study. Perhaps the most curious aspect of the struggle between political theory and quantitative methods was its unintellectual nature. Differences were much less frequently expressed in journals and papers than they were in private conversations and department meetings. The nature of this debate had its own debilitating consequences, as we shall see. But, as we shall also see, political theory grew in a strange way because of this controversy; a flurry of new work appeared, particularly in the middle sixties, that was a most curious blend of insight and isolation.

Nothing adheres so steadfastly as mistaken assumptions, it would seem. The technology of survey research brought to the study of democratic politics the promise of both badly needed technical competence and a new level of sophisticiation. At long last the inner workings of democratic politics could be visualized. It seemed very much like the technological equivalent of the introduction of X rays into medicine. The voting studies, however, produced results that were much more ambiguous.

The components of voting, and political participation generally, were examined in much greater detail and with much more exactitude than had been heretofore possible. A raft of fresh information quickly became available—books, articles, papers appeared by the score, each reporting new data and previously unspecified relationships. But the stream of original information opened up by the voting studies confused much more than it clarified. The voting studies made a botch of the central themes of democratic theory, and, as luck would have it, political theorists found their positions such that they were unable to help out. Rather than developing together in order to produce some fascinating research or joining in a dispute notable for its rigor and insight, those who worked the voting studies and students of political theory settled down to a protracted cold war.

Ironically, American politics was a casualty of the voting studies too. Although the studies made steady advances in the amount of individual political behavior that could be explained, the political significance of voting became less certain. The voting studies seemed to bring to the fore all the weaknesses inherent in the study of American politics, but seemed unable to draw upon any of its strengths. Misbegotten assumptions had begun to congeal. Layer upon layer of empirical work began building up, making it ever more difficult to locate those flawed foundations. Very soon the analysis of American voting behavior seemed unrelated to American politics.

CHAPTER 3

Problems in
American Politics

To those inclined to study it, American politics is a rich and enchanting field. The constitutional design of government in the United States proceeds from a more consciously elaborate theory than is true for most national governments. Catching the last breath of the Enlightenment, American government accentuates the major themes of the period, flaws and virtues alike. In a sense, the United States created political realities about which Europe could only dream.[1]

The American landscape heightened these feelings of uniqueness. Here freedom was not an idle hope, but a vast and unsettled wilderness. Power did not have to be amassed in order to attack the feudal order, class did not have to battle class. "This shattering of the time categories of Europe, this Hegelian-like revolution in historic perspective, goes far to explain one of the enduring secrets of the American character: a capacity to combine rock-ribbed traditionalism with high inventiveness, ancestor worship with ardent optimism."[2]

The land did seem to be sculpting the people, the land being ours before we were the land's.[3] If the westward expansion was a romance, the industrialization of the United States seemed like a morality play. Raw entrepreneurial skill and the workings of unbridled scoundrels somehow created a national market. The city replaced the country as the creative center of American life, as wave after wave of immigrants labored in their passionate and single-minded struggles to obtain their share of the American dream. American history seems irregular when set beside the categories of the European experience.

Even the disorder and confusion in the organization of American politics seem special. The muted conflicts and the incoherent party coalitions have been successful in a way that seems to defy explanation. Students of American politics have hungered for general theory and broad understanding if only to organize the profusion of themes and as a matter of self-explanation. Yet at the same time they cling to the feeling that the United States is unique, to the theory of American exceptionalism.

Whether in Louis Hartz's emphasis on the political theory, or Daniel Boorstin's on social history, or David Potter's insistence on affluence, or Seymour Martin Lipset's argument about value patterns, great care has been taken to differentiate American politics from the politics of all other nations, particularly from the political patterns found in Europe.[4] For Paul Lazarsfeld and his associates to conclude that voting decisions were socially determined was bound to incite students of American politics. Stunned by and angry with the results from the first voting studies, these scholars invested a disproportionate share of concern in invalidating those findings.

The Index of Political Predisposition Disproved

Warned V. O. Key, Jr., and Frank Munger:

> The style set in the Erie County study of voting threatens to take the politics out of the study of electoral behavior. The theoretical heart of *The*

People's Choice rests in the contention that "social characteristics determine political preference" . . . Yet almost inevitably from this basic view, which is usually not put so explicitly, there develops a school of analysis that tends to divert attention from critical elements of electoral decisions.[5]

The point that Key and Munger were making went far beyond the narrow question of the index of political predisposition's technical validity. They were arguing that variation in electoral politics occurred much more rapidly than changes in individuals' social characteristics. Therefore, the study of voting behavior had to be extended so that it included "an analysis of the factors that bring particular social characteristics to the level of political consciousness."[6]

In a curious way, this was closer to Lazarsfeld's original intentions, wherein social characteristics were a variable matter. What Lazarsfeld lacked was a feel for the political, an appreciation that in different elections the same array of social characteristics could be drawn into voting decisions in different combinations to produce altogether different choices. Key and Munger's effort was not so much an attempt to deny the influence of social forces as to refocus their analysis in political terms.

Most analysts, however, took the index of political predisposition at face value. In undoubtedly the most important effort at disconformation, Morris Janowitz and Warren E. Miller were able to show, using data collected by the Survey Research Center (SRC), that the index had virtually no explanatory power when the national electorate was considered.[7] By comparison to the relationship between the IPP and voting in Erie County, the relationship at the national level seemed insignificant. (Compare table 3.1 with table 2.1)

This was no small finding. Because it was based on data gathered in a national sample, the relationship between voting and social characteristics in *The People's Choice* appeared to be an isolated "case study" that was lacking in generality. Irreparable harm was done to Lazarsfeld's position in this regard. Not only was a principal theme of his work damaged, but the ability of the Bureau of

TABLE 3.1

*The Index of Political Predisposition in the 1948
Election for the Nation as a Whole*

IPP Scores:	1&2	3	4	5	6&7	Total (%)
Democratic	15	32	23	42	47	31
Republican	50	28	21	22	15	28

SOURCE: Morris Janowitz and Warren E. Miller, "The Index of Political Predisposition in the 1948 Election," *Journal of Politics* 14 (November 1952): 799. This table is percentaged down; it has been altered to omit two rows, "other" and "non-voters." Reprinted with permission.

Applied Social Research to compete for funds also suffered. The community-oriented surveys might be fine for most sociological purposes, but in political matters national samples were superior. Having experience in taking national surveys, the Survey Research Center's stock rose perceptibly with the publication of these results.

But the 1948 election study was surely the least reliable survey conducted by the Survey Research Center. Surveying only 662 people, the study was not organized with great care or rigor.[8] It is quite likely that the results reported by Janowitz and Miller are inaccurate. Using data from the 1952 SRC election study, the relationship between individual voting decisions and the IPP compares very favorably with the data presented in the Erie County study.[9] In turn, these data report a much stronger relationship at the national level in 1952 than did the analysis of the 1948 data. (See table 3.2.) These differences at the national level are themselves reason for discounting the 1948 study. Truman and Dewey battled for votes along the established lines of social cleavage much more so than Eisenhower and Stevenson did four years later.

Often the significance of a relationship is less a matter of statistics than it is a matter of judgment. The data presented in table 3.2 indicate a moderate degree of association between voting and the index of political predisposition. The IPP is certainly not

TABLE 3.2

The Index of Political Predisposition in 1952

IPP Score	1952 Voting Behavior		Total N
	Eisenhower	Stevenson	
Strongly Republican 1,2	72.1	27.9	(290)
Moderately Republican 3	63.6	36.4	(236)
Moderately Democratic 4,5	55.0	45.0	(364)
Strongly Democratic 6,7	30.8	69.2	(133)

NOTE: Morris Janowitz and Dwaine Marvick, *Competitive Pressure and Democratic Consent* (Ann Arbor: University of Michigan Institute of Public Administration, 1956), 91. Copyright © The University of Michigan, 1956.

determinant, but neither is its influence negligible. The judgments that students of American politics were wont to make emphasized the variance left unexplained. In this case, Janowitz and Marvick wrote that the index had "some predictive power. For voters not under cross pressures to any marked degree, the index accounts for voting preference correctly in seven out of every ten cases."[10]

There are those who would say that this is not all that bad. But attention was focused on the middle ranges of the index, where its explanatory power was weakest. Thus M. Brewster Smith, Jerome S. Bruner, and Robert W. White argued that the index was unsatisfactory on purely methodological grounds. Lazarsfeld, in their view, had created a simple "ranking matrix" that in essence placed pure types (urban, lower class, Catholic, upper class, rural, Protestant) at the extreme ends of the index while pushing people with mixed social characteristics into the middle of the scale. This made the IPP appear more powerful than it in fact was, for these middle categories contained fully half of the people in the sample. Yet this was where the index had very little predictive capacity.[11] This was precisely what Lazarsfeld had set out to do, of course. But somehow the index was viewed as badly flawed from a methodological perspective as well.

The central findings of the Erie and Elmira studies were simply not accepted then. While there was good reason to dispute the notion of social determinism, there was less justification for ignoring the manifest influences of social characteristics on political behavior. It would take awhile for the validity of this relationship to sink in, much less to be understood.

Primary Group Influences on Voting Decisions

Perhaps the clearest formulation of the influence social characteristics have on political behavior emerged from a survey conducted by Herbert McClosky and Harold Dahlgren on the Twin City area of Minnesota.[12] The results from that study are particularly interesting because, while the research was designed specifically to examine the influence of social groups upon voting, it did not contain the normative assumptions of Lazarsfeld and his associates or those of the Survey Research Center. Social characteristics were defined in a purely descriptive way as primary group influences.[13] The family, McClosky and Dahlgren's data strongly suggested, served to transmit political traditions and preferences. People learned to orient themselves in the world of politics through the socialization process, just as they acquired other social skills and dispositions. "The family is a key reference group which transmits, indoctrinates, and sustains the political loyalties of its members," concluded McClosky and Dahlgren bluntly.[14]

Family was not the only influence on an individual's political behavior, however; as the "social distance" between children and their parents increased, people were likely to alter their political orientations to accord with a new social reality. Social distance was defined in terms that closely paralleled the components of the index of political predisposition. But the authors used this measure in a much more clever way, computing one score as a measure of "life style," but, more important, computing another based on the respondents' accounts of their current social characteristics and earlier when they were "in their teens." McClosky and Dahlgren were able to establish "social mobility"—changes in individual social characteristics altered political preferences independently of family influences.[15] And in the same way, spouses and peer groups influenced voting choices, irrespective of the other social factors at play.

All in all, the stability of individual political preferences was a function of the degree to which family orientations were reinforced by the other social attributes of people's lives. (See table 3.3.) The cumulative effect of primary group influences on voting behavior in these data is unmistakable. Furthermore, people preferred situations where the group norms were mutually reinforcing.[16] And where political norms are reinforced by a variety of primary groups, political choices tend to be very stable indeed. Even when people have altered family political traditions, the influence of other reinforcing primary group ties is considerable. Or to look at these data the other way about, discordant family and group influences tend to produce unstable voting patterns.

Party identification was transmitted by families also. But just one step removed from the family's influence in this regard was the influence of social groups. Partisanship does not usually exist in isolation. Like other political attributes, it tends to be formed in a social environment that is mutually reinforcing. Goldberg sums up his study of family influences on party identification: "[T]he present study strongly suggests that there is a rational component to party identification rooted in group norms. At least in retrospect the notion is an obvious one."[17]

Soon it was apparent that a whole range of political attitudes and behaviors was controlled by the socialization process—by family, school, peer group, and workplace.[18] If these relationships seemed obvious in the end, their political significance continues to be uncertain. Political orientation is rarely a matter of individual decision. Most people do not make conscious choices in this regard; rather they inherit a variety of attitudes, behaviors, and predisposi-

TABLE 3.3

*The Combined Effect of Four Primary
Group Influences (Family Reinforcement,
Social Distance, Spouse, and Peer Groups)
on Voter Stability*

Respondents are:	Number of Favorable (+) Reinforcements* (%'s Down)			
	1+	*2+'s*	*3+'s*	*4+'s*
Stable Voters	17.6	35.7	58.1	70.5
Moderate Voters	17.6	32.1	27.9	23.5
Unstable Voters	64.7	32.1	13.9	5.9
Sample Size	17	28	43	17

*Favorable or (+) = association with a primary group whose party loyalties are congruent with those of the respondent.
SOURCE: Herbert McClosky and Harold E. Dahlgren, "Primary Group Influence on Party Loyalty," *American Political Science Review* 53 (September 1959): 773. Reprinted by permission.

tions. But the question V. O. Key and Frank Munger raised remains unanswered. How are social characteristics translated into political decisions? What is their political relevance for the individual and for the political system as a whole?

The Political Consequences of Social Stratification— The (Somewhat) Special Case of the United States

The social process forms the matrix of a person's political life by molding a variety of individual perceptions and behaviors. The precise nature of the transmission processes and their relative impact on the individual are still a matter of controversy and research, but in its broad outlines the main features of individual political socialization have been established.[19] Family, school, peer group, and workplace are the principle sources of influence. Each of these sources of socialization exerts an independent influence on the individual, but, for most people, various political socialization processes tend to be mutually reinforcing and to have a cumulative impact.

An extremely wide range of political perceptions, values, attitudes, and behaviors are controlled by the socialization process. The most important characteristics of politics are usually not so much matters of individual choice and conscious decisions as they are matters of social training. Furthermore, this seems to be the case everywhere. Political socialization is a process that is cross-national and cross-cultural in its implications. To be sure, the principle agents in the socialization process vary, but the *functions* that they serve are the same. (The notion of structural functionalism originated from the earlier findings of anthropologists. The various practices they observed varied widely from place to place, but the functions that these widely diverse structures performed were remarkably similar.)[20]

It is the inherited nature of political values and behaviors that is of most significance, of course. For, as Lazarsfeld and his associates believed, in the rhetoric of self-conscious decision making, political participation is most often thought of in terms of individual choice. But the weight of evidence on this matter is overwhelming. To think of most aspects of political participation as matters of individual choice is to misunderstand their function.

The socialization process itself is not neutral in its political consequences. It transmits into politics the established system of social stratification and the prevailing political culture. This process of social transference takes place at three distinct levels. The influence of primary groups is the most important, as we have seen. Herein is found the everyday and highly personalized influences that Lazarsfeld found originally, influences that McClosky and Dahlgren subsequently elaborated and verified.

Primary groups are formed out of an individual's immediate social milieu, an attribute that gives them immense political power.

But looked at in the aggregate, they are a representation of the established system of social stratification. Primary groups constitute the operational units of the social process. It is in the process of primary group socialization that most political objects are given their characteristic shape and meaning. This is particularly true for political values and fundamental beliefs. But it is also here that individuals learn about the political system and adopt an orientation toward it.[21] Similarly, individuals acquire characteristic modes of participating in politics. The range of their political activities is likely to have been established in their primary group, as is their individual propensity to vote. Certainly partisan ties are formed within this context.[22] It is also these primary groups that control the flow of communication and establish the meaning of current political events. In short, primary groups act to weave screens of selective perception for individuals and to give people characteristic ways of participating, so that by the time people are old enough to participate, most questions of political substance and style have already been determined. The political influence of primary group associations appears to be a very general phenomenon, describing patterns of political socialization in the United States just as much as it does in other nations and in other cultures.

At another level there is the influence of secondary groups—formal groups, group memberships, and group loyalties. The political meaning of group influence is, again, quite regular. The mere existence of group divisions translates into political differences, irrespective of whether or not people belong to any organized manifestation of that group or feel any group identification. This has been most clearly documented with religious differences,[23] but it is no less apparent with ethnicity.[24] Obviously the degree to which people feel they are a member of a group—the intensity of their group loyalty—increases the behavioral significance of that group.[25]

However, the number and political significance of group associations does vary from nation to nation. Since de Tocqueville, people have remarked on the propensity of Americans to organize and join groups. This characteristic has been verified by the electoral studies, although not quite in the way that had been expected. It turns out that people in the United States are much less likely than Europeans to belong to political organizations. Conversely, Americans are much more likely to belong to religious, civic, and fraternal groups than are people in other nations.[26] The effect of group memberships is to increase political activity, and the effect is strong indeed. "[I]t would be difficult to find another social characteristic that would have as strong an association with political participation after one had corrected for such characteristics as social status, race, sex, and age," concluded Sidney Verba and Norman Nie[27] after an examination of this relationship notable for its rigor and precision.

Two consequences of secondary group memberships are notable. In the first place, such group activities act to align individual attitudes and perceptions more closely with group norms. Behavioral psychologists are fond of showing that individuals, in fact, will alter their perceptions of reality to conform with those of the group.[28] Secondary groups act to reinforce the system of social stratification. In the second place, secondary group memberships act to reinforce inequities in political participation generated by the system of social stratification. Group memberships act to increase participation, as we have just seen. But the propensity to join groups is extremely class biased. Secondary groups not only act to reinforce the system of social stratification, then, they also act to increase the disparities between strata.

At the third and most distant level of analysis, there is the question of how closely inequalities in the system of social stratification are represented in politics. For the influence of the existing web of social relationships on individual political behavior can no longer be doubted. The question is not whether social stratification controls the substance and style of political participation but what difference do these relationships make. The question is one of equity and fairness. Or more bluntly, is participation in electoral politics systematically biased by social class?

The question challenges the fundamental validity of the electoral process, for if political participation is a systematically class-biased process, then the electoral process amounts to a delusion, a means of promoting privilege and protecting inequities of wealth and status. Conversely, if participation in the electoral process is intrinsically unbiased, then elections stand as an alternative to the inequities of social stratification, as a process whereby each person can participate in the formulation of the public good. Needless to say, a great deal rides on the answer to this question.

In the United States, the relationship between the propensity of individuals to vote and social class is fairly pronounced. (See figure 3.1.) Furthermore, the class bias apparent in voting behavior in the United Sates is much stronger than that in any other nation for which we have data.[29] This is cold comfort, in a way, for it leads

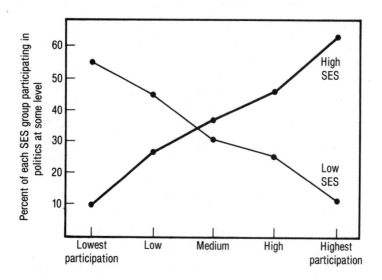

FIGURE 3.1 *Socio-Economic Status and Political Participation*

SOURCE: Data from Figure 20–1 from *Participation in America: Political Democracy and Social Equality,* by Sidney Verba and Norman H. Nie (New York: Harper & Row, 1972), 337. Copyright © 1972 by Sidney Verba and Norman H. Nie. Reprinted by permission of Harper & Row, Publishers, Inc. The authors divide their sample into five groups of equal size according to level of participation (base line); socio-economic status (SES) is divided into three groups of equal size: low, middle, and high. Only low and high are presented here.

to the inference that it is not individual participation in electoral politics that is intrinsically biased, but rather that there are factors in American politics that cause this relationship to be unusually strong.

Ironically, the most pressing reason for the disproportionate amount of class bias in American political participation is the relatively muted nature of class issues in American elections. Elections in the United States are relatively free of class or social group conflicts. (See figure 3.2.) The influence of social characteristics on voting decisions in the American electoral process pales in comparison to the politics of every other nation for which data are available. Nor is there some alternative social conflict in American politics to mobilize voters in the absence of class-related issues.[30]

The furor over the influence of social class upon voting decisions that so preoccupied the voting studies was misdirected from the first. While the studies correctly identified the influence of social characteristics, they failed to observe that, in comparison to other nations, the most notable characteristic of the American data is the amount of variance left unexplained, not the amount of voting behavior for which social characteristics could account. If the studies correctly identified the massive influence that social characteristics had on the style and substance of individual political participation, they failed to focus this knowledge on the appropriate dependent variable.

Several other qualities in figures 3.1 and 3.2 should be observed. In neither case is the amount of variance that social class explains very high. While the problem of the class bias of electoral politics has an importance all its own, there remains a great deal of latitude for other explanations. Indeed, with so much unexplained variance, additional explanations are almost required.

More important, the relationships between social class and participation, on the one hand, and voting behavior, on the other, vary considerably from year to year. What causes these variations? This, it will be remembered, was the question that V. O. Key, Jr., and Frank Munger asked in the first place.[31] What brings particular

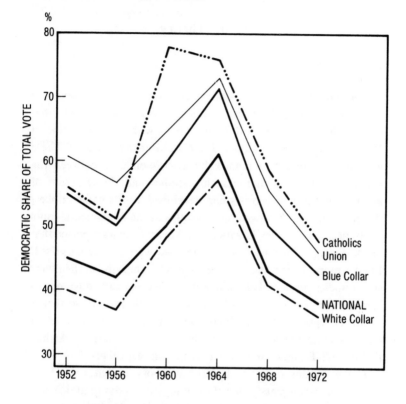

FIGURE 3.2 *Presidential Voting Behavior, 1952–1972:*
Selected Components of Democratic Coalition

NOTE: Peter B. Natchez, *Issues and Voters in the 1972 Election* (Morristown, N.J.: General Learning Press, 1974), 18.

factors to the level of political consciousness in some elections and not in others? The voting studies had a much more difficult time dealing with this question than they did with understanding the influence of social characteristics in general and the process of political socialization in particular. But even after all these years, it is difficult to see why students of American politics had, and continued to have, such a difficult time understanding these relationships.

Group Theory

At the time the first voting studies were appearing, the prevailing philosophy among American political scientists was "group theory," a theory that reached its apotheosis with the publication in 1951 of David Truman's book *The Governmental Process.*[32] There was, on the surface, a remarkable correspondence between the conclusions reached in the voting studies and the structure of analysis that group theorists had developed. As its name implies, the group approach viewed social groups as the fundamental units of politics, so that when Lazarsfeld and his colleagues reported that "people vote in groups," group theorists were hardly surprised. Furthermore, Lazarsfeld and Berelson relied heavily on the diversity of social characteristics along with a widespread adherence to "rules of the game" in remolding "democratic theory" so that it could incorporate their findings. Both these themes are used in almost identical fashion by group theorists, particularly by Arthur F. Bentley, Truman, and Earl Latham, among others.[33]

The group approach, as an effort at theory, operates at a level of depth and complexity that the voting studies did (and do) not. At one level, group theory was a philosophy of human behavior (indeed, it began as an effort to comprehend politics in these terms).[34] It was also a system of values, including the argument that it was not predisposed to any particular system of values. Group theory contained a coherent theory of representation (as well as some less coherent ideas about the structure of government). It developed its own methodology—the case study method. And, finally, it certainly had definite ideas about what was politically relevant and how politics defined in such terms should be studied.[35]

Any discussion of the merits and defects of group theory in these various domains is fully its own specialized concern.[36] However, from my perspective it is necessary to focus attention on one aspect of group theory, even though by doing so I approach this strand of thought selectively. For in addition to all the various levels at which group theory operated, it was also a theory of public opinion and political behavior—the predominating view, for that matter. Arthur Bentley may have thought of his book as "an attempt to fashion a tool." But it was a tool that in the hands of others provided the basis for understanding "political interests and public opinion."[37]

In a sense, group theory was the first systematic effort by political scientists to incorporate the consequences of voting and elections into constitutional politics. The trouble with the formal/legal approach (which until group theory had served as the basis of understanding in American politics) was that it did not account for the influence of public opinion on government, nor was it able to comprehend the competition among pressure groups for control of public policy. The struggle between pressure groups was particularly important, for it often gave both opinion in the mass public and the organization of public policy its distinctive characteristics. In this sense gains and losses in the mass public reflected the relative strengths and weaknesses of groups as they approached the legislative and administrative machinery of government.[38] Of course, pressure groups and public opinion were not the only concerns of group theory—legislative behavior and party organization received a great deal of attention also—but they certainly were there. More important, prior to group theorists' efforts to develop these themes, they had been largely unexplored.

Group theory's understanding of the mass public and political behavior is neither terribly elegant nor very complex. Beginning with the anthropological observation that groups form the organizing units of society,[39] groups attempt to expand the etiology of this concept so that it can explain politics and policy in mass society. The problem lay in discovering an expansive definition of the group, one that could work at dramatically different levels of analysis—individual and political, formal and informal.

Bentley did this by defining groups in terms of action, which in turn was conceived of as an expression of individual interest. Originally the chain of assumptions began with the concept that groups represented manifest actions in the world of politics; action presumes individual self-interest; without group politics individuals are bereft of interests; interests require the group as an expressive vehicle.[40]

Interests became an empirical problem. The extent and significance of different interests could be measured and compared. Finally, the study of politics could be systematic. "If we can get our social life stated in terms of activity, and nothing else," Arthur Bentley argued, "we have not indeed succeeded in measuring it, but we have at least reached a foundation upon which a coherent system of measurement can be built up."[41]

In constructing his definition in this fashion, Bentley was attempting to specify groups so that they would have both objective and subjective meaning. While being a valid representation of individual interests, groups also could be observed in the political process. It was a double-entry accounting system. But despite the considerable advantages this definition has in principle, it is implausible from a methodological perspective. How in a complex society does one render the actions of groups? Clearly, in most instances a group in its organizational form will not be acting with the foreknowledge of its membership.

David Truman resolved this theoretical lacuna by shifting the definition of groups away from behavior to group norms, which quickly became synonymous with shared attitudes. This view had the advantage of being distinctly appropriate for the mass public while at the same time it preserved the empirical quality of the definition.

    . . . [I]t was indicated that from interaction in groups arise certain common habits of response, which may be called norms, or shared attitudes. These afford the participants frames of reference for interpreting and evaluating events and behaviors. In this respect all groups are interest groups because they are shared-attitude groups. In some groups at various points in time, however, a second kind of common response emerges in addition to the frames of reference. These are shared attitudes toward what is needed or wanted in a given situation, observable as demands or claims upon other groups in society. The term "interest group" will be reserved . . . for those groups that exhibit both aspects of shared attitudes. . . . The shared attitudes, moreover, constitute interests.[42]

Shared attitudes, then, became the criteria for identifying groups in the mass public. It has become commonplace to object to this definition because it leaves an empty distinction between "groups" and "potential groups." Since attitudes are the basis of group formation, every group has the potential of being infinitely expandable. Suddenly any norm can sweep across the public landscape, capturing the sentiments of one and all.

From a philosophical perspective, this is not the most valuable distinction that has been drawn. From the perspective of group theory, however, the differentiation between groups and potential groups made the position of any group in the political process truly an empirical proposition. Furthermore, it was a definition that emphasized the dynamic elements of politics—the competition between groups, the struggle to enlarge memberships, the strategies to gain influence.

For group theory, public opinion is a battlefield between group interests, each attempting to extend its appeal and to maximize its political influence. Every method of political organization and all the techniques of political propaganda are relevant to the struggle. People and opinion are not easily persuaded; group loyalties and political opinions are established features in the distribution of influence and policy. If change is to occur, it must be in the competitive fires of existing patterns of influence, and, conversely, established interests must struggle against all challengers to maintain their position in the public and their influence in the political process.

Such techniques will maximize the possibility of ensuring perception, but they are by no means infallible. Particularly in dealing with those whose existing attitudes are hostile, the propagandist is likely to find that this message is neither seen nor heard. For example, in their 1940 voting study Lazarsfeld and his associates found that even those who had not decided how to cast their ballots but whose social characteristics indicated a predisposition toward one party or the other exposed themselves predominantly to material consistent with those predispositions. . . . The most obvious way of dealing with pre-existing attitudes, of course, is to alter the message so that it will arouse those appropriate to the aim being pursued.[43]

The promise of group theory was that common patterns of influence could be discovered, that there would emerge a systematic understanding of the various ways in which groups mobilized their resources and generated support, and that the connections between group activity and the governmental process would be clarified. Group theory, in truth, failed in precisely these terms. The case study method failed to produce meaningful generalizations. Rather a seemingly endless stream of cases began to flood the literature, some intriguing, some interesting, but all lacking any indication of cumulative results.

More deeply, some disturbing assumptions were embedded in the heart of the group approach. It was assumed that the competition between groups was unbiased, that every group had access to "the public mind," that hence each had an equal opportunity to maximize both its potential constituency and its influence on the policy-making process. It was here that group theory found the essence of democratic politics—in the great diversity of groups and in the unbiased competition between them. Diversity ensured competition, which itself was of enormous value for democratic politics. It also promoted multiple and overlapping group memberships, which were a further source of stability and compromise. Of course, there had to be a general adherence to "the rules of the game," both among leaders and the mass public, lest the competition between groups get out of hand. But the intrinsic ability of each group to compete was one guarantee that the system as a whole would succeed.[44] Unfortunately, all of these assumptions collapsed before the mounting pile of evidence from the voting studies.

Group Theory and the Voting Studies

The voting studies amassed a great quantity of evidence that indicated that the assumptions group theory made about the nature of the mass public were altogether inappropriate. From the first it was apparent that group memberships were not as extensive as had been presumed. Nor were there a sufficient number of multiple group memberships in the electorate as a whole to provide the diverse sorts of influences that were stressed by group theory. Moreover, where there were multiple memberships, they tended to be mutually reinforcing so that rather than receiving a diversity of appeals, multiple group members tended to receive redundant messages. And, most seriously, the group process mirrored—in fact, accentuated—inequities in the system of social stratification.

It was this last finding that was fatal to group theory. The other findings from the voting studies need not have been as damaging to group theory as they appeared. To be sure, group theorists waxed eloquent on the extent to which groups appeared in the mass public. The clash of groups each vieing for the public's interest provided a very pleasing metaphor. It conjured up the hurly-burly of the American frontier, the race for land and riches. It was a metaphor in which it was easy to lose a sense of proportion.

The data, looked at with expectations that were less grand, were not devastating on this score. There were still an impressive number of group memberships in the electorate as a whole, even quite a large number of multiple memberships. In comparative perspective, the United States did quite well in these terms. The voting studies and group theory might have worked very well in combination were these the only difficulties involved.

But the heart and soul of the group approach was the argument that in the struggle of groups for opinion and for influence everyone benefited, that the governmental process was inherently fair. To find that the group process incorporated established social inequities—that group theory was class biased—was a devastating piece of knowledge. Little wonder, then, that adherents of the group approach would cast about for some alternative to Paul Lazarsfeld and associates' voting studies. As luck would have it, this rebounded to the credit of the Survey Research Center at the University of Michigan.

Of Arguments and Institutions

In retrospect, the Bureau of Applied Social Research compiled an impressive record in the charting of individual voting decisions. If there were errors in theory and in interpretation, it must be said also that this research was truly being done for the first time. No group of scholars could have been expected to get everything right at once. With the passage of years, it is the quality of the effort that shines. Not only have the Erie and Elmira County studies, for all their considerable flaws, stood the test of time, but the secondary work of those associated with the Bureau is equally, if not more, impressive. Seymour Martin Lipset's *Political Man*, Herbert Hyman's *Political Socialization*, Robert Merton's study of the war bond drive, Merton and Lazarsfeld's edition of *Studies in the Scope and Method of the American Soldier*—all come to mind.[45] The Bureau was an institution that seemed to be unusually productive and imaginative in promoting original research.

Yet the Bureau of Applied Social Research would never again do a major voting study. After 1948 it was squeezed out of the field because of an inability to obtain funding for additional political surveys. A number of factors were at play here. Paul Lazarsfeld perhaps was not as aggressive as he might have been in seeking funding. By contrast, the Survey Research Center was very attentive to the problem of funding its surveys. With its ability to conduct national samples of unusual quality, the SRC was able to make a formidable case that it should be the institution to continue the systematic study of voting. In one sense, then, there was a simple competition for funds in which the Bureau did not do as well as it should have.

But students of American politics were casting about for an alternative to the voting studies conducted by the Bureau. Its theme of social determinism alone was enough to put people off. V. O. Key, who was a most influential figure during these years, was drumming up support for alternative surveys. David Truman was equally anxious for fresh evidence. Both men were members of the Social Science Research Council's Committee on Political Behavior, and they were instrumental in assisting the Survey Research Center to obtain funding for a national survey of the 1952 election.[46]

But as much as the nagging hostility to social determinism helped to promote these efforts, it was the influence of those associated with the group approach that proved decisive. It is not merely that the SSRC Committee on Political Behavior was particularly unfavorable to the Bureau, for with David Truman (as chairman), Avery Leiserson and Oliver Garceau as members, the group approach was certainly well represented. It was much more that group theory had provided the prevailing categories of analysis. The Bureau of Applied Social Research did not make any friends by providing evidence that the central premise of group theory was untenable.

It is probably correct to say that the Bureau of Applied Social Research was forced from the field of political behavior because of the opposition of those associated with the group approach. But it is equally true that the Bureau had sounded the death knell for group theory. Unable to establish satisfactory levels of generalization from its own case studies, and against the mounting evidence of class bias in the process of group formation, group theory began to sputter and fade. This was again a rather unconscious process, or at least an unpublished one, very much like the dispute between the voting studies and quantitative methods.

With the quiet fall of group theory, however, students of American politics seemed to become unglued. It was almost as if everything that had been learned about the political process had to be abandoned as the waves of electoral surveys advanced. True, group theory contained some monumental misperceptions about the mass public, but quite a bit had been learned about the political process because of the group approach. Parties, machines, administrative politics, the legislative process, the vagaries of state politics were all coming to be understood much more clearly and with a much greater sense of sophistication. There was no reason to lose command of these hard-earned pieces of knowledge. But lost they were.

From the early 1950s and for the next twenty years, almost every understanding of American politics was derived from the voting studies, or from the application of similar techniques to political elites. This was, in Donald Stokes's marvelous phrase, "analytic reduction" on a grand scale.[47] Everything was to be explained in terms of individual political behavior—voting, parties, elections, groups, lobbies, legislatures, policies, the functions of the political process as a whole.

There is enormous irony in this. Students of American politics were prisoners of their own making. Although the Survey Research Center made its own share of impressive discoveries, the thrust of its analysis was not different from the Bureau's. The SRC, too, concluded that voting decisions are controlled largely by nonpolitical forces; that these forces reflect an individual's "immediate social milieu, in particular his family."[48]

But in promoting the interest of the Survey Research Center, students of American politics gave these conclusions a position that they had lacked originally. It would take the better part of the next twenty years to sort out the confusions and misunderstandings that had been created in the study of electoral politics.

CHAPTER 4

The Psychological Bases of Democracy

There is no doubt that the progress of psychology has sent the older intellectualist theory of human conduct to the scrap-heap, or perhaps only into the dry-dock for repairs and equipment with modern machinery for use in a limited capacity. In reading some recent discussions one would almost gather that human beings hold no opinions and perform no acts by means of reasoning faculties.

A. LAWRENCE LOWELL,
Public Opinion in War and Peace

The voting studies can be said to continue after the Bureau of Applied Social Research with the work of the Survey Research Center. It was the surveys and analyses from this institution that came to dominate the study of political behavior, just as the controversies that raged in the discipline, particularly over voter rationality, are associated with the SRC's work. There is, however, a second strand of research that was very much concerned with applying the technology of survey research to problems in democratic politics. These studies focused on the problem of "the democratic personality"—or, more accurately, on the problem of undemocratic values in the mass public.

Unlike the work of the BASR or the SRC, this strand of research has not stirred lasting controversy or even provoked minor disputes (with the exception of one monumental flap over *The Authoritarian Personality*).[1] Research in this domain is not associated with any institution, nor are its conclusions attributed to any particular group of people. Rather, as a consequence of the efforts of a variety of scholars, there has been a steady flow of evidence that has formed something on the order of a professional consensus. Although the leading inference was slow to be made, the inescapable conclusion is that the quality of political participation by mass publics, even in the most highly industrialized nations, is quite low.

Prejudice and Authoritarian Personalities

Political analyists have never widely appreciated psychology, despite the fact that Freud and his followers had systemized the notion of the unconscious and unconscious aggression well before the outbreak of the First World War. It was not until that conflict that concern was expressed about the psychological underpinnings of the democratic idea.[2] But if that conflict provoked concern, the turmoil and persecution in European politics during the thirties, and the world war that followed as a consequence, impelled political analysts to inquire directly into the relationship between personality and politics. How, in the midst of the manifest irrationality of governments and the apparent inability of "the common man," could the concept of popular democracy be maintained? What caused some people to behave with such unrelenting inhumanity toward other people? Why were other people steadfastly tolerant?

The problem, then, was to determine what characteristics distinguished democrats from authoritarians. What sorts of personality disorders made some people persecute others? And, conversely, what personality traits were exhibited by democratic citizens and how were these to be measured? These were questions asked about mass publics, and obviously the tools of survey research were essential in responding to them.

Research on the relationship between personality and politics did not begin slowly with the cautious blending of method and theory. Rather like Lazarsfeld's surveys on voting, work began all at once with a single, large, inclusive project. As early as 1944, the American Jewish Committee expressed interest in funding research on anti-Semitism. A conference had been organized at the behest of the committee, which suggested several avenues of investigation that might be pursued. Out of this conference the decision to study the problem "scientifically" was taken, and research that led to the publication of *The Authoritarian Personality* was commissioned.

The working hypothesis of this study, undertaken at the Berkeley Public Opinion Study (at the University of California, Berkeley), was "that political, economic, and social convictions of an individual often form a broad and coherent pattern, as if bound together in a 'mentality' or 'spirit'; and that this pattern is an expression of deep-lying trends in his personality."[3] The problem was how to approach such a complex question.

Two broad types of evidence were brought to bear on the problem. First, an extensive questionnaire was developed. It was administered in various forms to different samples of "the population," providing a total sample population of 2,099. Embedded in the questionnaire was an Ethnocentrism Scale. Those scoring either in the top or bottom quartile on this scale were selected for more intensive study. The second stream of evidence was of the clinical variety. Subjects were given the Thematic Apperception Test (TAT) as well as a battery of other projective tests and questions. On the basis of these interviews, a more complete portrait of authoritarian and democratic personalities was to be painted.

The sample itself was a somewhat peculiar affair, and later it was to be a source of much criticism. As the authors noted at the outset, it was not a random sample of the American population, or of any population for that matter. Rather it was an effort to develop a "cross-section" of people. College students from a variety of different schools were used first. The other "samples" were drawn to include a variety of different types of groups—teachers, labor unions, service groups.[4]

Substantively, the questionnaire was constructed on the basis of four elaborate indicies—the Anti-Semitism (A-S scale), a scale of Ethnocentrism (the E scale), the Political and Economic Conservatism Scale (PEC), and the scale for Potentiality for Fascism or Implicit Antidemocratic Trends (the F-Scale), the two titles being used interchangeably. Although these scales were richly augmented with data developed in the nonstructured interviews, it is not unfair to say that they constitute the heart of the analysis.

The Anti-Semitism Scale was constructed from fifty-two questions that were formulated on the basis of the assumption that most people would not express overt prejudice and that hence statements of prejudice had to be given a democratic varnish.[5] Many of the questions in the index were bland and overly general ("There are a few exceptions, but in general Jews are pretty much alike"). It was decided to make each item in these scales as "appealing" as possible, in the sense that the prejudice contained in the questions was always qualified and conditional. In all cases, agreement with the new question (respondents answering positively, "yes") was recorded as an indication of prejudice, this being yet another way that the authors sought to make the expression of prejudice easier for people. Each of these decisions in questionnaire design was a serious source of error.

But the A-S scale as a whole, and the various subscales contained therein, performed very nicely from a statistical point of view. The correlations between them was remarkably strong, ranging from between 0.74 to 0.94. A "split-half" reliability test, wherein the original fifty-two items were divided into two groups of twenty-six each, produced a correlation of 0.92, which again was very strong. If these estimates were biased in that they encouraged the expression of prejudice, the prejudice that these questions recorded was internally consistent.

Ethnocentricism was also measured by a broad array of ques-

tions, thirty-four in all. These were divided up to form three separate subscales: racial prejudice, prejudice against various ethnic
minorities (in this case Japanese-Americans), Oklahomans (in
California), and Filipinos, as well as various cultural minorities
(Zootsuiters, criminals, the insane), and finally prejudice was conceived of as irrational patriotism ("the blind attachment to certain national cultural values, uncritical conformity with the prevailing group ways, and rejection of other nations as
outgroups").[6]

Again, the split-half reliabilities for the E-Scale were high (0.91),
as they were for each of the three subscales (between 0.80 and
0.91). Most important, the intercorrelations between the subscales
and the E-Scale were quite strong. The correlations between ethnocentrism in its various forms and anti-Semitism was equally impressive. (See table 4.1.) Prejudice, it seems, tends to be a highly
generalized phenomenon.

There is a tendency to think that prejudice is a highly selective
and idiosyncratic phenomenon, that it is sharply focused on a
particular group. However, these data suggest that, while there is
some variation among individuals, a person who discriminates
against any one group will harbor similar biases toward all social
minorities—Jews, Blacks, Zootsuiters, draft resisters.[7]

TABLE 4.1

*Correlations of E Subscales with Each Other and with the Total
E Scale and with the Total A-S Scale*

	Negroes	*Minorities*	*Patriotism*	*Total E*	*Total A-S*
Negroes	—	.74	.76	.90	.74
Minorities	.74	—	.83	.91	.76
Patriotism	.76	.83	—	.92	.69
Total E	.90	.91	.92	—	.80
Total A-S	.74	.76	.69	.80	—

SOURCE: T. W. Adorno et al., *The Authoritarian Personality* (New York:
Norton, 1969), 113, 122. Reprinted by permission of Harper & Row,
Publishers.

A primary characteristic of ethnocentric ideology is the *generality* of outgroup rejection. It is as if the ethnocentric individual feels threatened by most of the groups to which he does not have a sense of belonging; if he cannot identify, he must oppose; if a group is not "acceptable," it is "alien." The ingroup-outgroup distinction thus becomes the basis for most of his social thinking, and people are categorized primarily according to the groups to which they belong.... An ethnocentric individual may have a particular dislike for one group, but he is likely nonetheless to have ethnocentric opinions and attitudes regarding many other groups.[8]

This was a very substantial contribution, indeed. Furthermore, this conclusion has held up surprisingly well, given the multitude of methodological errors that were made in the research design. Writing almost twenty years later, Gertrude Selznick and Stephen Steinberg came to exactly the same conclusion: "There is a tendency for persons prejudiced in one way to be prejudiced in another." They concluded on the basis of much sounder data: "Anti-Negro, anti-Jewish and anti-Catholic prejudice are all highly interrelated and form an empirical syndrome."[9]

Had the authors of *The Authoritarian Personality* been content merely to establish the validity of this relationship and to explore its empirical dimensions, their research might have been an unqualified success. Unfortunately, they were determined to establish the validity of their entire argument, indications from the data to the contrary notwithstanding. Social prejudice—ethnocentricism and anti-Semitism—were viewed as manifestations of underlying personality disorders. But authoritarianism tended to be expressed through political ideology, through political and economic conservatism, to be specific.

Yet another scale was devised to measure political ideology. This index operated with considerably less efficiency than those measuring social prejudice. The pattern of intercorrelations between the sixteen items revealed a wide range of variation, 0.14 and 0.86, and the reliability tests reported evidence of instability. These statistical warnings were ignored. But in view of the evidence, many of the items that formed the initial scale were dropped and various "short forms" of the scale were tested. The authors, with some misgivings, finally settled on a five-item PEC scale on the grounds that it worked best, "that it made possible the comparison of groups and the study of this scale and the others."[10]

The appropriate strategy would have been to halt the analysis at this point and to look more closely at the data in order to understand what was going on. Had the authors done this, they would have found that political ideology in terms of a liberal/conservative continuum did not exist in the mass public at the level their theory presumed. Even with their determination to press on, the authors came very close to making this discovery.[11] But blind to the warning signals from the data, the analysis proceeded exactly as planned.

Unfortunately, there were similar measurement problems with the effort to identify the characteristics of authoritarian personalities. The capacity of survey research to identify latent personality traits is somewhat tenuous in the best of circumstances.[12] But the specification of authoritarianism in this case was particularly awkward from a methodological point of view. Authoritarianism was conceived as a complex syndrome consisting of nine different psychological dimensions. These were measured by a series of fixed-response questions, thirty-eight in all, which again would be represented in index form.[13]

In its first trials, the F-scale performed no better than the Political and Economic Conservatism scale. The reliabilities were low (0.74), and the dispersion between items was high. Again, an opportunity to revise the research design was ignored. The defects in the concept of authoritarianism reported by initial analyses of the data were remedied by selecting a subset of items that were more compatible with each other.[14]

The analysis in *The Authoritarian Personality* is decidedly weaker than it might have been, weaker than it should have been given the originality of findings concerning the tendency of social prejudice to generalize. But from the discussion of social prejudice onward, the analysis tends to deteriorate. The originality of this finding is made more in spite of the quality of the data than because of it.

The Authoritarian Personality, because it focused on a question of such importance, quickly received the critical attention of a great number of scholars. Errors in sample design and in the preparation of the questionnaire were examined in excruciating detail, as were the mistakes in inference and analysis.[15] The F-scale, in particular, seemingly established itself as a permanent feature on the methodological landscape.[16] As attention to these methodological issues continued, new substantive, although quite tangential, inferences were made about personality, and these in turn tended to spawn still more methodological arguments.[17] The entire exercise makes excellent reading as a case study in methodology and research design.

But it was the substance of the problem—the relationship between politics and personality—that gave this research a sense of urgency. In performing so poorly methodologically, the study dealt this relationship a very nearly fatal blow. Political analysts, on the whole, have not been sympathetic to psychology either as a tool or as a focus of concern. This is one of those lingering professional biases that exists without explanation or justification, a bias that simply continues, so that a number of intriguing problems never are addressed adequately. The impact of the discovery of the unconscious on democratic theory, a theory that depends inordinately on the human powers of reason, has never been fully understood. Nor have the psychological bases of the democratic idea in the mass public or among the political elite ever been established, despite the fact that a growing number of biographies of political leaders suggest the necessity for work along these lines.[18]

Clearly if any systematic inquiry was to be made along these lines, political analysts first would have to be convinced that the psychological approach bore fruit. But the work on *The Authoritarian Personality* seemed to establish the opposite result. This effort seemed to yield precious little while at the same time creating a huge methodological morass. The Survey Research Center was quick to demonstrate that the F-scale had no explanatory power in national politics. Representing the sentiment of the profession,

V. O. Key, Jr., observed with unconcealed glee that this was one of the more positive things that the SRC had accomplished.

Not the least of the utilities of the national sample survey is its capacity to debunk fantastic readings of the mass mind that gain currency among the sophisticated. A common source of such misreadings is the amateur Freudian—even on occasion the professional Freudian—who, extrapolating from his clinical observations, concludes that the country is hysteria-ridden, frustrated, authoritarian, rootless, or in a parlous condition because of mass neurosis. Among the questions treated in a discussion of personality factors in voting behavior (Chapter 18 [of *The American Voter*]) is the supposition that persons of lower educational levels have marked authoritarian tendencies. The finding is that, with various methodological artifacts controlled, only a trace of this relationship can be isolated in the 1956 sample.[19]

Would that the findings about social prejudice could have been so easily dismissed.

The Problem of Undemocratic Values
in the Mass Public

One of the arguments used by constitutional theorists in the eighteenth century against political equality was that most people were not capable of maintaining suitable value systems—values that would sustain "the rights of man." Because the people could not be trusted, for this reason among others, constitutionalism developed with an emphasis on "mixed" systems of government. Governments would at once be rooted in the "consent" of the governed, in "the people," but at the same time the implications of the idea of political equality, voting and elections, would be avoided. Nowhere was this logic more articulately expressed than in the formulation of the Constitution of the United States; and paradoxically, nowhere did the idea of political equality advance more quickly than it did in American politics.[20]

The worry that constitutional theorists expressed over the values that most people maintain was not resolved with the extension of the franchise, unfortunately. The most casual foray into the political history of the United States, or into the history of almost any people, for that matter, reveals a perfectly inglorious record of discrimination, bigotry, ignorance, and persecution—in short, a grand variety of undemocratic outcomes of virtually every sort. For the United States, the Second World War muted this sense of history and seemingly cleansed the self-inflicted wounds of the past. This war was fought for principle. It was fought against regimes that were openly hostile to the fundamental ideas of democracy—freedom, liberty, and law. But most of all, the war was fought by the people—in the armed forces, of course, but equally in the mobilization of national resources, in production schedules, and in consumer scarcity.[21] There was, as Carl Friedrich phrased it, a new belief in the common man.[22]

It did not take this belief very long to run into a wall of social prejudice; in this case the mass public seemed to acquire a taste for anticommunism, a disregard for civil liberties, an intolerance for diversity (particularly on religious and political matters), and to demand a high degree of political conformity.

In 1955 Samuel Stouffer reported the results from surveys conducted under his direction documenting the existence of a substantial amount of prejudice in both the mass public and among the political elite.[23] Although the data showed that anticommunism was a widespread sentiment and was characteristically irrational in its focus, that support for personal liberties was negligible, and that people exhibited little appreciation of political diversity, Stouffer found reasons in these data for optimism. Political leaders were noticeably more inclined to express democratic sentiments than was the mass public. Since political action required leadership, this meant that those "especially responsible and thoughtful citizens" were in a position to give the impulses of the mass public "a sober second thought."[24]

There were trends in the mass public that were encouraging too. Prejudice in all of its manifestations varied inversely with education. The more people experienced diversity, if only in the diversity of ideas, the less likely they were to express social prejudices. Furthermore, older people were decidedly more likely to harbor undemocratic sentiments than were more youthful members of the community, even when the effects of education were taken into account. This should be attributed, the data indicated, to the less "authoritarian" patterns of child-rearing. Geographic mobility also seemed to produce tolerance, as did exposure to the media. Thinking sympathetically of the American people, Samuel Stouffer concluded, "Great social, economic and technological forces are operating slowly and imperceptively on the side of spreading tolerance."[25]

Looked at retrospectively, however, these data seem more discouraging than Stouffer imagined. There appears to be very little latitude in the mass public for deviant opinions—for the fundamental rights of "socialists," "communists," "atheists," for political and religious beliefs that fundamentally contradict the dominant view. The material in table 4.2, a composite of different pieces of Stouffer's analysis, provides some estimate of the depth and pervasiveness of undemocratic sentiments in the mass public and among the political elite as well.

The mass public presents scant evidence that it can be relied upon in times of trouble and stress. One is struck by the simple magnitude of intolerance that Stouffer recorded. This is not to say that prejudice and pressure toward political and religious conformity are people's dominant concerns. There is a mercurial quality toward prejudice, at least as it is expressed in response to survey questions. Much depends on the question's wording. The basis of the data presented in table 4.2, for example, is designed to elicit attitudes about a person who admits being a communist, socialist, or whatever. When asked some of the same questions about someone who denied being a communist and so forth, respondents were much more likely to give tolerant answers. In such cases intolerant positions were taken by 10 to 20 percent of the population, depend-

TABLE 4.2

Mass and Elite Attitudes on Selected Items from the Stouffer Study

	% Giving Intolerant Responses	
	Mass	Elite
A Socialist has the right to give a speech	41	14
An Atheist has the right to give a speech	60	34
A Communist has the right to give a speech	68	47
Should a book written by a Communist be removed from the library?	66	54
Should a Communist be permitted to teach high school?	91	89
Should a Communist be fired from a job as a clerk in a store?	68	51
Should a Communist lose his citizenship?	77	77
	% Giving "More Tolerant" Responses	
Scale of tolerance toward nonconformists	31	66

SOURCE: Samuel A. Stouffer, *Communism, Conformity and Civil Liberties: A Cross-section of the Nation Speaks Its Mind* (Gloucester, Mass.: Peter Smith, 1963), 31, 33, 40, 41, 43, 52.

ing on the question. Similarly, the mere possession of undemocratic attitudes does not mean that people will act on those attitudes. The impulse toward action seems to follow its own logic.[26] There is also the question of how salient undemocratic sentiments are in comparison to other political concerns. When asked what kind of things they worried most about, people's predominant response was in terms of economic problems and concerns about their own health and that of their family. Less than 2 percent of the mass public mentioned the problem of domestic communism, compared to 5 percent of the political elite. Where respondents were asked a second time to list the things that worried them most, so that secondary worries might also be expressed, 6 percent of the mass public, compared to 14 percent of the political elite, spoke of fears of communism.

Still, once people had their attention focused on the problem of dissent, there was very little room to maneuver. Undemocratic sentiments seemed to dominate. More unsettling was the rather weak hold that the political elite had upon democratic values. The drift of Stouffer's interpretation was to take solace in the relative improvement in democratic norms as one moved from the general population into the strata of the political elite. Yet it must be remembered that these were the years of the McCarthy terror, an era in which people were penalized for their beliefs. Rather than being a source of protection, various segments of the elite seemed instrumental in enforcing the prevailing view and in focusing the attention of the mass public on the problem.[27] Even in terms of the data Stouffer presented, there is the forbidding realization that fully one-third of the political elite took undemocratic positions at the slightest provocation and that this proportion climbed steadily as the questions became more difficult.

The behavior of the political elite in Stouffer's study is a source of concern. Clearly, they should form a bulwark against spasms of prejudice and intolerance in the mass public. Although the political elite were to do better in subsequent surveys, as we shall see, their opinions surrounding the anticommunism question, not to mention the political history of this issue, stands as a strong warning that political elites provide insufficient protection for the fundamental principle of democratic politics.

Whatever the attitudes of the political elite, they were more than matched by the mass public. Most people in the United States had little familiarity with the democratic idea, and in response to survey questions many people expressed sentiments that were openly hostile to it. In a clever survey, James Prothro and Charles Grigg asked a sample of people a series of highly abstract questions about support for democratic principles (for example, "every citizen should have an equal chance to influence governmental policy").[28] Respondents, of course, gave overwhelming approval to this important but distant principle. But when it came to applying these general principles to specific situations, another set of questions revealed that a substantial segment of the public possessed no understanding of the lofty principles that just a moment earlier they had so heartily endorsed. More than half of the people questioned would restrict the right to vote to the informed, or in another example a majority of those sampled would restrict the franchise to those who pay property taxes.

In surveys conducted in 1956 and 1958, the problem of undemocratic values in the mass public and among the political elite was examined by Herbert McClosky, who formulated the design of that research with characteristic rigor and attention to detail.[29] These data did nothing to increase confidence in the mass public.

> The findings furnish little comfort for those who wish to believe that a passion for freedom, tolerance, justice and other democratic values springs spontaneously from the lower depths of the society, and that the plain, homespun, uninitiated yeoman, worker and farmer are the natural hosts of democratic ideology. The mystique of the simple, unworldly, "natural" democrat has been . . . assiduously cultivated. . . . Yet every one of these intuitive expectations turns out, upon investigation, to be questionable or false.[30]

While there is no doubting the validity of this conclusion, it is the specific pieces of evidence that are most damaging, for the questionnaire contained a series of questions designed to probe a number of different aspects of the democratic idea. The notion that there existed a popular consensus on "the rules of the game" was put to the test in one group of questions, as was the idea that there was a highly generalized "faith in democracy." The level of support for the procedural guarantees of the Constitution was examined, and readings were taken on the level of "Ethnocentricism," "Tolerance," "Elitism," and a variety of other democratic concerns. (See table 4.3.)

At every turn, the mass public performed poorly. The values presupposed by democratic politics seemed to find precious little support in the mass public. By contrast, the political elite did significantly better. Democratic politics seemed to be maintained by the political elite acting pretty much on their own. This explanation was the only one that the evidence from these surveys seemed to permit.

TABLE 4.3

Political Influentials vs. the Electorate: Percentages Scoring High and Low on Democratic and Anti-Democratic Attitude Scales*

Scale	Political Influentials (N=3020)	General Electorate (N=1484)	Scale	Political Influentials (N=3020)	General Electorate (N=1484)
	(%s down)			(%s down)	
Faith in Democracy			**Elitism**		
% High	40.1	18.5	% High	22.8	38.7
% Low	14.4	29.7	% Low	41.0	22.4
Procedural Rights			**Totalitarianism**		
% High	58.1	24.1	% High	9.7	33.8
% Low	12.3	31.3	% Low	60.1	28.4
Tolerance			**Right Wing**		
% High	61.3	43.1	% High	17.5	33.1
% Low	16.4	33.2	% Low	45.3	28.9
Faith in Freedom			**Left Wing**		
% High	63.0	48.4	% High	6.7	27.8
% Low	17.1	28.4	% Low	68.7	39.3
Ethnocentrism			**California F-Scale**		
% High	27.5	36.5	% High	14.7	33.5
% Low	46.9	36.3	% Low	48.0	23.5

*For explanations of High and Low, see footnote 12 in McClosky. The middle group has been omitted from this table. Differences between the influentials and the electorate on all the scales in this table are, by Kolmogorov-Smirnov and chi-square tests, statistically significant at or beyond the .01 percent level of significance.

SOURCE: Herbert McClosky, "Consensus and Ideology in American Politics," *American Political Science Review* 58 (June 1964): 368, Table IV. Reprinted by permission.

Values—The Missing Units of Analysis

The discovery that the mass public lacks the strength to bear the weight of the democratic idea need not have been as disappointing as it was. Nor should this discovery have led to such an uncritical reliance upon the political elite. In all of this research on values there was a general failure to appreciate the complexity of democratic theory. These surveys would have been most correct had they begun by observing that a specification of values in democratic theory has never been accomplished.

In part, this failure to be specific about essential values originates in the writings of eighteenth-century constitutional theorists. In addition to an articulate theory of individual rights, these theorists presumed that the political elite would have acquired, by birth and by training, a certain code of conduct. These attributes of character were never systemized in the way that institutional characteristics were. Rather it was assumed that a proper arrangement of institutions could rely upon these behaviors and attitudes in the day-to-day business of government.[31]

What is a difficult problem in constitutional theory was further complicated by the addition of the electoral process to the constitutional design of government. This was accomplished with very little theoretical justification. Rather the logic of voting and elections was hammered out in the pages of political history as various groups contended for power and privilege. If the values presumed by constitutional politics were unclear in the first place, the problem became doubly confused by the addition of the mass public. Even presuming that a good estimate of the values implicit in constitutionalism can be made, there remains the question of what share of these responsibilities now belong to the people, not to mention whether the electoral process presupposes a new range of values and beliefs.

The question of the distribution of democratic values in the mass public, then, is hardly a simple research problem. It would have been highly beneficial if students of political theory and those designing electoral surveys could have worked together on this problem. But the intense, silent hostility that existed between these two groups of scholars precluded this possibility, even in the form of cogent criticism of each other's work, much less in the form of shared research. It is impossible to redesign research that has already been conducted, of course. But one way of looking at the results of these surveys is from the perspective of the questions that were not asked.

Followers, Leaders, and Institutions

There is nothing wrong with the distinction between leaders and followers, either from a theoretical perspective or an empirical one, as we have seen. The more difficult problem is deciding, both in theory and in practice, where this distinction is most appropriately drawn; where it is a sound and secure division of responsibility and where it is an artificial distinction that is likely to collapse under the pressure of undemocratic sentiments in the mass public.

The data, particularly those reported by Herbert McClosky, seem to indicate that partitioning responsibility for the democratic idea between mass and elite works best on matters related to government and procedure. In short, the elite are uniquely responsible for maintaining the good order of the political system. Elite responsibility begins with an appreciation of the principles of government themselves, what appear in the data as "faith in democracy," and extends to an application of those principles in terms of "procedural guarantees" and individual rights and liberties particularly against the state. The special responsibilities of the political elite in this regard seem to include the cultivation of an appropriate spirit of government. Again looking at McClosky's data, this means that government should be "antitotalitarian" and "unauthoritarian" in its character.

While popular support for constitutional protections is always to be encouraged, there are good reasons why it cannot be expected. Many constitutional guarantees to the individual are not intuitively obvious, and it is not always a simple matter to apply those protections in specific situations. A substantial amount of education and training appear necessary in order for people to master the rudiments of democratic theory. Elites in general are likely to have had the requisite educational training. More to the point, the political elite in particular should have acquired a special feeling for the democratic idea beyond what could be expected by education alone. For it is they who must minister to the system on a day-to-day basis and who must maintain its operating assumptions in good working order.

The data on the capacity of the political elite to fulfill the special obligations that they have acquired is not very reassuring. At the heart of the relationship is the influence of education. In an important secondary analysis of the data collected by Samuel Stouffer, Robert Jackman pointed this out quite astutely for elites in general.[32] With the effects of education held constant, the mass public actually does a little better than the political elite in support for democratic ideas among those who have been to, or graduated from, college, while in the lower ranges of educational experience elites do somewhat better than the mass public. The ability of elites to do significantly better than the mass public occurs because elites are disproportionately more highly educated.

When political elites are singled out of the data, the same relationship obtains. Political elites do not do notably better than the average for elites as a whole, and they do markedly worse than other types of leaders, most notably newspaper publishers. Local political officials (mayors) did terribly as a matter of fact, much less well than their colleagues on the school and library boards. Party leaders do somewhat better than do local officials, but they still are not much better than the average for nonpolitical elites.

Several additional points should be inferred from these data. First, it is extremely important to note that the data are Stouffer's and that the focus of the study is anticommunism and nonconformity in the fifties. During these years the political elite probably could have been (certainly *should* have been) much more articulate in their support for fundamental democratic guarantees. The most interesting aspect of their behavior is that, as a group, they chose not to be. Rather than speak to the democratic ideal, various segments of the political elite sought competitive advantage by appealing to the mass public for support. In these circumstances, the concept of individual rights and liberties sank like a stone. Furthermore, the position of that segment of the elite who wished to apply these constitutional protections to individuals was compromised. The point of emphasis here is not the failure of the mass public to protect the operating principles of government (although any support they can lend is to be appreciated), rather it is that an operating consensus on the fundamental principles of government among the political elite is necessary precisely because of the existence of a substantial undemocratic sentiment among the people. When this operating consensus breaks down, the political equivalent of Gresham's law takes effect wherein unprincipled leaders drive their more principled counterparts out of the political arena, using public opinion and the electoral process as sanctions against political leaders who refuse to abandon the working assumptions of democratic government.[33]

That it was the problem of anticommunism and the intolerance of differences in politics and religion that unprincipled leaders used indicates some of the limitations of undue reliance upon the political elite. While elites may be able to preserve the integrity of democratic procedures, they are no protection at all against the more virulent strains of social prejudice in the mass public. Given an intense social prejudice and given its immediacy (its saliency) as a political concern, there is very little that a political elite can do, even in the short run. If the political elite refuses to bow to wishes of the mass public, then the electorate will recruit a new set of political leaders. One need look no further than the race issue in contemporary American politics for evidence of this point.[34]

In this regard, social prejudice should be seen as one element in the constellation of public values. Such prejudices are particularly dangerous because they have the characteristics of fundamental beliefs; indeed they *are* fundamental beliefs. Two arguments, both made by Seymour Martin Lipset, are essential to understanding how such belief patterns operate in electoral politics.

In examining the relationship of antidemocratic attitudes and social class, Lipset noticed an intriguing paradox. Social prejudice, intolerance, and anti-civil libertarian attitudes in general are located disproportionately among the working classes. This was true in all the nations on which Lipset had data. Yet unions in all of these nations had not only acted counter to these attitudes, union leadership had been in the forefront of efforts to produce change.

Despite the profoundly antidemocratic tendencies in lower-class groups, workers' political organizations and movements in the more industrialized democratic countries have supported *both* economic and political liberalism. Workers' organizations, trade-unions and political parties played a major role in extending political democracy in the nineteenth and early twentieth centuries. However, these struggles for political freedom by workers, like those of the middle-class before them, took place in the context of a fight for economic rights. Freedom of organization and of speech, together with universal suffrage, were necessary weapons in the battle for a better standard of living, social security, shorter hours, and the like.[35]

In this way, the organizational context in which working-class political behavior is formed compensates for the intrinsic weakness of democratic values among the people who compose this social strata. Merely because values are firmly held does not mean that they are politically relevant. In this case, the political consequences of working-class authoritarianism were muted, indeed reversed, by a more pressing value, the desire for economic improvement. This is not to say that working-class values cannot become the basis of antidemocratic regimes. The following quotation from Lipset argues that the belief system of *any* group may provide the basis for authoritarian politics. Fascism, Lipset concluded, draws sustenance from every class—and from left, right, and center groups.

> The analysis of modern totalitarian movements has reflected the old concepts of left, right, and center. . . . But antidemocratic groups can be more fruitfully classified and analyzed if it is recognized that "left," "right," and "center" refer to ideologies, each of which has a moderate and an extremist version, the one parliamentary and other extra parliamentary in its orientation. It is also necessary to recognize that a left extremist movement that is working class based and oriented also may be militaristic, nationalistic, and anti-Marxist.[36]

Lipset's emphasis is on the politically active component of undemocratic movements. Ideologies rarely extend to the mass public, however. Where such antidemocratic ideologies can find support is in their capacity to identify with undemocratic values. Thus a number of studies have made it reasonably clear that most Germans did not understand the political philosophy of the Nazi movement. But in their virulent anti-Semitism, the Nazis were able to identify with a more general sentiment among Germans.[37]

If the distribution of values provides political elites with room to maneuver, it is also clear that the quality of the values that the mass public maintains is of vital concern. Unfortunately, very little effort has been made to estimate the composition of values in the mass public. To be sure, social prejudice and intolerance were studied in a variety of different manifestations. But there was no effort to extend this line of inquiry into other domains, to the distribution of values on such essential political matters as personal economic values or fundamental feelings about justice, inequality, or diversity. When political philosophers wrote about the popular basis of democratic politics, they tended to touch on such themes.[38] It can be wondered whether the direction taken by survey research on these matters would have been different had students of political philosophy been involved actively in the studies.

Doubts about the Quality of Political Participation in the United States

The voting studies—using this term now to cover a wide range of political surveys—were not friendly messengers. Coming during the years when students of government were particularly anxious to explain the special virtues of American politics that had enabled democracy to triumph over fascism, survey after survey failed to find the genius that Americans had for democratic politics. Instead, data emphasizing serious flaws in the American character began piling up.

A spate of studies suggested that there were strands of cynicism, anomie, misanthropy, and alienation in the American electorate, and each of these regrettable psychological conditions was independently associated with a lack of interest in politics and with nonvoting.[39] So much for the enthusiasm and initiative of the American psyche. Moreover, there was a painful level of apathy in the general population, a lack of information, efficacy, and seemingly a general indifference to politics among a substantial segment of the population. It was less political activism that characterized the mass public than it was political passivity.[40]

The American Voter, published in 1960 as the Survey Research Center's first comprehensive report, seemed to confirm political analysts' worst fears about the American mass public. The quality of political participation was uniformly low, social identifications were strong, and issue voting seemed to be infrequent. Instead, party identification, in the form of strongly held psychological identification with a political party, was the dominant influence in the electoral arena. The inference that most voters behaved irrationally was inescapable.

If all this was not a sufficient burden, there was the added weight of the discovery that there was no consensus among the American people in support of "the rules of the game," nor was there very much support for any of the fundamental principles of democratic government. Rather, the electorate seemed to consist of a raft of social prejudices and undemocratic predispositions. It is easy to appreciate why the mood of political analysts had become perceptibly less buoyant. The voting studies, the most exacting examination of the inner workings of democratic politics, seemed to indicate that the system did not work or at least did not work all that well. Against evidence that was increasingly bleak, Gabriel Almond and Sidney Verba published *The Civic Culture*.[41] It was as if a breath of fresh air had swept the voting studies clean. No matter how dour the list of previous findings, there was in this book reason to believe that democracy worked and that the practice of the American democracy was sound. The earlier results had not changed, of course, but somehow Almond and Verba saw them in a better light.

CHAPTER 5

The Civic Culture
and Its Discontents

The Civic Culture to the Rescue

The most influential book among the voting studies was surely *The American Voter*.[1] It specified the critical relationships in electoral behavior and established the broad empirical generalizations for the period. As such, this was the book that influenced everyone's thinking. But *The American Voter* was never much loved, or even liked. Poorly written—ponderous in theory and containing huge arrays of data—it is a book that is slow going even for the most dedicated of readers. But the inadequacies of style were not the book's primary difficulty. The larger problem lay with its conclusions, for *The American Voter* confirmed in excruciating detail the political poverty of the American electorate. Whereas one could always quarrel with earlier voting studies—over their design or over their analysis—it was now apparent that most people in the American electorate cared very little about politics or about political participation. This lack of enthusiasm was reflected in the quality of information that people possessed about politics—their superficial appreciation of candidates and their ignorance of issues involved in campaigns. The electorate was pervasively dull and uninterested. *The American Voter,* then, confirmed all of the unhappy findings discovered previously, but it did so with such methodological purity and analytical precision that it seemed that little else could be said.

But if the flow of data and inference from *The American Voter* were bleak, *The Civic Culture,* by Gabriel Almond and Sidney Verba, was a breath of fresh air.[2] To begin with, it presented political participation in the United States in a much more favorable light. Almond and Verba had uncovered a range of political attitudes and behaviors that could explain why the American democracy was successful. Psychology is not supposed to play a role in political analysis, certainly not during this formative period when so much attention was being given to the objectivity of survey research. However, among American political scientists, *The Civic Culture* was a most welcome addition to the literature, for it seemed to capture the qualities that made American politics distinctive and triumphant.

Furthermore, the book seemed to provide a substantial amount of evidence for the prevailing theories of political development.[3] *The Civic Culture* is composed of surveys of political participation conducted in five different countries—the United States, Britain, West Germany, Italy, and Mexico. Not only did these surveys rescue American voters from the deeper recesses of political despair, the data also seemed to confirm that the advice the United States was giving developing nations was manifestly correct.

So *The Civic Culture* played to audiences that, while straining for objectivity, were decidedly pleased with the structure of the book's analysis and the conclusions that followed from it. There were other reasons to be happy with this book. Almond and Verba were expansive and literate in their analysis. Where other survey analysts tended to be dull and plodding, these authors mixed theory, data, and political history with apparent ease. The book was fun. While it had been a difficult project to plan and execute, Almond and Verba had administered it well, and the excitement that they shared in bringing *The Civic Culture* to a successful conclusion carries over into each chapter.

The theoretical heartland of *The Civic Culture* is really quite simple. Each nation, it argues, possesses a distinctive political culture that is expressed in terms of the "internalized . . . cognitions, feelings and evaluations of its population."[4] Political attitudes— how people feel about politics and about political participation— represent the key to understanding political culture and in turn its relationship with the stability or instability of democratic governments.

In making this theory more concrete, four different classes of attitudes were specified: feelings about the political system in general (system as object), attitudes about opportunities to participate in the system (input object), attitudes toward the performance of the system (object output), and feelings about oneself as an active participant in the political system. On each of these dimensions attitudes could range from parochial (nonparticipating and distrusting) through subjective (feeling favorable toward the performance of the system but not coupled with any personal sense of political efficacy) to participant (active and self-confident citizens who feel that their participation makes a difference).

National political cultures are obviously mixed affairs. Populations contain a diversity of orientations toward politics with significant and distinctive subcultures being readily apparent. Similarly, any particular government may be incongruent with the underlying political orientations of its people. Such a situation is likely to promote political instability, just as political stability is more likely to accrue in those circumstances where the people and the government share the same fundamental orientations toward politics.

The categories described in *The Civic Culture* are no longer highly regarded. Theoretically, this classification has its problems, as we shall observe more closely, and over the last fifteen years there has been a pronounced inability of this theory to maintain itself against the tide of events. Indeed, reading Gabriel Almond in 1980, I found him struggling to salvage the concept of a "civic culture."[5] While these problems are quite real, it should be observed that Almond and Verba's definition of political culture was a marked improvement over anything that had preceded it.

National character is an old and venerable idea. More important, it was an idea that was in full vogue in the United States during the fifties and early sixties, as Americans tried to understand what about them had brought such success and power. Almond and Verba lent to the idea of national character a precision and meaning that it lacked even among the most skillful of impressionistic accounts. If, with the passage of time, the categories in *The Civic Culture* seem slight, it must be remembered that they are far richer and much more systematic than anything that was available at the time—that, indeed, these categories made comparisons between national characters meaningful for the first time.

One additional point should be made about the theoretical structure of the book. In developing the phrase "the civic culture," Almond and Verba had something very definite in mind. This concept shared with other definitions of participation the notion that citizens should be active in politics and that their political choices should be guided by the voice of reason—the "rationality-activist" model of participation, as the authors so aptly label it. But in addition, "the civic culture" was intended to mean "an allegiant participant culture. Individuals are not only oriented to political input, they are oriented positively to the input structures and the input process."[6] This highly positive component of the civic culture was the crucial ingredient in blending different political orientations harmoniously—the participant with the nonparticipant and less participant and traditional political orientations. In this manner political attitudes and feelings were critical elements for the maintenance of successful democracies.

Given this theory, the data seemed to work wonderfully. Take, for example, the questions of how citizens perceive the political system and how much they know about it. Where other surveys had amassed evidence on the political ignorance of American voters, particularly on campaign issues, Almond and Verba found that people in the United States, Great Britain, and Germany had a fairly comprehensive knowledge about the operation of the political system itself, while people in Italy and especially in Mexico did much more poorly. It was understood in the United States, Great Britain, and Germany that both national and local governments had a substantial "impact on daily life," and in these nations people were most apt to characterize the consequences of government as positive. Similarly, people in the United States were concerned about the conduct of politics, and they were the most able to identify political leaders by name:

In general our findings on political cognition show the British, Americans and Germans to be predominantly oriented toward their political systems in both the political and governmental sense. Or to use our jargon, they are cognitively oriented toward the political system in its output and input aspects.[7]

The data seemed to tell the same happy story when the participatory side of the equation was examined. People in the older, more established democracies (the United States and Great Britain) were more active in politics and felt more positively about their political activity than did people living in countries where democracy was less secure. Furthermore, feelings of political conflict in the United States and Britain were much less apt to spill over into personal relations and social affairs.[8] And there was a more fully developed sense of civic (nonpolitical) cooperation in the United States than elsewhere. All in all, Americans and Britians were possessed of the idea that they could act in politics and that their actions have meaning and consequence in the political system.

People in Germany did not have nearly as positive an orientation toward politics on the input side of government as they had on the political output side. This finding fit nicely into the argument Almond and Verba had developed: Germany, with its disparate history of the Weimar Republic and with the rise of Nazism, had monumental difficulties with the stability of its political participation. Yet the nation's economic and political recovery during the post–World War II years was little short of phenomenal. Hence it seemed to Almond and Verba that this was a case where the civic culture was incomplete. Citizens were doing extremely well as subjects, in their feelings that government worked for them, but they were doing much more poorly as active participants in government.

The German case was not an isolated example. One of the most striking features of *The Civic Culture* is the way political history and the analysis of survey data seemed to go hand in hand. The British tradition of parliamentary democracy and self-reliant individualism seemed to account for apparent satisfaction with government as well as an active sense of participation in its affairs. The United States inherited this tradition, of course. But the openness of the frontier was added to it, as well as the unparalleled economic opportunities of rapid industrialization and an almost total absence of social class and political hierarchy. So it was hardly surprising that the United States should often exceed Great Britain in political participation.[9] What came as something of a surprise was that Mexico should outperform Italy in so many of Almond and Verba's categories. But here too, the data seemed to point to a historical interpretation. The Mexican revolution apparently created an enduring heritage for its people, a legacy that was incorporated into a wide range of political attitudes and feelings where contemporary circumstances seemed to make them inappropriate. By contrast, Italy's long history of political turmoil was reflected in the cynicism of its people.

For every twist in the data, then, there seemed to be a corresponding explanation in the unique political history of the nation in question. But if the presence or absence of the civic culture was rooted in the past, in shared political experiences, it was a political culture that was transmitted through the process of political socialization in very much the same fashion as previous surveys had described. Again, the heart of the process was located in "nonpolitical human relations." Almond and Verba were quick to add, however, that intentional teaching of political attitudes in the family and in the schools produced a noticeable impact. The civic culture, they stressed, could be learned. Where families, schools, and job situations promoted democratic participation, the evidence indicated that the appropriate political cognitions developed. These influences were not of equal strength, of course: "There appears to be a rank order in the strength of connection between nonpolitical types of participation and political competence: the connection becomes strong as one moves from family to school to job participation."[10]

This was an important finding for two reasons. First, at a theoretical level, these data emphasized that the civic culture was more than the sum of historical experience. It was also a learned set of attitudes and feelings. If history established the point at which a people started, they nonetheless could acquire a more democratic political culture if they chose to. Second and equally important was the raw empiricism of the result. The amount of influence that family, school, and workplace had on promoting changes in political attitudes was exactly the opposite of the influence that these factors had in molding general political orientations. Family is much more imposing in molding a person's general political orientation than is school or peer group. But with political change, proximity seems to be the determining consideration.[11]

These were the sorts of inferences for which political analysts had longed. At last a political survey had discovered some of the distinctive characteristics of popular democracies. There was finally some hard evidence that explained how democratic orientations were formulated and maintained. The particular genius of *The Civic Culture* was that it achieved these results without disputing the central findings of previous surveys. Rather, Almond and Verba created an explanation that seemed to penetrate more deeply. It was not information about specific candidates and issues that mattered. Electoral behavior itself was never considered. More important were people's feelings of political competence, their general knowledge of the political system and its leaders, whether their political orientation was positively or negatively associated with the political system and with participation in it, and the general sense among citizens that their participation was meaningful, that they could change an unjust law. These orientations toward politics, rather than the specifics of participation in election campaigns, lay at the foundation of democratic politics.

But there were two problems with this line of thinking. In the first place, many of the more important inferences that Almond and Verba made did not hold up upon reanalysis of the data. And second, the idea of a civic culture is itself badly flawed. Ironically, the difficulties associated with the data have led to very fruitful consequences. Each subsequent analysis and every additional study has added to our understanding of how political participation in the mass public works (or fails to work). The argument for a civic culture may have been damaged beyond repair, but in its place is an extremely solid body of evidence on the structure of political participation.

Unfortunately, this has not led to corresponding advances in theory. Indeed, there has been no theoretical advance at all, and perhaps there has rather been a net loss, for nothing has emerged to take the place of the civic culture as an organizing concept. The data, and the empirical relationships that have emerged from their analysis, have been left to speak for themselves. This would be fine if the data provided a theory. But, unfortunately, while *explaining* a great deal about participation, these data create substantial problems for democratic theory. These problems have not been widely examined or discussed even though the questions they raise are of the most fundamental order. Why, with ever better evidence to work with, both data analysts and political theorists have ignored problems of fundamental theory is itself an intriguing question.

Good Data, Bitter Findings

Almond and Verba had wanted to establish the causal primacy of the civic culture in establishing and maintaining successful democracies. On reanalysis of their data, however, it soon became apparent that individual attitudes and feelings about political participation do not have nearly the independent significance that were attributed to them initially. And the significance of individual attitudes was not the only problem to emerge. Subsequent studies, the best of which have involved Sidney Verba as a principal investigator, have had difficulty in identifying the distinctive characteristics of democratic political participation itself. Data that are stunning in their analysis confound the search for the fundamentals of democratic theory.

Far and away the most impressive reanalysis of the data from *The Civic Culture* was conducted by Norman Nie, G. Bingham Powell, Jr., and Kenneth Prewitt.[12] Working first by aggregating the data at the national level, these analysts discovered that two factors—social status and organizational involvement—accounted for a disproportionate share in the variance in participation, so much so that the differences between nations became trivial when these factors were considered.

In short, idiosyncratic differences between countries do exist, but they are very small when compared to the extremely strong pattern revealed in [the data]. With a few important exceptions *individuals with similar social statuses and similar organizational involvement display similar absolute levels of political participation no matter in which of the five nations they live.* This finding confirms once again the hypothesis that the two components of economic development, expanding middle-class and growing organizational infrastructure, sharply affect levels of mass political participation.[13]

Thus, on reconsideration, Almond and Verba's data showed that political participation was a consequence of economic development. Or stated more directly, participation is the political manifestation of the industrial revolution. This is not the first time that political analysts have reached this conclusion. Seymour Martin Lipset, most notably, created a brief stir in the early sixties when he observed the unmistakably strong correlation between economic development and democratic government.[14] But others argued that Lipset ignored the values necessary for a "democratic revolution."[15] These divergent viewpoints could have generated an extremely interesting discussion, for the two arguments—the one for industrialization and the other for values—lie at the heart of the problem of mass participation in politics.

Unfortunately, it was an argument that was never joined. Rather it drifted off into the corners of political science until Almond and Verba raised it again in *The Civic Culture.* By first reassessing differences between nations, Nie, Powell, and Prewitt produced an array of incontestable evidence testifying to the influence of industrialization. By shifting the analysis to the individual level, they were able to show *how* industrialization had its impact on participation. Social status and organizational involvement continue to be the causal agents. But it was found that social class has its influence on individuals *primarily by affecting political attitudes.* That is, citizen duty, efficacy, political attentiveness, perceptions of governmental impact—indeed the entire range of attitudes that were thought to compose the civic culture—are controlled by social classes. Organizational involvement, on the other hand, operates directly on political participation and does not alter the distribution of attitudes. To summarize:

The basic finding is both simple and important. Virtually all the relationship between social status and political participation is explained by the intervening linking attitude variables. The high social status citizen does not just participate in politics; he does so only when he has attitudes such as efficacy and attentiveness which are postulated as intervening variables. Social status, then, affects rates of political participation through its effect on political attitudes. This does not mean, it must be emphasized, that the correlation between status and participation is spurious; on the contrary, it means that intervening attitude variables explain *how* a citizen's social status affects his political activity.

On the other hand, a very large part of the relationship between organizational involvement and participation *is unexplained by any variable in this model.* In every case, about 60 percent of the correlation between organizational involvement and political participation is accounted for by the direct link, that line that does not pass through social class or the attitudinal variables.[16]

Once again it is economic structure that appears as the principle cause of political participation. This is an extremely important finding at the empirical level. Just documenting the influence of industrialization on political participation constitutes a significant advance. So too, specifying this relationship now gives us a fairly good idea of how industrialization creates changes in participation and the variables through which it operates. But industrialization, and its individual manifestation in social class and organizational involvement, is not distributed in a population by egalitarian principles. Herein lies a central problem for democratic theory.

The hope of political participation is that it creates a meaningful form of equality—the political equality of individual preferences. One person, one vote, and so forth. Clearly the evidence from these surveys places this ideal in jeopardy. Social class is manifestly inequitous in its political consequences. This appears to be universally true, in all nations and for all kinds of governments. Organizational involvement does not provide a remedy for the political defects of the class system. As Verba and Nie discovered during their analysis of a subsequent survey of participation in the United States, organizational involvement usually extends political inequalities among people, rather than shrinking class differences. The one notable exception to this finding is identification with a political party. This is an exception of singular importance, as we shall see.[17] However, in general, the finding is one of political inequality.

Industrialization promotes political participation, to be sure. Yet it is participation that is intrinsically unequal. Needless to say, democratic theory proceeds with a different set of expectations. On the matter of industrialization, democratic theory has precious little to say, a circumstance that does its ideals no favor. But one of the small advantages of leaving out the most important historical phenomenon of the eighteenth, nineteenth, and very probably the twentieth centuries is that democratic theorists could assume that political participation and political equality were one and the same.

This argument developed out of necessity, as electoral systems refashioned constitutionalist designs for government. While constitutionalism was openly hostile to the mass public and unalterably opposed to its participation in politics, the pressures of history installed the mass public as sovereign. Democratic theorists coming after the various nineteenth-century enfranchisements had little choice but to adjust their thinking about the mass public. This occurred in two ways. First, political participation became a virtue in and of itself. The idea of the more participation the better arose, a strand of thinking that leads to an argument for "participatory democracy."[18] Second, there was attributed to the mass public a wide range of political virtues and values of the sort that are necessary for good, wholesome, democratic politics. As with the constitutionalists, specific values varied from theorist to theorist, thus giving this question a certain elusive quality, but the central thrust of the effort is clear. Its purpose was to find in the mass public the attributes necessary to support democratic regimes.

Needless to say, this is not particularly easy or pleasant literature. It is populated by romantic visions of human nature, with confusions between what is and what is needed, and by a desperate effort to attribute the manifest evils of politics to "political conditions" rather than to the mass public.[19] But if the substance of these theories is poor, their central thrust is absolutely correct. Democracy depends to a substantial degree on the values of the people. Locating which values are essential to democratic politics and describing how they are distributed in the mass public forms one of the great unresolved problems in political science.

What made *The Civic Culture* an exciting book, in large measure, was the authors' willingness to attack this problem systematically. Unfortunately, the theory of a civic culture did not hold up against the very evidence on which it was predicated. But finding that industrialism, and all the inequities associated with it, is the principle cause of political participation does not reduce the importance of the theoretical problem at all. The question of democratic political values remains very much alive, even if it is a question that is not very near to resolution.

Much to his credit, Sidney Verba has explored the central conclusion to emerge from the reanalysis of *The Civic Culture* with great diligence and considerable imagination. In collaboration with Norman Nie and often Jae-on Kim, he has directed a series of stunning surveys aimed directly at the relationship between political participation and political equality.[20] Many of the findings have already been mentioned, while others will be mentioned later. But one result of this work bears special attention here, both because of the universality of what was found and because of the additional complications that these findings create for democratic theory.

These studies focused directly upon the inequalities in political participation, inequalities that were produced by industrialization. The aim of these surveys was to explore the magnitude of these inequalities in all their various political manifestations and to locate those aspects of political participation that were ameliorative in nature. Ambitions of this sort obviously required better and more refined measures of political participation. To accomplish this, all of the different measures of political behavior—questions about voting, campaign activities, community involvement, and so forth—were analyzed together in order to see if there was a common underlying structure. The hope was that the various forms of political behavior could be reduced to a simpler set of dimensions. The specific technique used was factor analysis, which from a methodological point of view is the appropriate technique.

A simple structure in the mass of data on political behaviors did appear. Indeed, it appeared with a vengeance. Four characteristic types of political behavior were located—voting, campaign activity, communal activity (that is, cooperative acts and good works in the community), and particularized contacts with governments (personal initiatives taken with representatives or with government). Conceptually each of these is an extremely important form of political behavior. But of more immediately interest is the generality of these results. These four dimensions seem to *define* political behavior.[21] They are the categories into which all of the various questions asked in the post-civic culture surveys fall. These same factors emerge no matter what country's data are analyzed. Political behavior in such diverse polities as India, Yugoslavia, Japan, Austria, Mexico, and the United States takes exactly the same form.[22] That is, the same four categories describe all of the political behaviors in these countries. Of course, the frequency of individual participation within these categories varies from nation to nation. There are higher turnout rates in Mexican elections than for those in the United States, for example, but "voting" remains a distinctive form of political behavior in both nations.

So the categories of political behavior have been settled by the force of data analysis. But although it has been much less noticed, the very generality of these findings places an additional strain on democratic theory. While the raw empiricism is intriguing in and of itself, the larger purpose involved, indeed the justification of the entire enterprise, was to discover the distinctive attributes of democratic politics—of which political participation is presumably an essential element.

The net result of finding the same modes of participation in so many different polities is to challenge this presumption. As of this writing, it is a distortion to call India, Mexico, Nigeria, and Yugoslavia practicing democracies, although it is certainly possible that these nations may become so. Still, to include these countries at this time is a misleading analysis that stretches the idea of democratic government.[23] That these nations have the same modes of political participation as do the United States, Japan, the Netherlands, Canada, Norway, and so forth poses a terrible theoretical dilemma, for the very distinctiveness of political behavior in democratic politics seems to be lost.

The major inference that these common modes of political behavior carry is that political participation is, indeed, formed by industrialization. The force of industrial economics, which is what all the nations surveyed have in common, gives political behavior its characteristic forms. Although in completely different locales and with vastly different resources, they are all engaged in the process of economic development—in industrialization, by another name.

What the data have not explained as yet are the characteristics of popular participation that distinguish democracy from other forms of government. This is not so much a problem in data analysis as it is one in political theory. Unfortunately, both data analysts and students of political thought have created more confusion than clarity in this domain. It is important to an understanding of the progress (or, more accurately, the lack thereof) in the voting studies to understand why this has been so.

Further Adventures in Democratic Theory

From a theoretical vantage point, "the civic culture" was a bad idea. That is, the idea itself was not a useful addition to democratic theory, and further, it promoted a confused and unproductive set of inferences from the data. In saying this, I do not mean to treat Almond and Verba unfairly. Their book is probably the best that this period (1950–1980) has to offer. Certainly the concept of "civic culture" was light-years ahead of everything else in the field in terms of its sophistication and systematic approach—qualities I have tried to describe in the first section of this chapter.

But the quality of political thought during these years was uncommonly poor. And, unfortunately, "the civic culture" reflects this too. Indeed, because of the considerable virtues that Almond and Verba bring to their book, the harm that a bad idea can do shows up all the more clearly. One can see quite vividly how a bad theory stifles other ideas, how it detracts from the immediacy of a problem, how it becalms the turbulence of nagging questions, and how it distorts data analysis.

Of course, this puts quite a bit of emphasis on the importance of ideas. Generally speaking, it is my feeling that ideas are undervalued, that a category of thought like "democratic theory," although it gets all the plaudits it can possibly bear, is considered an unnecessary luxury or an undesirable intellectual burden. One of the central purposes of this book is to demonstrate that democratic theory is not a finished intellectual history, one populated by ancient manuscripts and dreary texts. Rather it is a domain in which vital questions remain unanswered, where, to an important degree, the success of our own government depends on increases in our ability to understand the democratic idea. If this seems hopelessly idealistic, then the matter can be looked at in terms of the terrible damage that poor theory does. I think that these observations are applicable generally, a conclusion supported by the dismal quality of contemporary politics. But certainly, on a smaller scale, the voting studies offer indisputable proof of the point.

As a category in democratic thought, the civic culture manages the difficult feat of being at once too narrow and too broad. It is too narrow in that it focuses only on political attitudes and feelings. Remember, Almond and Verba use the term to mean "an allegiant participant culture" whose individuals are not only positively oriented to "political input" but also "oriented positively to input structures and the input process." What is missing from this definition is any reference to democratic *values,* to the distinguishing beliefs fundamental to democratic politics.

On the other hand, the civic culture is too broad a category in that it never examines how people function in specific political situations. It is all well and good to know that people feel positively about the voting system and about their capacity to participate in it. But the critical test is whether they are able to use the voting system to express their issue concerns.

It must be stressed that these are not small deficiencies. The civic culture leaves out the central ingredients of democratic theory. By failing to include an articulate set of democratic values, Almond and Verba exclude the most likely remedy to the systematic influences of industrialization. What distinguishes democratic participation from political participation found in other types of regimes is in good measure a distinctive set of values. But everything depends on the definition given to this set of values. As we have seen, constitutionalism was transformed into democratic politics without any accompanying work on this question. The question of values presents enormous difficulty in its own right, but from an empirical standpoint the question is even harder. Not only does a minimum set of values have to be identified *in theory,* but once identified, the data analyst then has to cope with the problem that the mass public is often alarmingly unprincipled in its politics—a circumstance that previous surveys have thoroughly documented. Nevertheless, the fact that the problem of democratic values in the mass public is a formidable one does not in any way lessen its importance.

Similarly, asking only how people feel about their participation in politics misses the point. The central question is whether or not people are able to use the methodology of the voting system to accomplish their political objectives. Highly generalized feelings about politics obviously play a role in this. But it is a role secondary to actual accomplishments. This can be seen by the sudden demise of the civic culture in the United States during the seventies. With the system under pressure from the civil rights movement and from protests against the war in Vietnam, the indicators that Almond and Verba used plunged down.[24] If the theory had been correct, the civic culture would have supported the system precisely during this period. People would have drawn upon their positive feelings to produce desired changes. That this failed to happen seems to indicate that Almond and Verba measured popular satisfaction with performance of the economy during the fifties and early sixties, and not a resilient political culture.

The civic culture was not a terribly potent addition to democratic theory, then. Yet both the concept and the book were enormously popular, for the civic culture mirrors the hopes and beliefs of the period. It is important to stress that *The Civic Culture* was not the source of these ideas, although it did help to stabilize them in the face of disconcerting evidence from the voting studies. Rather, Almond and Verba reflected the currents of belief that were around them. Theirs is a particularly well organized and articulate presentation of themes that were everywhere, a highly intelligent edition of the mindless faith in democratic politics that was so prevalent through the fifties and sixties.

Of course the democratic ideal is to be highly valued. But what is peculiar about this period is that almost no thought was given to intellectual tradition associated with democratic ideals; nor was much attention given to the historical evolution of these principles. Instead there was the assumption that democracy was already in full flower, that the United States had achieved in practice what in theory was an elusive ideal. The problem for political analysts was to formulate valid categories that described what already had occurred. *The Civic Culture, The Liberal Tradition in America, The Genius of American Politics,* and *People of Plenty* were extremely creative efforts toward this end.[25]

In truth, the practice of democratic politics in the United States was emerging from a deeply troubled period. Postwar America, 1946–1958, was most notable for its strand of virulent anticommunism. It was an interest that was only tangentially related to policy; it was a state of mind, as Richard Nixon, Joseph McCarthy, William Knowland—indeed as virtually every politician then practicing—was to prove.

Anticommunism was a form of ideological prejudice, a belief that functioned to suppress other values and ideas. Interestingly, this was a prejudice that was strongest among the elite, those highest in income and education. This makes anticommunism unusual among prejudices. Unlike other forms of bigotry and intolerance, anticommunism amounted to an item of genuine consensus in American politics. It was a form of prejudice that was immensely popular in the mass public, and it was a prejudice that was enforced by the social, economic, and political elite. To be sure, elite segments of opinion were more conscious of the limits of anticommunism as a value than the Stouffer surveys (mentioned in chapter 4) showed. That is, the elite were more likely to respect the rights of individuals. But support for constitutional principles, as the Stouffer data also show, did not occur to any degree that students of democratic theory could find encouraging.[26]

Intellectuals generally, and certainly academics, do not like to think of themselves as subject to the cultural predisposition of the times. We are a fiercely independent sort, who, if nothing else, all value the freedom of the mind. Yet nowhere are scholars as free as they imagine. Beginning in the forties and continuing into the sixties, the political system exerted tremendous pressure on everyone, academics included, to conform to the doctrine of anticommunism and correspondingly to believe in the native integrity of democracy in the United States. These views came with much force. Not only was the mass public looking for examples of deviation in and around the universities and colleges, but the elite, very likely including the administrators and chief officers of those institutions, were looking to enforce the very same sentiments.

This is prejudice with power. And its effects were remarkable. The striking aspect of writing in the fifties and sixties is the absence of any critical quality. For the most part, I believe this reflected unconscious adjustments on the part of the authors. Certainly no one can question the diligence and integrity of the people involved with the voting studies. One does not have to know Sidney Verba, Warren Miller, Philip Converse, or Robert Dahl very well to realize that these are scholars of considerable magnitude. Yet they all yielded, however unconsciously, to the prevailing and anticommunist prejudices of their time. Whatever the authors' political views and personal opinions, the influence of this strand of prejudice appears quite plainly in the scholarly products of the period. It appears equally, I should add, in the work of the best political analyst of the period, V. O. Key, Jr. All this is strong testimony indeed to the power of ideas and values.

Precisely because anticommunism was such a manifestly undemocratic value, it was difficult to acknowledge its position in the mass public and among the political elite. Doing so would have focused the strength of that prejudice on those who asked the questions. Serious students of politics avoided the subject instinctively. In *The Civic Culture* the subject is never discussed; there simply is no mention of McCarthyism or anticommunism. Nor were Almond and Verba unusual in this regard. Avoidance was much the better part of valor.

Ironically, the underlying concept of the period was "consensus." Every interpretation of the democratic idea used it. It even drifted into the political arena, there to be seized upon with a vengeance by President Johnson. As an idea, consensus was used to signify the unique and special ingredients that made the American democracy (and others like it) work, the essential stuff that made democratic politics operational.

As I have been saying all along, the values of the mass public as well as those of the political elite are essential elements of democratic politics. In developing the idea of a "democratic consensus," the voting studies could have gone a long way in exploring the values underlying the American political system. However, the starting place during the postwar period would have had to be the business of anticommunism. There was an enormous amount to learn by coming to grips with the underside of consensus, the power of antidemocratic values and how they operated in the mass public and among the political elite. But to open up this area to inquiry required a level of critical intelligence, a precision of thought and analysis, that itself would have to confront the power of this undemocratic prejudice.

Still, one cannot elaborate a concept like the "democratic consensus" and leave out essential elements of reality without incurring a terrific cost in the validity of the idea itself. Once universal agreement on "the rules of the game," the consensus on elements of constitutionalism, had been discounted by survey researchers, the idea of a democratic consensus became increasingly vague. It had a magical quality. Democracy lived by general agreement on the practice of democracy—on the national genius of particular nations.

In Almond and Verba's minds, "the civic culture" is most of all "allegiant." People trust each other; they have a strong faith in their governing institutions. This permits a relatively high level of political involvement, and concomitantly, of political cleavage, by subordinating these

to a more general overarching set of social values. As the data . . . suggest attitudes of interpersonal trust and cooperation are more frequent in the United States and Britain than in the other nations. More important, these general social attitudes penetrate into the realm of politics. The role of social trust and cooperativeness as a component of the civic culture cannot be overemphasized. It is, in a sense, a generalized resource that keeps a democratic polity operating.[27]

Thus is an underlying political consensus formed. But notice that it is a consensus without substance. Trust and cooperation appear as a social gift, nurtured by national histories and in turn nurturing national institutions. It is a consensus achieved without reference to other democratic values. It exists without reference to any specific elements of belief.

Trust and cooperation result from accomplishment. They are the result of shared values from specific political achievements—in this case, from the tremendous economic gains that followed the Second World War. Almond and Verba had picked up an effect but treated it instead as a cause. Intellectually the result was to further separate an understanding of how the democratic idea actually worked from its contemporary political practice.

Notice too that a consequence of the civic culture as an idea was to distort important and troubling aspects of the data. The five nation survey showed that in fact "there exists a gap between the *actual political behavior* of our respondents, on the one hand, and their *perceptions of their capacities to act* and their *obligations to act,* on the other."[28] Further, there was a similar gap between perceptions of potential influence and a much lower level of actual influence. Rather than treating these shortfalls as real, as weaknesses within the civic culture, they were incorporated within the idea as theoretical strengths.

These two gaps—between a high perception of potential influence and a lower level of actual influence, and between a high frequency of expressed obligation to participate and the actual importance and amount of participation—help explain how a democratic political culture can act to maintain a balance between governmental elite power and governmental elite responsiveness (or its complement, a balance between non-elite activity and influence and non-elite passivity and non-influence). The comparative infrequency of political participation, its relative lack of importance for the individual, and the objective weakness of the ordinary man allow governmental elites to act. The inactivity of the ordinary man and his inability to influence decisions help provide the power that governmental elites need to make decisions.[29]

The idea is that "a citizen within the civic culture has . . . a reserve influence. He is not constantly involved in politics. He does not actively oversee the behavior of political decision makers. But he does have the potential to act if there is a need."[30]

Almond and Verba are expressing the sentiment of the period. Everywhere survey data was reporting that the mass public exhibited in varying degrees undemocratic sentiments, that it was prone to spasms of undemocratic behavior, and that, in the American case, it tended to be weak and inactive. Yet political analysts were loath to acknowledge these to be genuine problems. There was always a new category, a different variation in theory that explained matters, that preserved the mass public as both participatory and democratic. "I want to propose an alternative explanation," wrote Robert Dahl in the most widely read, and possibly the most overrated, book during these years,

namely that democratic beliefs, like other beliefs, are influenced by a recurring *process* of interchange among political professionals, the political stratum, and the great bulk of the population. The process generates enough agreement on rules and norms so as to permit the system to operate, but agreement tends to be incomplete, and typically it decays. So the process is frequently repeated. "Consensus," then, is not at all a static and unchanging attribute of citizens. It is a variable element in a complex and more or less continuous process.[31]

"Consensus," "process," and the compensatory effects of the political system were ideas that appeared with a frequency that is startling.[32] Berelson, Lazarsfeld, and McPhee, when confronted with "inconsistencies" in their data, said about the same thing.[33] Despite the great gains made in our understanding of the political participation of mass publics, this knowledge did not coalesce in such a way as to form new insights. All in all, the voting studies have made a neglible contribution to political theory.

The Retreat of the Political Theorists

The obvious question in all of this is: Whatever happened to students of political theory? They were presented with a situation where the history of ideas was woefully misunderstood, where new concepts were being formulated without meaning or substance, and where political theory itself was being badly abused. Why did political theorists not seek to clarify matters? Why did they not generate a storm of criticism? After all, ideas that had been their special concern were being all but destroyed.

Political theorists never have become involved with the voting studies, of course. They criticized the theories somewhat at the outset, in the early fifties. But thereafter, political theorists are most notable in their absence. By using their publications alone as a guide, one could never guess that there had been a singular increase in the power of electoral analysis, that the technology of survey research created new opportunity to ask old questions in a new form. Political theorists seemed to retreat from the revolutionary implications of the political survey.

Two factors explain this singular failure. The first is technical in nature. Despite all the brave talk about theory and method working best together, the fact is that they are each quite distinct traditions of thought with very little in common—save perhaps a compelling sense of rigor and a demand for detail. Political theory's concern is for ideas—ideas not as small hypotheses, but as unique concepts, each with a distinctive pattern of development and unusual blend of influences. Such concepts are not expressed easily in statistical analysis. Ideas in political theory are completed as abstractions, wherein the fullness of thought, subtlety, and variation in theme and an explicit sense of ambiguity are much valued.

Statistical analysis demands a different, but equally rigorous, quality of thought. Precision in this tradition is a narrowness of focus. Theories must be tested not in the fullness of their complexity, but in explicit and manifest relationships. Concepts must be stripped down to operational details. The techniques of measurement and analysis impose themselves on political theory; or, rather, two very different styles of thought are forced to live together.

Of course, political theory and quantitative analysis can be successfully joined. But it is a much more difficult union than is commonly supposed. Differences in the style of thought, then, go some distance toward explaining the prolonged absence of political theorists from the voting studies. Still, another reason must be emphasized, one that is more personal in nature.

From the outset, political theorists viewed the voting studies as a threat to their position in the field of political science. The issues here are not terribly intellectual in character, centering as they did on money, power, and jobs. Nevertheless, or perhaps because of this, the results were fascinating.

Political theory had long been the bedrock of the profession. It was the specialization that was first among equals, the area of study that attracted the best minds, the one subject every aspiring political scientist was required to study. With the quantitative revolution, this sense of primacy was lost, and more. Stock in political theory literally plummeted. From the ranking field in the profession, suddenly political theory was uninteresting. Nobody wanted to study it. In many graduate departments it was dropped as a requirement, and where the requirement remained, it was watered down. The market for political theorists collapsed under the strain. There were fewer jobs. Grants and foundation funding virtually disappeared.

Furthermore, there was a tremendous loss in prestige. This again was not an intellectual matter, not an honest difference of opinion over the value of political theory. It was much more an undercurrent of bitterness and hostility. It swirled in and out of professional gatherings, within departments, and among graduate students. Political theory has never been easy. And for those students who do not plan to make a profession of teaching it, examinations on political theory are a most fearful event. Many graduate students would postpone their general examinations for as much as a year in order to prepare this field, and no one outside of political theory was comfortable in it.

With the quantitative revolution, there was suddenly a convenient reason to avoid all this unpleasantness. The reaction against political theory was almost total. It was as if the resentment and difficulty of those graduate years could not be expressed freely and was expressed indirectly by the rejection of political theory. This was unjust, of course, but not wholly undeserved.

For reasons that are still not apparent, political theorists in the period following the Second World War ceased to do political theory as a creative enterprise and began to concentrate on the history of ideas. Theorists like Carl Freidrich and Louis Hartz began to fade from prominence. There was less an attempt to add to theory than to clarify the grand conceptions of others.

This had the consequence of making a discipline that contains, by its nature, a fair amount of formality excessively formal. There was much attention to detail. A spate of books appeared on the seminal names in political theory: John Locke, Jean-Jacques Rousseau, Karl Marx. Much attention was paid to the development of ideas—Leo Straus and his school or alternatively Sheldon Wolin, or Ernst Cassirer, or John Plamenatz.

Little wonder that those poor graduate students who did not intend a career in political theory (myself among them) trembled before general examinations. How could one possibly read the masters carefully, and be responsible for knowing the progression of ideas and how they influenced each other, while at the same time developing a primary field of specialization with its appropriate corollaries? And worse, there were a sufficient number of mean-spirited theorists who were only too willing to make the examination process a fairly brutal experience.

Political theorists, then, reacted to a declining market position by making things worse. They turned inward and nurtured their sense of injustice. Ironically, this resulted in some good work being done. Without concentrating on the electoral process, Hanna Pitkin analyzed the concept of representation; there appeared several excellent studies of the development of constitutionalism; Isaac

Kramnick wrote a fine biography of Viscount Bolingbroke and Betty Kemp added an extremely useful study of Sir Francis Dashwood. J. G. A. Pocock supplied a superb essay on English political ideologies in the eighteenth century.[34]

If these works lack a sense of grand adventure, a sense of exploration into the unknown, it is equally true that they provide insight and excitement of a different kind. They are careful contributions to an understanding of constitutional theory. A very systematic development of constitutionalism's many themes, and the host of variations upon them, is provided. It was almost as if political theorists reacted intuitively to the confusion of the voting studies by reexamining the intellectual basis of the democratic idea.

This body of scholarship is extremely useful in its own right, of course, as a guide to other scholars who wish to work on the democratic idea. From the perspective of the voting studies, however, it has two serious defects. In the first place, it does not address the changes that were made in constitutional theory by the electoral process. To concentrate on constitutionalism alone is to stop at the water's edge. Or, more properly, it is to halt political theory at the end of the eighteenth century. It leaves unaddressed the turbulent transformation of constitutional theory into democratic politics. As I have tried to point out, this area of political theory has yet to be charted. While a sound theoretical foundation in the development of constitutionalism is essential to such explorations, sound foundations are most useful when they are built upon. There was, alas, no effort by political theorists to move into this area.

The second major defect in this research was that it remained isolated from the voting studies. By and large, quantitative political analysts no longer read political theory. It was judged to be unnecessary baggage by the more senior members in the field, and younger recruits seemed to lack training in political theory altogether—this, undoubtedly, was a consequence of the changes made in graduate study programs. So among the quantitative researchers there was simply no appreciation that political theorists had anything to offer.

Political theorists, for their part, failed to appreciate the great potential of survey research, just as they failed to understand the importance of the voting studies. If quantitative political analysts suffered from a certain lack of depth and sophistication, political theorists suffered from a regrettable lack of imagination and insight. The break between theorists and the voting studies has been more or less permanent. In this regard, *The Civic Culture* forms something of a watershed.

Almond and Verba's work was an effort to explain an important aspect of democratic theory, namely how the mass public promoted or retarded the stability of democratic governments. It was the theory in their work that cried out for discussion and criticism. Implicit in it were all the unanswered questions involving the transformation of constitutionalism into democratic politics. Unfortunately, there is little evidence that political theorists read this book, or if they did, they failed to see in it aspects of their own special field of knowledge.

In this failure, an important opportunity was missed. For *The Civic Culture* is an easy book to read. It contains no elaborate pieces of data analysis; no special methodological training is required to understand the flow of the argument. After the book's publication the voting studies would become much more difficult to penetrate. *The Civic Culture* itself was responsible for this in a small way, in that its data proved so much stronger than its theory. But the larger reason was that a new generation of students, now fully trained in statistical analysis, was coming along. Also a new generation of large computers, the IBM 360 series, became available, and with them a new batch of sophisticated prepackaged programs, among them Statistical Package for the Social Sciences (SPSS).[35] The emphasis now was even more technical in nature.

If in the first instance political theorists had disdained involvement in the voting studies, now there were substantial entry costs. A working knowledge of multivariate statistics and data analysis was a prerequisite. Participation by the mass public in political life remains a quintessential problem in political theory, but it is a problem that cannot be addressed without prior methodological training.

The explanation for the failure to achieve a better understanding of the role of the mass public in democratic politics lies in this peculiar intellectual history. Theory and method have truly been separated. Political analysts have worked the data into ever more elaborate empirical relationships without being prepared to consider the theoretical implications of the results. Students of political theory, on the other hand, remain insensitive to the emergence of what is a powerful series of empirical relationships and unprepared to participate in any meaningful discussion of them. The popular basis of democratic politics, the essential ingredients that must be provided by the mass public, continues to be a mystery.

PART II

ISSUES IN ELECTORAL POLITICS

Rationality.—The democratic citizen is expected to exercise rational judgment in coming to his voting decision. He is expected to have arrived at his principles by reason and to have considered rationally the implications and alleged consequences of the alternative proposals of the contending parties. Political theorists and commentators have always exclaimed over the seeming contrast here between requirement and fulfilment. . . . In any rigorous or narrow sense the voters are not highly rational; that is, most of them do not ratiocinate on the matter, e.g., to the extent that they do on the purchase of a car or a home. Nor do voters act rationally whose "principles" are held so tenaciously as to blind them to information and persuasion. Nor do they attach efficient means to explicit ends.

BERNARD BERELSON,
PAUL F. LAZARSFELD, AND WILLIAM McPHEE
Voting

We have, then, the portrait of an electorate almost wholly without detailed information about decision making in government. A substantial portion of the public is able to respond in a discrete manner to issues that *might* be the subject of legislative or administrative action. Yet it knows little about what government has done on these issues or what the parties propose to do. It is almost completely unable to judge the rationality of government actions; knowing little of particular policies and what has led to them, the mass electorate is not able to appraise either its goals or the appropriateness of the means chosen to serve these goals.

ANGUS CAMPBELL ET AL.,
The American Voter

Introduction

Less is known about electoral democracy than we pretend. It would seem that this form of government is valued beyond our appreciation of the essential concept itself, certainly beyond our understanding of the way it operates. As a category of political discourse, electoral competition acts indiscriminantly—to obscure meanings, to hide underlying issues.

The resulting confusion about elections arises from the great popularity of what is an extraordinarily complex and ambiguous concept. Seeing this, George Orwell once recommended that phrases like electoral democracy be dropped. Let each person define the forms of government in operational terms, without borrowing misplaced meanings. This suggestion has its advantages. But too much intellectual and political history is lost by it. Formal categories are essential tools of analysis—both for the distinctions they supply as well as for the ambiguities they create. Better to be clear, precise, and honest in one's dealings with this most difficult concept.

I think the place to begin is with the understanding that electoral democracy as a theory of government, much less as a practice, is far from complete. This applies in two senses. Most important, the idea itself is not fully developed. It does not stand as a finished concept with all the pieces present and identified. Even if one sifts through the history of the idea and studies how it has been practiced, one still comes up short. Electoral democracy is preeminently a self-conscious concept. Yet electoral democracy also demands an inordinate amount of faith.

There is another, more immediate, sense in which electoral democracy is incomplete. Our understanding of the concept is limited by the manner in which it developed. In intellectual terms, the democratic idea was completed during the Enlightment. It was during this marvelously fertile period that the individual was made the basis of the state, that the concept of inalienable rights and personal liberties flowered, that the power of government was given limits, that the purposes of the state were enumerated, that public institutions were organized in functional terms—separated and balanced—and that the necessity of written constitutions was recognized. Each of these aspects of electoral democracy had been established by the time that the United States came to draft its Constitution.[1]

The electoral process, however, did not develop corresponding significance as a generalized method for conferring public power until much later. Insofar as this method was considered, it was either greatly restricted in principle or rejected outright—in both cases the explanation being that mass publics and electoral processes were inconsistent with the principles of individual liberty, "democratic" government, and the public good.

Elections and participation won their victories, not in pages of theory, but in time and through practice, in the fire of group conflict (between classes, between religious groups, between center and periphery, between regions, between states).[2] It was almost as if political history took one of the most precious achievements of the Enlightenment and returned it to democratic theory for major revision.

In principle, the criticism of history was quite to the point. The distribution of political power in constitutional theory was inherently unfair. Whether this was for the best of motives (to protect the public good) or for the worst (to protect class interests) is quite beside the point. Those systematic biases had to be remedied. The course of history rearranged the constitutional divisions described in theory so that there would be a more equitable distribution of power. One person, one vote—to amend the ill-considered wording by the United States Supreme Court of an otherwise valid proposition. The redistribution of public power through mass participation in the electoral process altered the entire theory of democracy as it emerged from the Enlightment. "Constitutional democracy" became an irrelevant formalism. It no longer described the distribution of power or the processes by which power is obtained. Under the pressure of group conflict, constitutional divisions acquired a meaning quite different from that which had been intended. Government had shifted forms.

These developments occurred without benefit of theoretical exposition. The sweep of history was clean, but quite silent. It can be said that, *in principle,* mass participation and the electoral process solved the problem of power in democratic politics. But this is an argument that cannot be made in principle alone. Political power, in the end, is essentially an empirical proposition. The question arises whether popular participation in the electoral processes produces results—whether, indeed, political power has been redistributed.

Robert Dahl's question, "Who governs?" is very much to the point. The electoral process has some very strong pretensions in this regard. But how are they to be evaluated? What are the critical tests that electoral politics must pass to be accepted as a valid solution to the problem of power in democratic theory?

As if this question were not burden enough, there is a further line of inquiry that must be pursued. Mass participation and the electoral process also must answer to the normative demands of democratic theory. What political values (and personality traits) must mass publics maintain to ensure the good order of democratic politics? It is one thing to conclude that "the people rule." It is quite another to describe how a successful electoral democracy functions.

These are grand inquiries, indeed. They demand that the logic of mass politics be made articulate and that the operation of the electoral process be a matter of conscious understanding. But these demands have been ignored for a very long time. Popular participation in elections as a form of government seems to thrive on romantic illusions—illusions that are remarkable primarily for their stubborn ability to cloud honest political analysis.

Of course, romantic illusions will no longer do. Perhaps as the electoral process was washing away constitutional barriers it was useful to be enchanted with "The People." But we have learned in a series of painful lessons that people can fervently support vile public policies, that they can choose leaders of unrelenting incompetence, and that they can be altogether insensitive citizens.

Once democratic theory had accepted this unhappy view of human nature but had sought to mitigate its political consequences by the "just" distsribution of power and by an inordinate faith in the power of reason among political elites. These remedies collapsed with the emergence of the electoral process but without there being corresponding advances elsewhere in democratic theory.

Electoral democracy, then, is composed of two unmatched halves. There is a venerable and sophisticated tradition of democratic thought, reaching its high-water mark in the Enlightenment but continuing as a standard of evaluation and method of inquiry into the present. But there also is the electoral side of the equation —mass participation, public opinion, and the electoral process. These came to power in the absence of articulate theory, without a body of critical intelligence by which they can be evaluated.

It would be nice if I could report that, over the years, substantial progress has been made in joining these two disparate elements, that there has been a cumulative trend toward explanation. But the present statuts of the concept is not nearly so pretty. The best efforts of contemporary political theorists have amounted to very little.[3] This is less a statement about the poverty of theory than it is a good estimate of the difficulty of the problem. Mass participation and the electoral process are too formidable to be worked out as "pure" theory—in one's head, as it were. These are problems that require both theory and data, where political analysis must have a reliable body of survey data and appropriate analytic techniques.

It is precisely here that the voting studies held such great promise. At the outset, however, the two major survey research institutions—the Bureau of Applied Social Research and the Survey Research Center—possessed little knowledge of politics and even less familiarity with political theory. At the same time, unfortunately, political scientists were equally unskilled in survey research and quantitative methods. The great promise of the voting studies dissolved amid a welter of theoretical complications and empirical misunderstandings. Political behavior became its own narrow speciality, noted for its technical virtuosity but quite isolated from questions of deeper significance.

In the preceding chapters I have considered the voting studies as a fascinating problem in intellectual history. This perspective permitted me to ask how such a marvelous set of research techniques could produce such an unsatisfying literature while, at the same time, these very techniques have located so many relationships of fundamental political importance.

In the chapters that follow I want to shift the emphasis to a more meaningful analysis of the study of elections and participation. By inclination and training, I am most comfortable working fairly close to the data of politics. But my intentions are no less theoretical. It is my hope that in my efforts I will have benefited from the relationships that others have found as well as from some of the mistakes that they have made.

Theory is both an overworked and an underdeveloped category at present. It is overused in the sense that people seem to delight in advancing new theories, in introducing major conceptual innovations. The voting studies have suffered for theorizing of this sort at every turn. I do not have anything so elaborate in mind. Rather, the questions that I want to ask are of an older vintage and do not seem to require much in the way of new conceptual apparatus.

There also is a sense in which theory is an underused form of expression. Empirical regularities warrant inferences. I am predisposed to make these. But inferences, if they are to be at all insightful, must exceed the data. With the voting studies, however, the data themselves constitute a serious obstacle. These limitations must be part of the discussion too. But the very thinness of the data makes "strong inferences" all the more essential.[4] If I have thought the voting studies often mistaken and negligent, it is well that I put my own ideas on the line.

CHAPTER 6

Party Identification
and Candidate Images

In view of the influence that the Survey Research Center has had on the study of electoral behavior, its contributions have been surprisingly modest. No general theory of electoral behavior has emerged as a result of its researches, and very few new relationships have been discovered. The SRC established the importance of party identification, of course, and the significance and the power of that discovery can hardly be overstated. It has also provided some excellent work on the flow of information, the components of electoral decisions, and the process of political socialization. But these strands of research, party identification aside, have been much more in the nature of systematizing relationships that had been previously discovered rather than in plotting a fundamentally new course of analysis.

Two aspects of the voting studies conducted by the Survey Research Center seem to stand out above all else. One is the consistent excellence of administration at the SRC. In its ability to organize and fund a series of complex electoral surveys, the SRC demonstrated an enormous institutional capacity. This is not a quality to be lightly considered. Simply in terms of its ability to obtain research grants, the SRC has shown remarkable strength and inventiveness. Equally important, it has maintained a steady flow of data that are of unquestioned excellence. The cost associated with maintaining these data has been borne by the Interuniversity Consortium for Political Research, which also ensured that these data have been available generally and that a succession of students have been trained in the analysis of these data (among them this author). Largely under the direction of Warren Miller, the Survey Research Center has been able to institutionalize the voting studies, ensuring that every national election since 1952 has been surveyed.[1]

A second notable trait that has characterized the SRC has been the consistently high quality of its publications. Both in methodological and in conceptual terms, analyses bearing the SRC's imprimatur have been notable for their precision. Data have always been analyzed thoroughly; arguments have been cogently organized; inferences have been sharply stated. The work of Angus Campbell, Philip Converse, Warren Miller, and Donald Stokes—whether writing in combination or writing alone—has been consistently strong. So too has the work of a succession of younger scholars who have been (or have become) associated with the Center's researchers—Merrill Shanks, Aage Clauson, Herbert Weiseberg, Arthur Miller, Jerold Rusk, Arthur Wolfe, Alden Raine. If their publications have often sown the seeds of controversy, this should be taken as a measure of their power and importance.

Yet the influence of the Survey Research Center has not been uniformly positive. Although as an institution it has become synonymous with the voting studies, there has always been a distinctly nonpolitical emphasis to its surveys. Or rather, the SRC consistently has failed to capture the essence of electoral politics, either as history or as theory. This has not been an accidental outcome, but rather it is a systematic consequence of the SRC's approach to voting and elections.

Approaches to Voting

The Survey Research Center began its study of voting without any clearly specified model of voting and elections, indeed without any clearly identified problem, in mind. Looking back, this seems very odd. But at the time, such an explicit focus was not required, and in view of the circumstances it would have only complicated matters. The SRC's association with the voting studies originated in its opposition to the work of Paul Lazarsfeld and his associates at the Bureau of Applied Social Research. Political scientists were looking for an alternative to the social determinism contained in those studies and were delighted to seize upon the opportunity presented by the SRC, as we have seen.

Angus Campbell of the SRC shared an abiding hostility to social determinism as a category of explanation. His commitment was to a different branch of sociology—social psychology. Between Lazarsfeld's emphasis on social structure and Campbell's emphasis on individual perceptions there lay a good deal of intellectual ground. The heart of social psychology beat to individual perceptions and subjective identifications. It was not the imposition of social structure that determined how people lived, rather it was how people perceived social structures that gave characteristic shape to their "life space."[2] Individual perceptions determined social structure, as it were. As applied to politics, the SRC wished to emphasize the immediacy of the relationship of individual "perceptions, values, and identifications"[3] to voting decisions in contrast to the influence of social and economic forces.

With a heavy emphasis on individual attitudes, and in an attempt to reinstate political variables as the foci for the analysis of political behavior, the Center executed a study [the 1952 survey] which gave short shrift to such time-honored variables as income, occupation, or religion. The main thrust of the argument was that individual perceptions, values, and identifications related to political phenomena can be the stuff and substance of political analysis; socioeconomic variables were by implication assigned a secondary role.[4]

The source of the misunderstanding among David Truman, V. O. Key and associates, and the SRC is easy to see, in retrospect. Speaking for political analysts, Truman and Key were asking that electoral surveys focus on the politically relevant characteristics of voting—individual perceptions, values, and identifications specially defined by the electoral process. Campbell and Miller, speaking for the SRC, had in mind a different range of individual perceptions, values, and identifications. Their interest was in the subjective definitions the individual gave to politics.

These two approaches sound closer than they are. The perspective of social psychology seeks to understand the individual's subjective representation of politics. But the focus for the political analyst is on the distinctive qualities that the electoral process imposes upon individual perceptions—elections sometimes producing one set of characteristics and at times imposing different qualities. The two approaches lead to an entirely different set of research questions.

But this is to state matters much more clearly than they were understood at the time.[5] The two become hopelessly ensnarled. It would take time—the better part of the next twenty years—to sort through the confusing interpretations of the electoral process and to understand the controversies that had developed. This is to focus on the results, however. As a practical matter, the Survey Research Center never missed so much as a step.

The approach to electoral surveys—the orientation of the research—has remained fixed; the social-psychological view guided the preparation of each survey. At the same time, the SRC has been remarkably indiscriminant in its attachments to theory. As Warren Miller observed with characteristic bluntness, "We were concerned with political phenomena, of course, but we did not have any theory which argued that political behavior was any different from social or economic behavior."[6]

Not surprisingly, the SRC shifted its interpretative model of voting decisions from one publication to the next, staying always within the social-psychological framework, of course. The 1952 study, for example, depicted voting decisions as the joint product of individual perceptions of party identification, candidate orientation, and issue orientation. It is important to stress that each of these variables was treated in terms of individual perceptions, in terms of general orientations as individuals impose their definitions on electoral politics. While this captures the mood of social psychology as a research orientation, it is not much of a theory of voting, as several reviewers were quick to point out.[7]

The authors of *The American Voter* were at pains, therefore, to correct this defect. They accomplished this in a discussion of the book's "theoretical orientation," which, as luck would have it, is less a model of voting decisions (much less the electoral process) than it is a description of the application of social psychology to the study of voting.[8]

Voting decisions continue to be seen as a function of individual perceptions. The substance of these perceptions is drawn from the vast array of political, social, and economic forces that form the "life space" in which people live. Of course, these political and social forces are given meaning only to the extent that people perceive them. The metaphor that is used to give shape to these ideas is that of the "funnel of causality," a representation of which is presented in figure 6.1.[9] Perceptions that have the greatest causal impact on voting decisions appear at the narrow end of the funnel. These are the perceptions, orientations, and values of which people are most immediately aware and which, in this case, turn out to be similar to those employed in the model of voting developed in the 1952 study.[10] These perceptions are then traced back to their origins, to ever more distant perceptions of political, social and economic factors.

This effort at theory did not receive a much better reception than did the first.[11] Rather than defend this approach, the SRC simply abandoned it, omitting it from the paperback abridgement of *The American Voter* altogether. The theory that has been used in its place rests on the concept of "the normal vote." This is theory, more or less, as raw empiricism. It uses the manifest power that party identification has in determining voting decisions as the

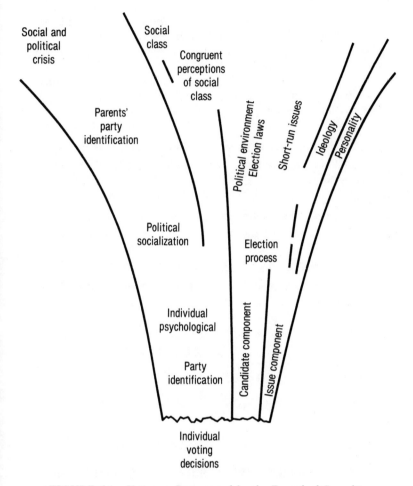

FIGURE 6.1 *Voting as Represented by the Funnel of Causality*

SOURCE: Natchez, Peter B. "The Reasonable Voter." Ph.D. diss., Harvard University, 1969, p. 562.

means for examining both long- and short-term influences on voting decisions.

The important point of our current purposes, of course, is . . . the utility of the normal vote construct in sharpening our analyses of the meaning of voting change. If citizens approached each election tabula rasa, then there would be no point in analyzing long-term components of the vote. . . . On the other hand, if all channels of political communication were to be shut off, so that citizens were obliged to go to the polls with no new political information to evaluate, there would be no short-term component to analyze. In reality, voting decisions involve a blend of these components, and it is illuminating to split them up analytically. The normal vote construct enjoys a sound operational base for this task.[12]

While methodologically the normal vote is a much more elegant concept than the funnel of causality, the conceptual distinction between the two is difficult to draw. The SRC has not altered its approach to research on electoral politics. Over the years it has merely shifted causal metaphors.[13] This research orientation is responsible for much of the misunderstanding that surrounds the relationship between issues and voting, as we shall see. But whatever the quarrel over electoral theory, there can be little argument about the power that party identification exerts on voting decisions.

The Social Psychology of Party Identification

Given the statistical significance of this concept, it is important to understand exactly what the SRC means by party identification. Political parties are conceived of as a type of social group, a group that happens to be political in character but is otherwise no different from other social groups. Identification with this group is psychological in character, resting on nothing more than personal perceptions of the group's importance. More distantly, the existence of parties is seen as a social phenomena, a political manifestation of more distant social and economic forces, no different from, say, labor unions or social classes. Parties are distinctive in that they are the groups most immediately relevant to politics, but they obtain no distinctive political characteristics. There is no sense that party identification results from a continuous flow of individual political concerns, values, issues, and events. Least of all is it a reflection of conscious choice, an expression of articulate political feelings. People can be said to choose their party identification only insofar as they can be said to choose their religion. Moreover, like religion, identification with a political party alters individual perceptions and puts pressure upon the individual "to conform to what he sees as party standards."[14]

The concept of party identification, as we have defined it, implies a personal sense of belonging to one or the other of the major political parties. We have proposed that this psychological attachment is one of the major forces which determines the behavior of voters on Election Day. We have also suggested that this factor will have effects not only on voting preferences but also in the stands the individual citizen takes on political issues. It is our belief that party serves a standard-setting function for its followers, that conformity to this standard will be most apparent on issues which are most clearly party-related, and that strong party identifiers will conform more closely to their "party-line" than will weak identifiers.[15]

Party identification as it is formulated here is "a concept in which the Survey Research Center has a strong and continuing interest," wrote Angus Campbell and Homer Cooper, actually understating matters.[16] But at the time when the SRC was just getting into the business of electoral surveys, it lacked an adequate indicator of party identification. Individual voting intentions ("if the presidential election were held today, how do you think you would vote?") were used at first, but this was an unsuitable measure for obvious reasons.

Actually, it was V. O. Key, Jr., who formulated the indicator that was later to become the bane of his interest in the electoral process. Writing to Angus Campbell about the SRC's initial efforts to measure party identification, Key observed that "the whole business strikes me as a most indirect way to get at the perhaps 'autonomous' political variable. 'Are you intensely, moderately, or only slightly loyal to the X party' might get you a better predictory than the other attributes."[17]

With a more valid and reliable indicator in place, party identification quickly established itself as the principle motivation in determining individual voting decisions. The impact of party identification in this regard can be gauged by the data contained in table 6.1 and figure 6.2. The data in the table simply report the distribution of party identification in the American electorate over time, from the 1952 through the 1978 elections, while figure 6.2 reports the direct, bivariate relationship between party identification and voting behavior.

The most impressive quality of these data is the relative stability of party identification over time. These data span seven presidential elections—elections that have seen a considerable amount of political turmoil. The most regular feature of the political landscape surely has been the distribution of party identification in the electorate.

Stability, of course, is a relative matter. These data also indicate that substantial changes have occurred in the composition and intensity of party identification. The number of people who think of themselves as independents has almost doubled during

TABLE 6.1

Division of Votes "Normally" Expected to Party

Party	Expected Proportion of Two Party Vote Democratic	Volatility of Votes by Party Types
Strong Democrats	.96	Low
Weak Democrats	.82	Medium
Independents	.49	High
Weak Republicans	.16	Medium
Strong Republicans	.04	Low

SOURCE: Philip Converse, "The Concept of the Normal Vote," in *Elections and the Political Order* (New York: Wiley, 1966), 27.

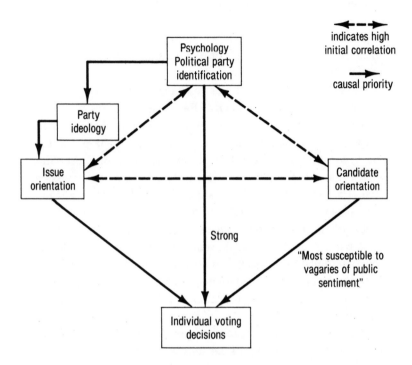

FIGURE 6.2   *The SRC's Preliminary Model of the Forces Causing the*
Voter to Decide

NOTE: Peter B. Natchez, "The Reasonable Voter." Ph.D. diss., Harvard University, 1969,
p. 561.

the period covered by these data, so that almost 40 percent of the
electorate now think of themselves in nonpartisan terms. Correspondingly, there has been a sharp decline in the number of people who think of themselves as strong partisans; the 1964 election
was a crucial indicator of this shift. There also has been a more
or less steady growth in the number of people expressing negative
feelings about both parties. While these shifts have affected all
segments of the electorate to some degree, they have been most
pronounced among young voters just entering the electorate. The

169

intergenerational transmission of party identification is declining in importance at this point, and the decline seems to be cumulative in that each successive generation of voters has been less likely to reproduce the levels of partisanship of the previous generation.[18]

Party identifications are not unchanging, then—a matter to which I will return in chapter 8. But these variations would not deflect attention away from the singular stability that the distribution of party identifications has maintained or the power that party identification have had in explaining voting decisions. Given that the American political system has seen the assassination of a president and of several political leaders, political agitation around the increasingly intractable problem of racial discrimination, mobilization against the Vietnam War, several third-party candidates and movements, a serious and prolonged economic inflation associated with rising interest rates and relatively high levels of unemployment, and a variety of significant group conflicts, party identifications have exhibited an amazing resilience.

One measure of the tenacity of party identification—the best measure undoubtedly—is its capacity to predict voting decisions. No other variable in American electoral politics exhibits the same analytic power. (See figure 6.2.) To be sure, the relationship seems to reach a peak with the 1960 election, and there is a noticeable decline in the relationship's power with the 1964 election and thereafter. But the relationship remained strong nevertheless. The capacity of party identification to motivate voting decisions is all the more impressive given the problems in intergenerational transmission of party identification; its statistical significance actually enjoyed a modest rise with the 1976 election. As Campbell and associates concluded, with every justification: "no single datum can tell us more about the attitude and behavior of the individual as a presidential elector than his location on a dimension of psychological identification extending between the two great political parties."[19]

Party Identification—Present and Past

The significance of party identification is not limited to its formidable influence upon voting decisions. It shapes individual perceptions and defines political attitudes. This means that the electorate's attitudes about politics and toward particular candidates and issues are largely a function of party loyalties, and thus beyond the influence of the electoral process, at least in the short run.

Party identification does not originate as a consequence of electoral politics. Usually it is a result of the process of political socialization, a matter rooted in the family and the family's perception of its immediate social environment. "It is apparent from this presentation," concluded Campbell and associates, sounding for all the world like Berelson, Lazarsfeld, and McPhee, "that an orientation towards political affairs typically begins before the individual attains voting age and that this orientation strongly reflects his immediate social milieu, in particular, his family."[20] Furthermore, these partisan identifications are often learned in a most casual and unconscious way. ("It is not much of an exaggeration to say that parents socialize their children [into partisan orientations] despite themselves.")[21]

It is the nonpolitical quality of this process that is remarkable. The significance of partisan affiliations is no different from the character of identifications with any secondary group. The political impact of party identifications is the greater only because such loyalties are always part of electoral politics. But the nature of the relationship is not intrinsically political.

If the political party, and psychological membership in it, fit a more general model for social memberships and political influence, it is equally clear that the party has a peculiar location in the space that the model encompasses. We have laid out with some care what seem to be the components of the relationship between any group and the world of politics. This effort was necessary because the secondary groups with which we dealt were not at base political, and this fact turns out to be a crucial limitation in the political influence they can wield. Now if we were to fill in the values that the scheme requires for prediction, we would find that in the case of party, proximity is at an upper limit, for the party has a central position in the world of politics. In all major elections, its salience is absolutely high: one candidate is always a group member, the prime group goal is political victory, and all controversial issues represent subordinate goals that the group has assumed. The legitimacy of its activity in politics goes without question for the major parties at least, and the communication of their standards is perfect.[22]

In normal times, party identification is a family matter. It is during times of crisis that this pattern is disrupted and that old identifications are altered and new ones formed. The very nature of these massive changes marks these crises as distinctive, and the elections that occur during them are "critical" in that the party loyalties for the subsequent political period are established at this time.[23]

But in the SRC's hands these upheavals are essentially nonpolitical events. Neither public policy nor the electoral process are thought to exercise an independent influence on the way in which voters perceive the crisis. Rather, an economic or social crisis befalls the political system, and, as one of its consequences, political affiliations are realigned.

From a classification of past presidential elections it can be suggested that it is only the realigning election, following hard on the heels of a major social or economic upheaval, which is intended by voters to convey durable dissatisfaction with the policies of the previous stewardship. And yet the American experiences with such realignments suggest that they are the product of what we have described as essentially nonpolitical antecedents.[24]

Thus from first to last, party identification bears very little relationship to electoral politics. Although it controls a substantial amount of political behavior, it is not itself controlled by the electoral process.

172

Political Issues and the Flow of Information

The damage done to the integrity of the electoral process by the nonpolitical character of partisanship was immense. An entire set of working assumptions about the meaning of political parties crumbled in the wake of this knowledge. But it was more than an understanding of political parties that was shaken. The very independence and validity of the electoral process suffered also, for party identification exhibited a strong capacity to regulate both the perception of political issues and the flow of information, this at the same time the Survey Research Center was demonstrating that there was precious little political information and only a fragmentary knowledge of political issues in the electorate to begin with.

By the time the SRC got around to it, observing that most voters were uninformed was nothing new. Yet this general finding was reorganized and presented so sharply that the inferences following from it began to seem inescapable. Two related pieces of analysis were central in this regard. By examining responses to open-ended questions about candidates and parties, the SRC was able to show that the level of political conceptualization with which most people worked was extremely low, lower than anything that had been imagined previously. A set of categories describing the quality of voter information was established, ranging at one extreme from an ideological frame of reference to no discernible issue content at the other extreme. A generous coding scheme was developed to sort out the response patterns and to permit classification.

The picture that emerged was not pretty. Almost half of the electorate operated without any meaningful level of political information. And an additional 27 percent of the electorate was capable of thinking of electoral politics only in the most shallow terms—in terms of single-group interests or vague group benefits. These results depend to some degree on the composition of the categories themselves. Other analysts—Klingemann and Wright working with the 1968 study, and Nie, Verba, and Petrocik reworking the 1956 study—report different distributions.[25] Still, the striking characteristic of these data is the political ignorance of most people.

Few analysts had expected (or had wanted) high levels of political ideology in the mass public. But to discover that most people were operating without any sense of generalization, without any sense of self-interest, was something else again. The distressing implications of this finding were reinforced by a second piece of research, which demonstrated that opinions on political issues tended to be fragmentary at best, and that frequently issue opinions were unstable.

At the center of this aspect of the evidence is a perfectly marvelous piece of research by Philip Converse, "The Nature of Belief Systems in Mass Publics." In Converse's skilled hands the data showed that, in addition to people being uninformed, there is little consistency between issue positions that they take, that there is very little "constraint between idea-elements."[26] Even in the best light, these data suggest confusion in the mass public, the type of inconsistent demands that lend themselves to exploitation in electoral politics.

Converse also suggested that individual issue positions exhibited a temporal instability, that people were likely to shift issue positions relatively freely. This aspect of the analysis was subsequently modified by the work of others. The issue positions people assume do not seem nearly so variable as was first reported.[27] But, unfortunately, political instability of a much more serious nature does seem to be a valid characteristic of mass publics. There is a strong relationship between irregular voting patterns and low levels of political information (see table 6.2). People who consistently identify with the same party are likely to possess inordinately larger quantities of information than do people who shift political preferences between elections. In turn, those people who voted in only one of the two elections are still less well informed, while those who failed to vote in either were desperately deficient in terms of political information.[28]

Party identification serves a standard-setting function for party

TABLE 6.2

The Association Between Stability or Change in Presidential Voting Over Time and Political Information Level, 1956–1960
(in percentages)

Information Level	Voted Twice and for Same Party (N = 712)	Voted Twice but Shifted Parties (N = 207)	Failed to Vote in One of Two Elections (N = 220)	Twice a Nonvoter (N = 20)
High	49	33	19	11
Medium	32	32	35	17
Low	19	35	46	72
	100	100	100	100

NOTE: Philip E. Converse, "Information Flow and the Stability of Partisan Attitudes," *Public Opinion Quarterly* 26 (1962): 581. Reprinted by permission.

adherents, just as the Survey Research Center said originally. It controls the flow of information to voters and regulates perceptions of issues. Those voters who stand outside of the influence of party, who lack enduring partisan ties, are largely unaware of the substance of electoral contests.

The political inferences to be drawn from these relationships are quite clear. Those voters most open to political change are those least identified with a political party. But they also are precisely those voters who know least about politics and who have the poorest idea of what is at stake in any election in particular. Therefore, these people are the most likely to respond to simple, manipulative appeals—to the images, slogans, jingles of political advertising campaigns. From the perspective of competing candidates, those voters likely to be decisive in determining election outcomes are most easily motivated by appeals to the "irrational," to candidate imagery. Public policy and political issues seem to make very little difference. Or as Warren Miller put it, "It seems that the multitudes pay little heed [to public policy], until calamity strikes."[29]

Candidate Images as Contentless Responses

These inferences appeared to be substantiated when responses to the open-ended candidate questions were categorized in terms of their manifest content. Six attitudinal dimensions were formed—attitudes toward each of the two candidates themselves but otherwise lacking any content, expressions of opinion that contain issue content either on foreign or on domestic policy, reactions to "parties as managers of government," and "group related responses."[30] Using these six dimensions as independent variables, a straightforward multiple regression was run with voting behavior as the dependent variable for each presidential election since 1952.

> The model treats the behavior of the individual voter as governed in an immediate sense by the direction and strength of his attitudes toward the several political objects he is asked to appraise, attitudes which we have probed in these presidential elections by asking a series of free answer questions about the parties and presidential candidates.[31]

The results of this analysis indicate that the most powerful components are attitudes toward the candidates themselves. Political change, in other words, appears to be governed by candidate imagery. By contrast, neither domestic issues nor foreign policy concerns seemed to make much of an impact, and group-related loyalties remained quite stable over the period covered by these elections. Only perceptions of the candidates seemed to vary widely, in fact. To understand why in 1964 Barry Goldwater did so much more poorly than did Dwight Eisenhower in 1956, one need only to know that Goldwater's net image fell 17 percentage points below that of Eisenhower's. Or to return to the more neutral language of statistics, the "net change" in attitudinal responses across these contentless measures of candidate orientation produced much more variation than did all the other components combined.

"The fluctuation of electoral attitudes over these elections have to a remarkable degree focused on the candidates themselves."[32] The preeminence of candidate imagery again emphasizes the shallow, nonpolitical nature of the electoral process in the United States. In constructing this variable, all responses related to issues and policy had been removed; there is nothing left in these indicators of candidate orientation but reactions toward the candidates themselves. Images of the competing candidates do not seem like the greatest hope for democratic politics. Yet the inference to be drawn from these data is that election outcomes, the crucial margin between victory and defeat, is controlled by people who see little else but the images that candidates project.

Candidate Images as Campaign Strategy

In focusing attention on the significance of the candidate dimension of electoral responses, the SRC was being both terribly insightful and splendidly obtuse. Profound changes began to occur in the system of electoral competition in the postwar period, changes that appeared at the presidential level for the first time in 1952, as luck would have it. For in this campaign the techniques of survey research and public relations were first incorporated on a systematic basis. Political competition would never again be the same. The systematic use of the mass media and all the tools of the advertising industry had entered the political arena.

The SRC's surveys were an ideal vehicle for monitoring the effects of these changes. Indeed, it is quite worth noting, with all the attendant irony, that this is the problem that Paul Lazarsfeld set out to study in the first place. But Lazarsfeld was ahead of his time. The political system operated on a different basis during the years that he was involved in its study—different from the generalizations that held in the marketplace and different from what the political process would later become. And as Lazarsfeld's knowl-

edge of American politics was not his strongest suit, these differences escaped his attention at the time and during the years thereafter. The Survey Research Center, however, had a golden opportunity to be more astute, the more so since its surveys proved to
be very sensitive in recording the influence of these changes.

If there was considerable insight in measurement and in analysis,
there was a corresponding failure to realize the significance of what
had been discovered. The systematic use of political advertising
was new to American politics. Even assuming that the development of these techniques was wrong on moral grounds, that political advertising and political democracy are incompatible, it was
important to follow the changes that these techniques produced in
the system of electoral competition. But in this regard Angus
Campbell and his associates were no more sensitive than were Paul
Lazarsfeld and his colleagues.

To categorize respondents' reports of what they like or dislike
about a candidate as candidate image is to miss the mark.[33] But it
is a summary judgment that, in the end, may be appropriate. An
accurate portrait of how the electorate is being influenced needs to
precede such a conclusion. The very power and technical virtuosity
of the SRC acted as a limitation here, for there is absolutely no
question that the data gathered by the various commercial polling
organizations is inferior in every respect, save one, to data collected
by the SRC.

Commercial pollsters—even the American Institute of Public
Opinion (Gallup polls), probably the best of the lot—lack the range
and sophistication of the questionnaire composed by the Survey
Research Center. The measurement procedures that commercial
pollsters' questions presuppose are often crude, and they offer far
less analytical flexibility. Nevertheless, they often contain much
more politically relevant information than do the SRC's in that
they focus explicitly on candidate attributes; the policies and performance of incumbent administrations are monitored continuously. If the data that comes from these surveys is inferior and if
it lacks depth and analytic richness, still these polls contain elements of electoral competition that their more elegant counterparts

from the SRC sorely miss.[34] Analytically, one wishes the SRC had been more attentive to the substance of the commercial side of the business. In retrospect, that would have produced a nice set of data to analyze from the perspective of the changing patterns of political competition.

It was hardly surprising that judgments about political advertising were made before its effects had been described. Most analysts were uneasy about its manipulative qualities. What is surprising is that so few people were interested in describing its effects at all, despite the fact that there was good reason to pursue the matter. Change was in the air. Advertising and its technicians—people in public relations—were gaining power and influence in the political process in highly visible ways. Stanley Kelley, in a fine and widely appreciated study, described these developments in a way that should have attracted additional work on the problem. Using the case study method, he observed that a rise of public relations in politics was unmistakable.

The possibility of the public relations man's rise to the policy level in politics might be viewed as only an occasional one, did not it develop quite naturally out of the conditions for the effective use of propaganda. It is hard to see why the same trends which have brought the public relations man into political life will not also push him upward in political decision making. His services are valuable because effective use of the mass media is one of the roads to power in contemporary society, and it is difficult clearly to separate strategic and tactical considerations in that use.[35]

But as often as Kelley's book would be cited, it did not stimulate further research. Most important, political analysts did not design electoral surveys to examine the problem. The history of the voting studies is littered with paradoxes and irony. But none is more remarkable than this. During the decade of the fifties, electoral studies gained power and prestige among political analysts and the voting studies dominated the study of American politics. Yet the studies are singularly devoid of information on what has been a fundamental transformation in terms of electoral competition. To be sure, these data do record the fact that the system has changed, and, as we will see in chapter 8, they have permitted some rough estimates of the consequences of these changes. But taken together, the voting studies failed to record the mechanisms by which those changes occurred, or how they operated in the mass public. From the perspective of political history, the loss is irreparable. Theories of electoral politics suffered too, of course. Data that are fundamentally flawed usually lead to prolonged controversies—disputes that, in the end, find that the wrong question has been asked.

The Rationality of Voters and the Stability of the Electorate

The terms of the controversy were established by the Survey Research Center's "theory" of voting. "Theory" is an inappropriate term, really. Work at the SRC has proceeded on the one hand from an enduring commitment to a research orientation, a philosophy of research which is no less important because it has drifted from an articulate strategy into the realm of unconscious assumptions. On the other hand, the SRC's voting studies have acquired strength from clearly established empirical regularities. Nevertheless, data and philosophy have never blended to form a coherent model of voting, much less of the electoral process.

Still, it is not pushing matters to present the SRC's analysis with more formality than analysts there have chosen to do. (See figure 6.3.)[36] The strength of party identifications operates as the lynchpin of this representation of the electoral process. Its direct effect on the formulation of individual voting decisions is considerable. But no less important are the indirect consequences of individual psychological associations with political parties, for individual party loyalties control the flow of information and perceptions of individual self-interest in politics. Political parties operating in a "group process" establish the political standards for individuals—they

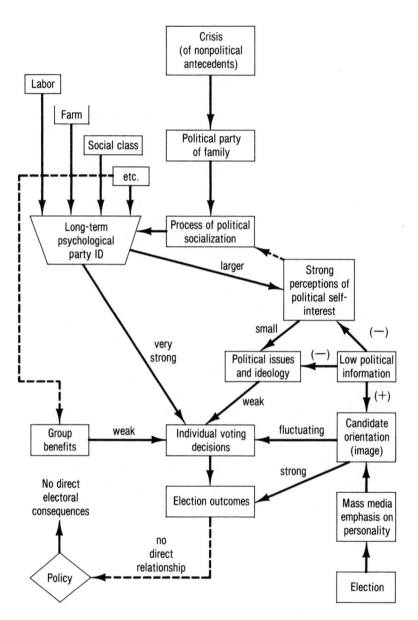

FIGURE 6.3 *A Representation of the SRC's Explanation of Electoral Decisions*

NOTE: Peter B. Natchez, "The Reasonable Voter." Ph.D. diss., Harvard University, 1969, p. 562.

mold positions on political issues and provide the basis for what little ideology there is in the electorate.

Compared to the influence of other factors, individual voting decisions pale beside the power of party identification. To a degree, other groups exercise an influence, and similarly, political issues exercise some independent effect. More impressive in this regard are the images created by the competing candidates themselves. Again, in comparison to the power of party loyalty, the significance of candidate orientation is not large. Candidate orientation obtains a special significance, however, because it is singularly related to the outcome of elections. The crucial margins between victory and defeat in electoral politics are explained disproportionately by the images projected by the competing candidates—an explanation that is placed in broad relief by the massive stability and influence of party identification.

It was a curious portrait of politics that the SRC had painted. The electoral system was best characterized in terms of its unbending stability. Yet voting decisions were molded by distinctly irrational characteristics.[37] It was the inference of voter irrationality that was unacceptable to many political analysts, none more steadfastly than to V. O. Key, Jr., the person who had been instrumental to the Survey Research Center during its formative years and who had painstakingly edited *The American Voter* while it was in manuscript form. But the controversy was not merely between Key and the SRC. It raged among political scientists for almost twenty years.

CHAPTER 7

The Problem of Voter Rationality

The main difficulty with unsystematic knowledge is that fundamental insights often go unheeded. In this category of intuitive
understandings belongs a great deal of the writing on American
politics prior to the quantitative revolution and, unfortunately, to
very nearly all of the published work of V. O. Key, Jr. The controversy over voting rationality was, in large measure, a result of the
inability of students of American politics to apply the body of
knowledge that they had developed to the data and inferences that
came pouring in from the SRC.

At the heart of the problem was the challenge by the voting
studies to the integrity of the electoral process. Voters, these studies
showed, lacked the tools for political analysis; the people were
ill-prepared to pass judgments on central questions of public policy; and, most important, the influence of party identification was
pervasive and controlling. Yet it would be odd indeed if the significance of party identification had gone unnoticed by political analysts during the years prior to the electoral surveys. The strength
of partisan ties in the United States had been observed, of

course. But somehow this discovery did not bring all thinking about electoral politics to an abrupt halt. Rather it was a circumstance whose political consequences, good and bad, required further investigation. Thus V. O. Key could write in *Politics, Parties and Pressure Groups,* already in its second edition in 1948, that:

> All students are agreed that the persistence of party preference is high, but how high is another question. It is probably not far wrong to estimate that from 75 to 85 percent of persons voting in two consecutive presidential elections support the same party both times. . . .
>
> Such conclusions may be drawn about the facts, but what is the significance of these facts?[1]

This suggests that the controversy over voter rationality could have been argued in much more broader terms; that is, emphasis could have been on how the electoral process functioned, and thus a wide range of information from previous work could have been relevant. But such was not the case. Rather than incorporating the data and inferences from the Survey Research Center into an existing literature, that literature seems to have been rendered meaningless. The one principle that could not be surrendered was that of the integrity of the electoral process and consequently the "rationality" of the outcomes that it produced. To conclude that voters were devoid of political motivations amounted to conceding that electoral politics was a series of empty gestures, not a distinctive and invaluable method of government. The controversy over voting rationality was fought by necessity much more than by desire. Yet, for all its complexity, the more difficult question for the practice of democratic politics may yet prove to be located in the value systems that inform the mass public generally. The failure of these two strands of research to converge bears a moment's emphasis. Throughout the postwar period, political scientists have been reluctant to discuss fundamental values. This reluctance has deprived the voting studies of an essential tool of analysis and renders an otherwise impressive array of data terribly incomplete.

184

The Problem of Voter Rationality

The Responsible Electorate

... [My] comments could, in the main, be lumped under the observation that the plan does not give, it seems to me, adequate explicit recognition to "the political." I hasten to concede that most of your data could be analyzed in those terms, but it may be that you ought to have a more deliberate injection of the political into the planning.[2]

Although Key had edited *The American Voter,* he remained unhappy about the structure of its argument and about the inferences that followed from it. Key's uneasiness put him in an awkward position. He was a strong advocate of survey research in general, and additionally he had been instrumental to the SRC in its search for funding.[3] Still, in a review essay, Key wrote critically:

Most of these findings . . . have been primarily of sociological or psychological interest. They have been about behavior in political situations, but only infrequently have they contributed much to the explanation of the political import of the behavior observed. This probably amounts to an assertion that a considerable proportion of the literature commonly classified under the heading of "political behavior" has no real bearing on politics, or at least that its relevance has not been made apparent.[4]

The text of Key's criticism, while cogent and incisive, is not as important as the reasoning behind it. For him the essential problem was that individual behavior in the electorate was being examined without reference to how the electoral system performed. The motivations and behaviors of voters should derive their definition and significance from the system of political competition. It is assumed, of course, that people, through the electoral system, exercise great influence on the political system. However, this is quite different from the belief that the structure of the system can be deduced from the ways in which people behave in it. "If the specialist in electoral behavior is to be a student of politics," concluded Key with his characteristic mixture of insight and imprecision, his major concern must be the population of elections not the population of individual voters. One does not gain understanding of elections by the simple cumulation of the typical findings from the microscopic analysis of the individuals in the system. The most plausible working hypothesis is that the electorate and elections perform certain functions in the system as a whole. The electorate responds in some way or another to great events, to competing candidates, or to the conditions of the times, and moves toward a decision which has both meaning and consequences in the context of the political system.[5]

But if it is to be argued that elections and the electoral process have consequences that reverberate throughout the political system, then it follows that manifestations of those consequences ought to be discernible in the behavior (and ideally, in the motivations) of individual voters. Otherwise, the electoral process becomes an illusion—an illusion that goes no further than the perceptual apparatus of the political elite.

The very murkiness of Key's general proposition suggests the difficulty of the idea. Elections and the electorate are described as performing "certain functions for the system as a whole"; the electorate "responds in one way or another" and it "moves toward a decision" that has "meaning and consequence." This is not a model of analytic precision.

Key wrote two books in an effort to give his intuition shape and substance: *Public Opinion and American Democracy,* and *Southern Politics.* The first represents an effort to rework data from the SRC into a more useful description of political opinions and to examine the ways in which those opinions are incorporated into the American political system. In many ways it is infuriating to read—brilliant and well crafted, but also overlong, plodding, and textbookish. It is as a description (rather than a theory) of political opinions that the volume is at its best.

As an elaborate essay on the characteristics of political opinions, Key's book remains an indispensible guide to the field. This is true not only in the specific descriptions of political opinions that he provides, but even more so in the structure of the analysis itself.

186

The Problem of Voter Rationality

Key seems to have had a remarkable knack for organizing research, for asking the right questions. This part of his art is heightened by the skill with which various aspects of a diffuse literature are joined together in combinations that frequently stimulate subsequent research.[6] Key's notion of political stratification, for example, presents a new and powerful way of looking at the participation of the mass public in politics. In this instance Key is arguing that participation has its own distinctive system of stratification that stands apart from stratification in the social and economic spheres. It is an intriguing concept, one that has already borne fruit in the work of others.[7]

In these terms—in its capacity to organize and to describe political attitudes and behaviors—*Public Opinion and American Democracy* is an easy book to praise and justly deserves the attention that has been lavished upon it. It is in answer to the question of how public opinion functions in an electoral democracy, the question that Key raised in criticism of the SRC, that the work becomes difficult.

Stylewise, Key was most comfortable working intuitively. This has a certain charm and humility about it, but the overall effect is often to obscure meaning and to avoid the presentation of a carefully reasoned theory. If among Key's tremendous gifts as a political scientist were his truly powerful sense of insight and a capacity to organize a difficult literature in original ways, his great failings were that he was never able to present his insights in a carefully reasoned way and that he avoided sharply defined causal arguments, as well as the controversies that these inevitably entail.[8] Thus in the second book, *Southern Politics*, there is a positively brilliant discussion about the causes and consequences of one-party factionalism (chapter 14). But the argument appears in such an intuitive and scattered form that much of its complexity and sophistication was actually lost or misinterpreted in the researches that followed.[9]

Key's reticence to formulate an explicit theory, present to some extent in all of his writing, is particularly apparent in the final section of *Public Opinion and American Democracy,* the four chapters on linkages. These chapters bristle with imagination. Yet they do not coalesce in any way that provides a systematic response to the question of how public opinion derives "meaning and consequence" in the political system.

In a halting, almost folksy style, Key's stress is on the critical role played by the political elite. "These remarks require reference again to the special ethical imperatiaves under which governing levels of democratic orders must operate," he writes in talking about the linking functions of political parties.

> The steps from the broad aspirations of a people to their effectuation in public policy are numerous and tortuous. Opportunities for humbugging the people are also numerous. Achievement of popular government consists, not in a simply leadership reflex in response to popular mandate, but in fidelity to the attempt to give definition to vague popular aspirations and in the search for technical means for their effectuation. The governance of a popular regime requires a powerful indoctrination of leadership elements with its special norms of governance. If exploitation is the object of governance, different rules of the game prevail.[10]

V. O. Key returns to this theme again and again as he pushes on in his effort to link public opinion to the conduct of government. But the more he concentrates on this relationship, the more the political elite become a mysterious force. Elites operate beyond the realm of public opinion. Leaders seem to be related to the electorate only by the highly specialized norms and belief systems that they possess:

> Repeatedly, as we have sought to explain particular distributions, movements, and qualities of mass opinion, we have had to go beyond the survey data and make assumptions and estimates about the role and behavior of that thin stratum of persons referred to variously as the political elite, political activists, the leadership echelons, or influentials. . . . The data tell us almost nothing about the dynamic relations between the upper layer of activists and mass opinion. The missing piece of our puzzle is the elite element of the opinion system. . . .

The Problem of Voter Rationality

The longer one frets with the puzzle of how democratic regimes manage to function, the more plausible it appears that a substantial part of the explanation is to be found in the motives that actuate the leadership echelon, the values that it holds, in the rules of the political game to which it adheres, in the expectations which it entertains about its own status in society and perhaps in some of the objective circumstances, both material and institutional, in which it functions.[11]

No one would quarrel with Key over the central importance of the political elite. Their position in the short run is surely determinate. However, the problem with *Public Opinion and American Democracy* is that the book does not develop a theory that isolates the ways in which the people and the political elite are linked through the electoral process to the conduct of democratic politics and to the actions of government. Both aspects of the equation are left incomplete. In the first place, Key is unwilling to discuss how the political elite should operate so as to fulfill its normative obligations; nor is he willing to describe the way the political leaders operate in American politics as a practical matter. Key uses the defense that he lacked data to extend the discussion any further. For someone as empirically oriented as he, this is not an empty excuse. Still, he could have been more specific about the sorts of things he was looking for and about the types of relationships he expected to find. And in the second place, Key is unable to make it clear how the popular side of the equation works—how the electorate is empowered to exercise its influence on political leaders by the electoral process. The problem of political issues is handled in structural terms alone. This is done first by examining public opinion in terms of alternative distributions (consensus, conflict, concentration) and then in terms of the properties of these distributions (intensity, stability, latency, interrelationships). The analysis moves slowly, topically, inconclusively.

It is difficult to be critical when it comes to V. O. Key, and it is especially difficult to be critical about *Public Opinion and American Democracy*. Key's contributions to the study of American politics are probably greater than those of any other political scientist, and he was surely at the height of his intellectual powers when he began work on this particular volume. This book is generally accepted as his major writing on the subject, and it soon was incorporated into the literature as standard reading.

However, it is important to understand that the book did both more and less than Key had intended. The volume exceeded its design in its speculative aspects, in its tendency to wax rhapsodic about the political elite. Given Key's other writings, particularly *American State Politics* and *Southern Politics,* this is an interesting twist, and frankly one wishes Key had been more specific and complete along these lines. But for Key this was already an excessively adventurous proceeding.

But the book was less than Key had planned in that it failed to delineate the defining characteristics of political issues and, more deeply, in that he failed to develop a framework that explained how such issues are incorporated into the politics of the American democracy.[12]

Key himself never thought that *Public Opinion and American Democracy* was as successful as his colleagues believed it to be. He grumbled about the book in his correspondence without being able to say quite what was wrong with it.[13] Finally Key decided that the problem was that the issue of electoral rationality had not been resolved, that he had evaded this question, and that as a result the electoral process lost its sharpness and integrity. Key believed that the reason for this, in part, was that he had relied solely on data collected by the SRC.

By using Gallup surveys from the Roper Center and by focusing exclusively on the question of political rationality, Key sought to remedy the defects of his earlier analysis. But in meeting the question of voter rationality directly, he was forced to think quite explicitly about the nature of political issues and how they functioned in a system of electoral competition. His efforts in this direction are actually more interesting, and in the long run much more important, than the specific argument he makes about the rationality of voters, although it is common to read the book the other way around.

The Problem of Voter Rationality

The Responsible Electorate is written in the same intuitive style that characterizes all of Key's theorizing. It is vague; there is a forced earthiness in the commonsense way that he speaks about popular preferences, elections, and democracy in the United States. Key maintains his disconcerting habit of hiding important conceptual distinctions in the sparest of sentences. It is virtually impossible in those pages to find Key making a cogent theoretical argument, much less building one in a systematic fashion. Yet, for all this, this book contains an intriguing line of thinking, one that becomes especially important when placed alongside that of the voting studies.

In its simplest form, the theme of *The Responsible Electorate* is that voters, on the whole, behave rationally; or in Key's phrasing of it:

> The perverse and unorthodox argument of this little book is that voters are not fools. To be sure, many individual voters act in odd ways indeed; yet in the large the electorate behaves about as rationally and responsibly as we should expect, given the clarity of the alternatives presented to it and the character of the information available to it. In American presidential campaigns of recent decades the portrait of the American electorate that develops from the data is not one of an electorate strait-jacketed by social determinants or moved by subconscious urges triggered by devilishly skillful propagandists. It is rather one of an electorate moved by concern about central questions of public policy, of governmental performance, and of executive personality.[14]

Ostensibly Key seeks to make this argument by dividing the electorate into categories different from those that had been used in the voting studies. Previously the electorate had been analyzed only in terms of its final voting decisions, with different independent variables used to explain the electorate's action. Thus votes were analyzed, first in terms of social characteristics (the approach taken by the Bureau of Applied Social Research) and then in terms of enduring psychological commitments (the orientation employed by the SRC). Key now argues that the electorate should be divided functionally in terms of the position occupied by voters as they move through successive pairs of elections. Operationally this means that voters are to be classified in terms of whether they continue to support the same party that they had four years ago ("standpatters"), or whether they had shifted parties from one election to the next ("switchers"), or whether they were voting for the first time or reentering the active electorate ("new voters").[15]

On the face of it, this does not seem like a major conceptual innovation. The idea is certainly introduced in a casual fashion, without any effort to distinguish it theoretically. "Obviously," Key observes, "if we are to see whether the voter may after all try to form sensible judgments on those questions relevant to his supposed duties as a citizen, we need to analyze the movement of voters across party lines from presidential election to presidential election."[16] And that is all that Key has to say by way of explanation. But it must be emphasized that partitioning voters in this manner is not obvious and that as an analytic device, it has important consequences for interpretations of electoral behavior and for probing the meaning of elections.

The primary virtue of this division is that it draws attention to voters as the electoral embodiment of party coalitions. Viewing the electoral process in this fashion places both parties and voters in a dynamic, political context. Parties, through their presidential candidates, compete for control of the government by appealing differentially to various segments of the electorate. Their problem is how to retain the loyalty of those who supported them previously, while simultaneously seeking to attract the support of people entering (or reentering) the electorate as well as encouraging discontented elements within the other party to alter their allegiance. Political parties must carry their campaigns to each segment of the electorate in order to maintain (and perhaps improve) their competitive position. Key's assumptions about the condition of political parties in the United States are a curious mixture of description, theory, and aspiration. In the following section, his ideas will be examined more carefully, for the aspirations that he had for political parties are largely a function of his argument for electoral rationality.

Issues of policy, performance, and executive competence become vehicles for mobilizing and maintaining popular support in the electorate. As such they obtain inherent meaning and significance in the electoral process. But they also give coherence and definition to the party coalitions themselves. No longer remote, political groups whose electoral significance lies in the symbolic identifications lodged in voters' psychology—political parties, in Key's terms—acquire meaning in relation to the issues that cause voters to adhere to them. This is very much an empirical proposition. All one has to do is to search through successive pairs of elections to observe the issues that characterize the enduring basis of support for each political party. Similarly, one can observe how the coalitions have shifted in emphasis and meaning as they make new appeals and modify old ones in the struggle for electoral predominance.

Key seizes upon the role that voters play in maintaining and reorganizing party coalitions as a vehicle for asserting the responsible nature of the electoral process in general and the rationality of voters in particular. The device he used to establish these conclusions is relatively simple. In Key's analysis, voting rationality becomes a question of whether the electorate as a whole participates in succeeding pairs of presidential elections in a manner consistent with its policy preferences and with the terms of the alternatives provided by the competing parties. Take, for example, the question of the policy of government toward organized labor in 1948, an issue that was vigorously contested by the candidates in that presidential campaign. If the electorate was to have responded to this issue rationally, there should have been, first, a clear difference between the continuing supporters of the Democratic and Republican parties; and second, this difference should have been carried through to those entering the electorate and to those switching parties. In table 7.1, reproduced from Key's original text, the pattern of electoral responsibility and, concomitantly, the rationality of voters individually, is affirmed. Using 1944 as a base year, D-D refers to voters who voted Democrat in 1944 and 1948; D-R refers to voters who voted Democrat in 1944 and Republican in 1948, and so forth. Working his way through the data, Key concludes:

> Party switchers move towards the party whose standpatters they resemble in their policy views. . . . The D-R's are divided in their policy views in about the same fashion as the R-R's with whom they join in the election, and the R-D's resemble the D-D's to which they attach themselves for voting. The nonvoters at the preceding election who join the D-D's or the R-R's also have an attitudinal resemblance to the standpatters with whom they ally themselves. Yet, . . . the switchers bear earmarks of their origin. The D-R's are not in quite the same degree as the R-R's attached to the party policy position, and the R-D's also bore traces of their Republican origin. Nevertheless, on balance each of these groups bore far greater resemblance to the standpatters of the party of their destination than to the faithful of the party of their origin.[17]

According to Key, the electorate is rational because the policy preferences that people incorporate into their votes have meaning in terms of party competition. It is a definition of political rationality that has two distinctly different parts, although Key never put it quite this way. First, voters are rational because they behave

TABLE 7.1

*Patterns of presidential preference, 1944–1948, in relation to distribution of responses to question: "As things stand today, do you think the laws governing labor unions are too strict or not strict enough?"**

Response	D-D	R-D	O-D	O-R	D-R	R-R
Too strict	31%	26%	27%	17%	15%	9%
About right	33	31	36	31	31	31
Not strict enough	19	28	20	35	38	46
No opinion	17	15	17	17	16	14
	100	100	100	100	100	100
N	(909)	(65)	(220)	(123)	(165)	(648)

*Based on AIPO 432, 11-1-48, a post-election survey (interviews were conducted after the election; the date is the "send-out" date).

NOTE: Reprinted, by permission of the publisher, from V. O. Key, Jr., *The Responsible Electorate* (Cambridge, Mass.: Harvard University Press, 1966), 55.

politically in a manner consistent with their policy preferences, as can be seen when one examines the distribution of policy preferences in succeeding pairs of elections. But more important, these preferences acquire meaning in the governmental system because of the competition between political parties in the electoral process. It is this second aspect of Key's argument that is crucial for this theory of electoral responsibility and that constitutes the more original contribution to the analysis of elections.

In terms of the analysis of elections, Key is able to shift the focus away from the purely microscopic study of individual political behavior to the collective properties of electoral distributions. This was the elusive quality that he had chased previously in *Public Opinion and American Democracy*. But in that volume he elected to begin by describing opinion distributions, and then to search for a linking mechanism between those distributions and public policy, a line of inquiry that is not fundamentally dissimilar to that of the voting studies.[18] Now, by arguing that the logic of electoral competition compels parties to use issues as an essential part of the methodology for maintaining traditional supporters as well as for appealing to new ones, the problem of linkages becomes less difficult conceptually.

Parties establish the terms in which the rationality of the electorate is to be understood. And by doing so, parties also link issues to the performance of government. This is done by the political elite, not in homage to the prerequisites of democratic theory but out of necessity, by the logic imposed on political elites by the system of electoral competition, for in elections, votes are the currency of power. Hence parties organize conflicts over policy for voters. By the continuing effort of parties to attract and hold voters, issues of policy and government are given coherence—for the electorate and for the policy-making process.

This is a fundamentally empirical proposition, for evidence of the effects of electoral competition should be apparent in the distribution of preferences among voters and in the types of voting choices that are made. Equally, the consequences of the electoral process should be apparent in the formulation and reformulation of public policies. These are strong inferences indeed. And since they are essentially empirical matters, how can their validity be maintained against the great mass of data set out by the SRC?

Political Issues as Retrospective Judgments of Public Policies

It will help clarify matters if two subsidiary points in *The Responsible Electorate* are articulated here. One of these concerns the definition given political issues, while the other has to do with how political parties function in organizing these issues for the electorate. These arguments have been largely overlooked in the debate over electoral rationality; yet they are crucial to the argument that Key was making. As with so many of Key's innovations, these are embedded in the analysis without sufficient effort to distinguish their originality or meaning.

Key's definition of political issues has its unusual aspects. In his initial phrasing of the matter, when Key is writing about the purposes of his "perverse and unorthodox argument" about electoral rationality, issues are described as consisting of "central and relevant questions of public policy, of governmental performance and of executive personality."[19]

What Key seems to have had in mind here is that voters are motivated primarily by the judgments they make of the policies and the performance of government that they have experienced during the last four years. Or as Key offhandedly observes:

> As voters mark their ballots they may have in their minds impressions of the last TV spectacular of the campaign, but more importantly, they have in their minds recollections of their experiences of the last four years. ... The impact of events from the inauguration of an Administration to

the onset of the next presidential campaign may affect far more voters than the fireworks of the campaign itself. Governments must act or not act, and action or inaction may convert supporters into opponents or opponents into supporters.[20]

Or as he argued somewhat more precisely:

What kinds of relations would be found if we assumed that the voter was a fairly reasonable fellow who voted to promote or to discourage public policies he approved or disapproved insofar as he could perceive the consequences of his vote? Obviously, all kinds of motives, attitudes, and concerns enter into the voting decision; yet analyses of the available information indicate quite marked correlations between policy attitudes and vote switching. In short, the data make it appear sensible to regard the voter as a person who is concerned with what governments have done or have not done and what they propose to do rather than one guided, unaware, by the imperatives of economic status or the tricks of Madison Avenue.[21]

While the data Key based this inference on are not as solid as he would have us believe, it is the specification of political issues itself that is interesting. The central proposition here amounts to a fundamentally different way of looking at the problem. His emphasis is on how people react to questions of governmental policy and performance. This is quite different from defining issues as responses to questions about what people think is the most important political problem facing them. Such questions ask people about interests and problems to which they want government to respond. The focus is solely on self-interests as they are defined by individual voters.

By conceiving of issues as central questions of governmental policy and performance, an important element of subjectivity from individual responses is removed. To be sure, policy evaluations remain subjective in that individual voters respond according to their own feelings and perceptions. However, the policies themselves are quintessentially acts of government. One may like or dislike the government's farm policies, but the visible presence of government is not to be denied.

Issues of policy and performance, then, contrast sharply with expressions of individual self-interest. They are established by the actions (or inactions) of government itself. From the individual's point of view, such questions may bear only a distant correspondence to self-defined political interests. Thus when Samuel Stouffer conducted a survey at the height of the McCarthy era, he found that less than 2 percent of the population responded that domestic communism was, in their mind, the most important problem. People were concerned about other things—about economic problems and matters involving personal and family health. Yet when people were asked to think about anticommunism as a policy issue, the distribution of responses was quite different. Unfortunately, in American politics this question was raised as an issue of policy and governmental performance.[22]

It is important to mention that, in Key's view, issues of policy and performance are intrinsically retrospective. The mass public is seen, not pressing demands upon government, but as the place where policies are judged and government is evaluated.

The patterns of flow of the major streams of shifting voters graphically reflect the electorate in its great, and perhaps principle role as an appraiser of past events, past performance and past actions. It judges restrospectively; it commands prospectively only insofar as it expresses either approval or disapproval of that which has happened before.[23]

One wishes that Key had been more specific about the nature of political issues as he saw them, but he left the ideas vague and incomplete. Nowhere are policy issues distinguished from other types of issues. Nowhere are the characteristics of performance issues specified. Rather, a new and powerful concept is introduced by assumption and discussed in bits and pieces. The entire idea is presented as if it were obvious. This quality of the argument has its defects—in limiting the discussion of political issues and, even more damagingly, in Key's discussion of how political parties function in terms of these issues.

Issues of policy and performance are rarely self-enforcing.

Rather, they depend in large measure on the system of electoral competition for their effectiveness. In pursuing his argument for the rationality of voters, Key is impelled to discuss how parties function. This aspect of electoral rationality is as important as the composition of the issues themselves, for the logic of party competition establishes the quality and clarity of the choices with which the electorate must work.

In Key's system, the party in power attempts to maintain its majority position by every means available—the tools of policy, programs, symbols, rhetoric. But every action and policy involves an element of risk. It seems impossible to produce satisfactory policies, for pressure groups make their demands and coalitions of minority interests seem to form almost by nature and threaten to undo the majority party at the next opportunity.[24] To remain in power requires great insight into the possibilities of government and enormous skill in the creation of policy.[25]

Thus the majority party is not given its position by events alone. Rather, once empowered, it must be sufficiently successful in the process of government so that it can endure the repeated testing of electoral competition. A majority coalition is not an abstraction, but can be examined in the policy preferences that cause voters to adhere to it.

As difficult as the problem of maintaining a majority position is, the problems confronting the minority party in its struggle to gain power are greater, for it must provide voters assurance that it will not disrupt their most favored policies while at the same time providing a strong and genuine opposition to the party in power.

The election of 1952 may illustrate the role of the electorate as judge and executioner. It, too, suggests observations about the requisites the minority party must fulfill if it is to play its role in a two-party system. We must have, the commonplace axiom goes, an active minority party so that when necessity arises an outraged citizenry can use it as an instrument to replace the majority and, incidentally, to punish by banishment. But not just any sort of minority will serve the purpose. If it is to be serviceable, the minority must not clearly threaten basic policies that have won majority acceptance.

. . . This is not to say that a serviceable minority must be identical with the majority; it must be different. It must be different enough in the appropriate aspect to arouse hope that it can cope satisfactorily with those problems on which the majority has flunked. It must not, though, so threaten accepted policies and practices that it arouses widespread anxieties.[26]

What Key is saying here is that, in order to take advantage of unpopular policies and poor governmental performance, a minority party must prove itself to be an acceptable alternative by not challenging fundamental values or popular policies. It must be successful in these terms in order to be able to capture discontented voters and to challenge the incumbent administration on its performance in office.

This conception of party competition dramatically alters the notion of responsible parties. Parties provide responsible alternatives insofar as they encourage voters to express their grievances over the way government has been conducted. Presenting clearly defined issue positions can impeded this process. Indeed, from Key's perspective, both Barry Goldwater and George McGovern were irresponsible candidates. Each insisted on challenging the electorate precisely where a policy consensus had been established; and in turn, each made it impossible for his party to capture the votes of those segments of the population that were unhappy with the performance of the incumbent party. The "irresponsible" element in these candidacies lay in the fact that the electorate was forced to choose among alternatives that were not responsive to their concerns. By giving voters a choice, not an echo, people were deprived of venting their real frustrations with the incumbent administrations and instead forced to decide on a set of issue alternatives that were imposed by the candidates.[27]

As the examples of Goldwater and McGovern illustrate, parties are likely to be responsible to policy and performance issues not out of any special concern to provide the electorate with meaningful choices, but because parties must compete successfully in the electoral arena if they hope to gain control of government. Operationally, this means that parties must nurture and maintain the support of diverse elements within their coalitions, while simultaneously appealing to new voters and to disaffected elements in the other party's coalition. Of course, issues are not the only means to this purpose; but they are inherently a continuing part of the process.

Parties, then, are forced by the electoral process to focus on issues of policy and performance. No party can afford to ignore the sorts of policy preferences that maintain the loyalty of previous supporters. Similarly, no party can resist an issue that will pull supporters away from the other party. Even if the defection is short term, it provides a real opportunity to gain power. Key's division of the electorate into standpatters, switchers, and new voters is particularly important in this light, for it makes the nexus between policy and party an empirical proposition. Policies take shape in the electorate through party preferences. The empirical strength and meaning of parties is available by simple tabular analysis. And in the same way, the popular evolution of party composition can be examined. In short, the idea of party coalitions is rendered operational.

I believe this to be the singular contribution of V. O. Key. But it is a contribution that Key refrained from making consciously. The consequences of policy and performance issues as they function in a system of party competition are never really examined. Or rather, Key maintains the fiction that parties in the United States during the modern period are archtypical examples of the argument he wants to present. Thus, in a passage that is both marvelously insightful and terribly inaccurate, Key writes:

> The only really effective weapon of popular control in a democratic regime is the capacity of the electorate to throw a party from power. Not only was Mr. Stevenson rejected; other Democrats also fell by the wayside and the party leadership collectively lost, at least for a time, the fruits of power. In effect, many Democrats felt the effects of public dissatisfaction with their party's performance. Had Mr. Stevenson not been saddled with responsibility for past Democratic performance—or were other like-situated candidates not usually so saddled—the electorate would be deprived of its most effective instrument for control of governments. Happily, too, this institutional custom probably permits the electorate to be utilized to best advantage in the process of popular government. The odds are that the electorate as a whole is better able to make a retrospective

appraisal of the work of governments than it is to make estimates of the future performance of nonincumbent candidates. Yet by virtue of the combination of the electorate's retrospective judgment and the custom of party accountability, the electorate can exert a prospective influence if not control. Governments must worry, not about the meaning of past elections, but about their fate at future elections.[28]

This is a piece of truly original thinking. But the assumptions that Key makes to establish its validity are outrageous. "The custom of party accountability," as Key so quaintly puts it, was extremely weak during the entire New Deal period, so weak as one can wonder about whether it existed at all. The party coalitions were too diverse and inconsistent—both at the mass and elite levels —for anything like party accountability to enter the system. The electoral system may have behaved "responsibly in 1952," but if so, it was the last election to have that characteristic. Rather one observed the increasing independence of candidates in the system irrespective of party.[29] This showed up first at the presidential level, in the inability of the Republican party to control Congress, and then among congressmen and elected officials generally.[30] The reality of American party politics in the New Deal and post–New Deal periods is not quite the picture that Key was trying to paint. The problem is that Key's ideas about issues and how issues function in the context of electoral competition are only part of the story —but a part that takes us a good bit further than the collective researches of the SRC.

The Survey Research Center versus Key

The Responsible Electorate, then, was intended to be a book about the rationality of voters. But in making this argument Key introduced a number of original ideas about how the electoral system functions. Undoubtedly the most important of these concerned the nature of political issues and how these issues work in a system of party competition. But at the time it was published, after Key's death, *The Responsible Electorate* played to distinctly mixed reviews.

Angus Campbell, writing in the *American Political Science Review,* expressed the feeling that the book would have been altered substantially had V. O. Key been able to revise it. Arthur Maass, then chair of the Harvard government department, wrote the Introduction to the book. This notwithstanding, Campbell argued that nothing in the volume resolved the question of voter rationality.

> Is political man rational as Professor Maass concludes from Key's data? If this statement is intended to mean that the average citizen carefully informs himself on questions of governmental policy and votes for the party or candidate who comes closest to his own ideological pattern, the answer is certainly no. The answer is still no if one considers only that minority of the electorate who move from one party slate to another from one election to the next. This has been the repeated finding of careful surveys of the national population, and the data Key presents do not challenge it.[31]

Another critic, thinking that Key had suggested nothing particularly new, concluded that Key would "remain one of the great contemporary students of politics, but that the fate which made this little, unfinished book his last contribution is unjust to the scholar he was."[32] No one seemed enthusiastic about the volume.

It is easy to appreciate the difficulty that *The Responsible Electorate* caused. Since the book was published posthumously, Key's draft manuscript was completed and edited by Milton Cummings.[33] Further, it was difficult for many to believe that Key had really intended to depart so radically from the paradigm established by the SRC—a paradigm with which he had been associated (at least indirectly).

Also, there were very real problems with both the data on which Key based his analysis and the methodology he employed in constructing his argument. He had relied heavily on data collected by the SRC in almost every respect. Further, from a methodological point of view, Key's argument about the relationship between issue preferences and voting decisions is specified rather loosely. Key asserts this relationship by presenting a series of tables in which issues are associated with voting behavior in the desired manner. But this relationship is never tested against other explanatory factors. Rather Key simply repeats the same correlation over a great many issues and elections as if the weight of repetition would establish the validity of the relationship. His analysis, however, required a more exacting response to the findings of the Survey Research Center, particularly with regard to the low level of information in the electorate, the absence of issue awareness, and the dominating influence of party identification.

So in addition to the feeling that the book was not quite Key's, there was the strong impulse to distrust both the data and analysis on which it was based. But, while the circumstances of the book's publication made its audience less than receptive, the largest reasons for its misunderstanding had to do with the internal structure of the argument. Throughout the first four chapters, Key introduces important and original concepts without pausing to distinguish them, much less to place them in articulate contrast to the framework developed by the SRC. Such matters as political issues, the analysis of electoral coalitions, the effect of issues in terms of party competition are treated casually, with the various aspects of their interrelationship scattered about the text most unsystematically, almost at random. The net result is to leave the impression that Key is talking about political rationality and the history of presidential elections in a very narrow way.

Had this volume been written by anyone other than V. O. Key, there is little doubt that it would have been ignored. But Key was a commanding figure among political scientists in a way that is difficult to appreciate now. His previous work had established something of a baseline for studies of American politics. Whether or not scholars believed Key was right on the question of voting rationality, the very fact that he had made the argument forced others to take it seriously. The Survey Research Center took up Key's hypothesis at the first opportunity: in its analysis of the 1968 election.[34]

In many ways the 1968 presidential election was ideally suited to the controversy over voting rationality. The turmoil of Vietnam and civil rights (as well as the concern over "law and order" that protests involving these issues generated) ensured that there was no shortage of relevant issues on which voters might draw. Further, in the Democratic primaries at least, issue differences between competing candidates were clearly stated. Although differences in the general election between Richard Nixon and Hubert Humphrey were more muted, these candidacies (along with George Wallace's) certainly represented different approaches toward government.

The survey data collected by the SRC reflected these changes. A heightened sense of issue awareness was recorded. Very simply, there was more issue voting. In this sense it was concluded that Key's work had provided a useful "corrective." But the SRC was at pains to stress that these were differences in degree, not in principle—that Key's findings "were hardly as discontinuous with earlier work as was often presumed, and that the 'corrective' nature of his argument is badly exaggerated at numerous points."[35]

Essentially what is meant by this is that the issue voting observed by Key, while more extensive than originally estimated, is largely superficial in nature, that people for the most part remain uninformed and unaware of the meaning of their votes, and that party identification remains the great anchor of the electoral universe. Using the issues in the 1968 election, particularly the Vietnam issue, the Survey Research Center labored to make good on these points. For example, voters in the New Hampshire primary did find expression for their dissatisfactions with Lyndon Johnson by supporting Eugene McCarthy in the manner Key suggested. But when the informational structures behind these votes are examined more closely, the results are more disappointing. People voted against Johnson *irrespective* of this issue position. Indeed, more often than not voters wound up supporting an issue position diametrically opposed to their own.

Such issue voting can be construed to be electoral rationality of a sort, but it is not the deep and purposeful rationality that Key had wanted to find.

. . . when we reflect on the rather intensive coverage given by the national mass media to Eugene McCarthy's dissenting positions on Vietnam for many months before the New Hampshire primary, and considering how difficult it must have been to avoid knowledge of the fact, particularly if one had more than the most casual interest in the Vietnam question, we might continue to wonder how lavishly we should praise the electorate as "responsible." Here, as at so many other points, *pushing beyond the expression of narrow and superficial attitudes in the mass public to the cognitive texture which underlies the attitudes is a rather disillusioning experience.* It is regrettable that none of the data presented in *The Responsible Electorate* can be probed in this fashion.[36]

The 1968 analysis further reaffirmed the strength of party identification in determining votes cast for either Nixon or Humphrey. Here "it is party that towers over all other predictors, and the central 1968 issues tend to give rather diminutive relationships."[37] Rather than issues, it is evaluation of the candidates themselves that is of secondary importance, the great and powerful issues in this election coming in dead last.

Votes for Wallace were much more likely to be issue motivated —Vietnam, race, and law and order all a part. Equally, this segment of the electorate was likely to feel "little capacity to influence government" while at the same time distrusting "the morality and efficiency of political leadership."[38] But even the Wallace phenomenon was not free from the effects of party identification. Wallace voters tended to be drawn from the youthful segment of the electorate. This was not because younger people were more sympathetic to his candidacy than were others in the electorate. Rather, older persons tended to have established party identifications and these loyalties inhibited people who would have otherwise defected to Wallace on the basis of their issue concerns. The unspoken inference here is that, from one point of view, the effects of party identification are not all that unpalatable.

Good or bad, the power of party identification is quite apparent in the 1968 election. It, along with candidate orientation, provides the motivational basis for most voters. It was Key's inability to control for the effects of these factors that led him to exaggerate the significance of issues in determining voting decisions. Or in the more exacting language of Converse and associates:

. . . if we set the Wallace phenomenon in 1968 aside and limit our attention in the Key fashion to two contrasting groups of "changers" between the 1964 and 1968 elections (Johnson to Nixon; Goldwater to Humphrey) we can show correlations with issue differences which look very much like those presented in cross-tabulations by Key for earlier elections: some strong, some weak, but nearly always "in the right direction." There are, to be sure, other problems of interpretation surrounding such correlations that one would need to thrash out before accepting the Key evidence fully. But our principal point here is the simple one that even with Wallace analytically discarded from the 1968 scene, the rest of the 1968 data seem perfectly compatible with the data Key used. The only reason that there may seem to be discontinuity, then, is due to the different nature of the question being asked by Key which, by focusing on marginal change from election to election, effectively defines party loyalty [and candidate orientation] out of the explanation and correspondingly opens the way for greater orienting weight for issues.[39]

It was by this logic that the controversy over issue voting was joined. For the decade that followed, this controversy became the cutting edge of research in electoral studies. In a multitude of articles and professional papers, in monographs and books, scholars presented an impressive array of data and data analysis in an effort to determine whether or not political issues occupied a significant place in the formulation of individual voting decisions.[40]

Taken together, this literature indicates that the text of controversy itself was by no means an artificial concern of otherwise idle intellectuals. Rather it has contributed substantially to our understanding of electoral behavior. Old arguments were made more solid and occasionally, at crucial places, reformulated. The passage of time alone brought new situations, and this, in turn, expanded our appreciation of how change occurs (and fails to occur) in the context of the American electoral process. And, of course, there was the crucial matter of issue voting to settle.

Much of democratic politics seems so simple and straightforward that systematic formulation of its inner workings is unnecessary. The nature of political issues seems to have the feel of simplicity. But the belief that we somehow know in the depths of us what political issues are and how they function dissolves as soon as an attempt is made to articulate such knowledge. The very length and sophistication of the controversy over issue rationality should be taken as a good measure of the difficulty of the problem.

If anything, the controversy over issue voting was too narrow in its focus. Both V. O. Key and the SRC—quite unintentionally, to be sure—conspired to limit the scope of the conflict. Key, because he had a marked distaste for critical discussion, for the systematic presentation of ideas, minimized the points of difference between his views and the work of the Survey Research Center. What is meant to be an alternative conception of the electorate is presented in a scattered, intuitive manner. But intuition is not magic, and the impression is left that Key is talking about issues and rationality in a very narrow way.

For its part, the Survey Research Center was quite willing to construe the problem of issues narrowly. Each of the principal investigators there were deeply indebted to Key, as much for the intellectual as for the financial assistance he had made available to them. But further, the SRC has always been weakest on the political aspects of electoral democracy and there was no desire to extend the controversy to its limits.

But although neither of the principals in the controversy wished to say so, the differences between V. O. Key and the Survey Research Center were primarily theoretical in nature. The crux of the problem lies in different conceptions of how party coalitions are organized and how they compete in the electoral process for control of government. Political issues become an important test of the electoral process only when the functions they are to fulfill are made clear.

Unfortunately, both Key and the SRC wished to ignore these deeper questions, with the result that the controversy over issue voting took place on extremely narrow ground. The question was examined in isolation, apart from other aspects of the electoral process. But examined it was. During the decade that followed, political scientists bore down on this question with all benefits of methodology and data collection that previously had been only new and uncertain techniques. The result was an outpouring of evidence that paradoxically reaffirmed the central relationships propagated by the Survey Research Center even as Key was proven quite correct on the matter of issue voting. Reviewing the evidence that had accumulated after a decade's work, Philip Converse would conclude that there was indeed much more issue voting among voters than had been estimated initially, but that its presence by no means established the rationality of the electorate.

To summarize, then, in my estimation Key failed to cope with his customary adeptness with the information problem, although he poked at it with the "echo chamber" idea, and he made the further mistake of importing the concept of rationality to the discussion while leaving it hopelessly undefined. His final and posthumously completed work has helped to legitimize a simplistic equation between rationality and "issue voting" which simply does not bear scrutiny. Some portion of genuine issue voting proceeds on misinformation, and hence demonstrations concerning issue voting cannot be used to show how well informed the public is nor can they be used to prove rationality, save in the sterile tautological sense in which rationality governs all behavior, which is to say the case in which proofs are irrelevant from the outset. All these problems would fall away if the focus were on issue voting *per se,* uncluttered by the rationality concept.[41]

The evidence that has accumulated has borne everything but fruit. It has extended our understanding of issues and of information in the electorate. And we know too how these aspects of electoral politics are related to candidate preferences and party identification. Yet the logic of electoral politics—the relationships that make democracies function well or cause them to function poorly—remains hidden.

CHAPTER 8

The Restoration
of Theory

One of the more attractive qualities of quantitative studies is that
once a problem becomes sufficiently important, it is approached
from a variety of methodological perspectives. This research is
often tedious and difficult to follow, and occasionally the larger
problem is lost altogether. But nonetheless there accumulates a
solid body of evidence that, because it lacks theoretical subtlety,
casts a nice diversity of methodologies and approaches on the
matter in controversy.

This is precisely what happened with the differences between V.
O. Key, Jr., and the SRC. In the truest sense, the issues between
them involved fundamentally different conceptions of the electoral
process and the meaning that voting has within it. However, the
problem was never stated in its boldest form. Rather, differences
in theory became more narrowly defined. The dominant view
among political scientists held that the SRC believed issues
counted for very little next to party identification, the electorate
thus being irrational. And conversely, Key's position was interpreted only to mean that voters were motiviated primarily by issues,
the electorate thus being quite rational.

It is easy to disparage the content of this dispute as well as the time and the effort that has gone into resolving it. The more honest response, however, is to observe how stubborn the problem has been. It is one thing to demonstrate, with a series of bivariate correlations in the manner of V. O. Key, that political issues have an important role in electoral behavior. It is quite another matter to establish the significance of issues in a multivariate context with, among other things, the power of party identification at play. Given that the problem of issue voting was vastly oversimplified, establishing its importance required imaginative manipulation of the data and all the methodological sophistication that could be mustered.

The Accumulation of Evidence and the Decline of Theory

Three important pieces of research served to establish the role of issues in voter choice. First is the work of Gerald Kramer, whose analysis of aggregate voting and economic data showed a clear relationship between economic conditions and voting at the national level.[1] Kramer's work created a controversy of its own,[2] one that had the unusual effect of clarifying the underlying controversy, through the second important piece of research.

Howard Bloom and H. Douglas Price demonstrate in a brilliantly polished piece of research that "economic downturns reduce the vote for the party of the incumbent President, but economic upturns have no corresponding effect."[3] They also found that voters use a remarkably short frame of reference in making their evaluation of the economy. The year immediately preceding the election seems to determine how people feel about the economy, the events of the preceding three years notwithstanding.[4] This fact suggests a situation where the short-term manipulation of the economy is irresistible to elected political officials. Unfortunately, a growing body of evidence confirms that politicians, particularly at the national level, operate in precisely this manner.[5]

Taken together, these studies and others[6] enhance the role that issues play in the formulation of voting decisions. But the benefit of having rational, issue-oriented citizens is weakened considerably by the knowledge of just how easy it is to manipulate them in the context of electoral competition. People may vote rationally in terms of their issue interests, but the same evidence establishes just as strongly that the electorate lacks the capacity to think independently about public policy and public outcomes.

Bloom and Price and Kramer produced their findings from the analysis of aggregate data; establishing the rationality of voters from survey data is a more perplexing problem. Nevertheless, the data provided by the Survey Research Center is rich in possibilities. David RePass showed that partisan perception of issues is quite strongly related to voting choice, even when the effects of party are controlled.[7] And Philip Converse used responses to sixteen closed-ended questions to lay bare the uncrystallized and inconsistent nature of the opinions of the mass public. His concept of "issue publics" was seized upon by other analysts as a vehicle for establishing rationality.[8]

But Richard Boyd produced the conclusive, and perhaps the most sound, piece of evidence.[9] Using Converse's model of "mean party identification" as a baseline, Boyd calculated the expected partisan component of each issue for a diverse array of self-anchoring scales and fixed-response questions, and then compared those expected values to observed behavior.[10] In every one of the fifteen issues he analyzed in the 1968 election, there were noticable departures from the proportion of the vote that the Democratic party could otherwise have expected to receive.

Professor Boyd's analysis collapsed the SRC's argument internally. In terms of analysis that were precisely those of the SRC, Boyd demonstrated that the same issues that Converse, Miller, and their associates sought to minimize had great significance on the vote. Returning to the concept of the normal vote as Boyd had conceived of it, the SRC's 1972 analysis conceded the presence of issue effects, but argued that the conditions for party realignment were present.[11]

From this controversy one gets the sense that the disagreement over the effects of political issues has been settled while the central problem has been suspended. The results that establish the role of issues in voter behavior represent hard-won gains in the field of voter research. Yet there is also a growing sense of both redundancy and incompleteness about the work now going on in the field.

The source of this confusion is twofold, I believe. In the first place, the debate over political issues has been resolved in its smallest dimensions—in terms of whether or not political issues exist. From a deeply political point of view, it is curious that the question should have ever been asked this way. The study of political issues took this form because of assumptions about the nature of democracy made by the people who study it. If it is objected that these people knew nothing about politics, political history, and democratic theory—and by and large the indictment is truer than it should be—and that theirs was a sort of imperialism of methodology—and to some extent it was—it must also be said that neither the students of American politics nor those of political theory knew enough to respond to these shortcomings strongly or successfully.

Yet it is my own feeling that the development of intellectual discontinuities of the size surrounding the voting studies is less a matter of narrowmindedness or scholarly perversity than it is a manifestation of important currents of intellectual history. This is the second source of the confusion in the current literature. The entire debate over the voting studies represents the grand and diverse assumptions that have been made about the nature of mass publics; it represents also how little was actually known about political behavior and about how voting worked in an electoral democracy.

In this light, the progress of voting studies is both remarkable and inherently interesting, as I hope the preceding chapters have shown. On the one hand, a considerable amount has been learned about how people behave in electoral systems, the attitudes they have, and the motivations that bring them to act as they do. But on the other hand, this knowledge has been expensive indeed. I do not mean "expensive" in the sense of the high cost of survey work and in the redundancy of effort, but rather in the sense that we have paid a high cost primarily in terms of assumptions that were made, too often inarticulately, and in the paucity of theory that has been gained. So very much effort and controversy for so very little.

It is fitting in a way that the voting studies should, after more than forty years of work, finish with a simple consensus that issues do, after all, matter. Lest these remarks be misinterpreted, it is important to note that the struggle to get this far has been a hard one. It is one thing to believe that issues play an important part in the political process; it is quite another to establish empirically that they do. Had the problem been a less difficult one, it would have been solved long ago by some graduate student. However, it has taken twenty years of concentrated research to develop the tools to demonstrate that political issues have a place in the system.

Where the controversy over political issues remains shallow is in the placid assumption that, because it has now been shown that issues affect voters, the problem of linking popular preferences to public policy has been resolved. Surely this is the correct assumption for politics in electoral democracies. However, the truly challenging question rests not with this assumption; the deeply difficult problem is to show *how* the electoral system works to produce these results.

Unfortunately, there has not been much progress on this problem since the work of V. O. Key, Jr. The little work that has been done on linkages has yielded very little, despite the success researchers have had in demonstrating issue effects. Rather, it has been weakly assumed that because issues affect the voting behavior of mass publics, they must then be linked to the behavior of the political elite. The model implicit in this assumption is that issues have a sort of "hydraulic effect" on the political elite, who respond because the pressure is there. Of course, there is an element of truth in this assumption. Given enough popular pressure in a specific direction, the elite *will* respond. But this is a long way from an adequate description of how the electoral system operates and the effects it has on public policy.

The reason the hydraulic model of issue effects could be accepted so uncritically stems largely from the context in which the research has been done, that it has focused on presidential elections in the United States, and that it largely uses data gathered by the SRC. With the 1964 election, certain issues that had not been present previously, or that had not been present so clearly, came to the fore. The significance of these issues continued in the elections of 1968 and 1972, so that in the McGovern-Nixon contest their significance could hardly be missed, even by the SRC. It is not coincidental that survey analysts began wondering whether the United States was in a transitional period, where political realignment demonstrated not only the power of issues, but also a reorientation of party identification. However, the paradox that increased influence of issues occurred simultaneously with a decline in the system's stability received relatively little attention.

The hydraulic model of issue effects, if correct, has some thorny implications for democratic theory. This simplistic conception and the corresponding ambiguity in defining issues rule out focusing on the special role of the elite in understanding the role of elections in democracy. If one conceives of the linkage between voter and elite as an automatic process, then one never asks the critical theoretical questions that lead to the dimensions on which the system can be evaluated. The hydraulic model would have us believe that the motor forces of policy making come from the electorate and the electorate can be understood by focusing on the psychological characteristics of individual voters. Taken together, the approaches of the voting studies hold in common the assumption that democratic politics rests on individual "psychological orientations towards social objects," that is, the orientation of mass publics toward government and politics.

This assumption receives strong support in political theory, particularly among contemporary writers.[12] And the concept, indeed, has intuitive validity. How can democracy be sustained without a supporting political culture? Moreover, comparative variations on the order of those discovered by Almond and Verba suggest that the different capacities of nations for democratic politics rest on differences in political culture.[13]

But the capacity for democracy does not derive directly, or hydraulically, from the psychological orientation of the masses. Theorists of this persuasion are silent on the question of how a democratic political culture translates into a democratic regime, or how the policy preferences of the masses are translated into the policy-making behavior of the elite.

Indeed, the elite has broad latitude for action independent of the context of the psychological orientation of the mass public. The elite can exercise its authority without regard to, and apparently in spite of, hydraulic pressure from the attitudes of the mass public.

A brilliant, and generally overlooked (by political scientists) study of authority suggests a fruitful approach to the role of authority in a political system.[14] The Milgram Experiments, behavioral experiments in the psychology of authority, present a challenge to the hydraulic model, and to my mind render this approach untenable.

The Milgram Experiments

Stanley Milgram, a social psychologist at Yale, originated the Milgram Experiments to study the relationship between national culture and personality. Initially, the research was designed to determine which personality traits separated Americans from Germans in authority situations. The atrocities of World War II concentration camps provided an ideal focus for Milgram's investigation. The experiments were designed with a view toward positing an authority relationship in which one individual was "ordered" to harm another, the expectation being that willingness to disobey authority would vary across cultures.[15]

The essential experiment involved three people: a "naive subject," the victim, and the experimenter (Milgram varied the structure and setting with no important variation in results). Naive subjects entered the experiment believing they were participating in a learning experiment. By a process that was made to appear random, one person was selected to be the "teacher" (always the subject), and the other was selected to be the "learner" (always an actor who was part of the experiment). The learning task consisted of paired words that the teacher would read to the learner ("blue box," "nice day," and so forth), and then the learner would be tested in terms of his (always the same male actor) ability to complete the original pairs. The learner was strapped into a chair; each time an error was made, the teacher was instructed by the experimenter (authority) to administer an electric shock to the victim. The shocks were administered in increments ranging from 15 to 450 volts in thirty steps, with the highest switches labeled "Extreme Intensity Shock," "Danger: Severe Shock," and two more switches labeled "XXX." All naive subjects were given a sample shock (45 volts), a procedure that served the double function of "strengthening the subject's belief in the authenticity of the generator" and reminding them that even a shock of 45 volts is not terribly pleasant.[16] To reinforce the expectation of disobedience, the victim always made mention of a mild heart attack that he had suffered several years ago.

In abstract, this is not a situation that seems to favor obedience. And indeed, when the experiment was described to different groups (psychiatrists, college students, and middle-class adults), each predicted that all would refuse to obey the experimenter at some early point in the "learning process." Unfortunately, this expectation was not fulfilled. Indeed, people were so readily compliant that there was essentially no variation in the experiment and, hence, no variation for purposes of analysis. The situation created by Milgram cried out for disobedience, yet everyone obeyed the authority. The results of the experiment confirm that, even in situations that are manifestly inhumane, people have great difficulty disobeying "legitimate authority."

218

In explaining the results of these experiments, Milgram develops a theory of "agentic shift," a theory that argues that in hierarchical systems of authority, people suspend their value system and no longer see themselves as responsible for their actions. Milgram is both specific and concise in his development of this notion:

> [T]here is a phenomenological expression of this shift to which we do have access. The critical shift in functioning is reflected in an alteration of attitude. Specifically, the person entering an authority system no longer views himself as acting out of his own purposes but rather comes to see himself as an agent for executing the wishes of another person. Once an individual conceives his action in this light, profound alterations occur in his behavior and his internal functioning. These are so pronounced that one may say that this altered attitude places the individual in a different *state* from the one he was in prior to integration into the hierarchy. I shall term this *the agentic state,* by which I mean the condition a person is in when he sees himself as an agent for carrying out another person's wishes. This term will be used in opposition to that of *autonomy*—that is, when a person sees himself as acting on his own.[17]
>
> . . . From a subjective standpoint, a person is in a state of agency when he defines himself in a social situation in a manner that renders him open to regulation by a person of higher status. In this condition the individual no longer views himself as responsible for his own actions but defines himself as an instrument for carrying out the wishes of others.[18]

Milgram's results can be interpreted as a strong case for the position that the entire idea of focusing on the psychological basis for democratic politics represents a misplaced emphasis. As the critics of the *Authoritarian Personality*[19] argued, psychology washes out at this level. Placed in a system of authority, individuals enter the state of agency, thereby holding their preferences in abeyance. The attitudes and values of the individual—his or her psychological profile—are present in the individual characteristics that Milgram identifies as an independent effect, but these variables have no role in the state of agency itself.

A second implication is that the idea of locating the basis of democracy in attitudes about participation, as did Almond and Verba, is to probe the wrong area. It is vastly more important to know an individual's attitudes about authority. In this connection Harry Eckstein's orientation to comparative politics contains a lesson for students of voting behavior.[20] While authority is not the only concept that could be fruitfully employed in voting surveys, Milgram's work provides compelling evidence that understanding attitudes about authority is more important than understanding attitudes about participation for the development of democratic theory. The focus of such research should be to assess independent effects on the state of agency: the individual's values and attitudes toward authority; the nature and impact of group effects in reinforcing authority relationships; and perceptions and attitudes of voter and elite about the nature of the exercise of authority.

Of course, the source of authority relationships is an additional research question of importance to democratic theory. It is largely through experience and familiarity that authority relationships gain legitimacy. Family and school authority systems, for example, identify and reinforce understandings of authority relationships.

But the most important source of understanding authority relationships is via the values of culture. Democratic political culture includes some particular values and excludes others, thus placing constraints on the range of conceivable authority relationships. Almond and Verba's emphasis on political culture is completely correct in this sense. Yet they focused too narrowly on participation. That itself is one value, but a more fruitful approach would emphasize the values that participation expresses. The important point is that participation is an expression of the fundamental democratic values of tolerance and civility, and perhaps even of the norm of disobedience, at least in certain types of situations. Indeed, it is values that we must talk about when we consider democracy, and a great deal of effort has been expended to avoid that fact.

The failure of the voting studies is their failure to study values. Almond and Verba chose to seek the determinants of participation in individual attitudes rather than the meaning of participation in individual values. They simply did not ask about values. Nor, more importantly, did the Survey Research Center, the institution that came to dominate the field of political behavior. The group theorists came closest to centering voting studies on values and norms, but they were proportionately displaced by the rise of the Survey Research Center.

Finally, it would be false to conclude that Milgram's results subvert the ideal of democracy. The conditions of Milgram's experiments did, indeed, cry out for disobedience. The willingness of the subjects to transfer responsibility for their choices, and thereby their individual freedom, is disconcerting in the extreme. His results tell us the conditions under which subjects are willing to give up responsibility and freedom, but his explanation does not state, or even imply, that such results are in any sense absolute, that they can be generalized to all cultures or for all subjects. To the contrary, his explanation is an agenda for the application of survey research to the development of democratic theory: What is the nature of the independent effects on the shift to the state of agency? When the questions on this agenda are answered, the conditions under which responsibility and freedom are forfeited can be understood and democracy's possibilities understood as well. Those who cherish democracy understand that freedom and responsibility are the ends of democracy, not its preconditions.

The point is that disobedience is a choice, and choices are framed by values. To be able to disobey is to be able to respond to values contrary to authority. The freedom to exercise such a choice requires acceptance of responsibility for one's actions, which, in turn, can lead to the conclusion that one ought to exercise freedom.

As opposed to the study of issue rationality and the social psychology of voting, the question of the distribution of values in mass publics has barely been included in the voting surveys. However, the absence of this dimension is surely not for want of its importance. It is perfectly clear in both democratic theory and the history of democratic institutions that the problem of values is central. The differences between mass and elite value systems mark an important distinction to draw; but by no means does this resolve the problem—it only locates the functions of values in democratic theory. This evidence should be taken to mean that mass and elite value systems serve different functions.

In particular, it is clear that the bases of democratic politics rest more in the hands of the political elite than of the mass public. This is true in a variety of ways, as Key and McClosky have noted.[21] However, the data do not indicate that mass values are therefore unimportant; they indicate only that mass values are of secondary importance in terms of responsibility for maintaining the political system. In this regard, Key's reliance on the short-term influence of the political elite was precisely right—a conclusion made definite by the Milgram experiments.

Yet, political elites are not infallible, nor are their value systems always to be relied on. Hopefully, there is a reservoir of democratic sentiment in the mass public that serves as a basis for remedying the worst errors of the political elite, as, for example, with the issue of Vietnam or the Algerian question, where political elites (or at least substantial portions of them) were insensitive to the moral dimension of policy.[22]

Of course, the capacity of mass publics to remedy the errors of the political elite is entirely an empirical proposition. It is certainly not a principle that can be taken for granted. This is one reason why systematic investigations of value systems in mass publics are highly desirable. The possibility of comprehending where "public values" are strong with regard to democratic practices and where they are vulnerable is one that should have been fulfilled by survey research. That the area of values has not been pursued systematically represents one of the fundamental intellectual failings of the field of electoral behavior.[23]

In principle, there is no reason why "the public philosophy" cannot be estimated by survey research at regular intervals. And there is every reason that such estimates should be made. Not only are there the secondary functions that mass values serve for the system as a whole, but it is also true that mass values change over time,[24] and that some values are more enduring than others.[25] But, most importantly, in many areas the democratic values that mass publics express are weak and inadequate. We have seen that the main difficulties lie in the areas of social prejudice and cultural intolerance. However, there is also a problematic inability of mass publics to appreciate democratic procedures.[26] It is quite important to know how active people's concerns are in these areas. This is doubly true: first, in the sense that these are areas in which the learning process—formal and informal—plays an important role,[27] and second, in the more immediate sense that social prejudice and cultural intolerance can form the basis for voting decisions in the electoral process.

The Theory of the Reasonable Voter

In these final sections, I want to develop a theory of political issues and explore how this theory functions in the American political process. Much of the confusion that has enveloped the voting studies is due to a persistent lack of thought on these basic matters. Issue voting has been handled as if it were solely an empirical problem. Always the assumption has been that the form political issues take is self-evident, that the place to consider issues is democratic theory, and that the functions they are to serve are firmly established. Nothing, I believe, is farther from the truth.

Elections and voting, it must be remembered, were added to democratic theory as a historical afterthought. Unlike the development of constitutionalism, there exists no body of theory that describes these innovations or that explains, at least in principle, how they can be expected to function. The electoral process was hammered into constitutional theory by the repeated blows of group conflict. In political systems where the concept of the individual survived, voting and elections became the vehicle for modifying the inequities of constitutional designs, while at the same time rescuing the essential elements of constitutional theory. But these revisions operated at the practical level only; they were not extended into the realm of theory.

This has produced an extremely untidy arrangement of ideas and practices. Voting depends on constitutional theory for its fundamental assumptions—assumptions about the individual, the limited nature of government, and the proper design of institutions. Similarly, the moral and ethical principles implicit in the idea of voting—the nature of political obligations, the meaning of law and of political power, indeed the working assumptions about human nature itself—are derived entirely from constitutionalism. Yet constitutional theory is explicit both in its distrust of voters and in its opposition to the primacy of the electoral process. It was never the intention of constitutionalists that the public good would be derived from the perceptions or preferences of the mass public.

The changes imposed on constitutional theory by the electoral process reverberate throughout the governmental system. From the expression of individual interests to the definition of the public good, the entire flow and emphasis of the constitutional design has been altered. But by the same token, constitutional theory imposes its principles and assumptions upon electoral politics. This can be seen in the moral obligations acquired by the electorate, in the special burdens of the political elite, and in the definition of political power itself.

In the tangle that has grown out of the intermixing of these ideas and practices, one very important question has never been asked: What are the functions that the electoral process fulfills in constitutional theory, and more narrowly, how are political issues supposed to function in this process? I do not mean to imply that there is some latent, mysterious element in either the electoral process or constitutional theory that heretofore has gone undiscovered. Rather I feel that the meaning of the electoral process has rarely been considered on its own merits, that its functions always have been assumed rather than stated clearly.[28] But without such a clear description of purpose, it is impossible to examine the capabilities of the electoral process or to evaluate its performance.

The electoral process functions to provide political choices. This seems quite simple and direct. And indeed, from the voters' perspective, it is. Electoral systems are fairly easy to operate, and they accept any decisions that voters make no matter what the electorate's motivations. But from an analytic perspective, electoral choice is a considerably more sophisticated proposition. Choice in the electoral process extends over the full range of powers and responsibilities that have accrued to citizens by virtue of modifications in the constitutional ideal. Rather than speaking of electoral choice, it would be more accurate to describe a range of distinctive types of choices. Elections are not merely an opportunity for voters to assess their interests in politics. They equally ask voters to evaluate the policies and performance of government, to choose between competing elites and parties. Every election involves a moral dimension also, in the underlying values and beliefs assumed by voters. The electorate makes a variety of different choices in every election.

To think of elections in terms of popular control of government misrepresents the nature of the choices provided by the electoral process. Such a view assumes that elections consist of representations of self-interests—the implication being that the positions people take on issues are expressions of their interests and that therefore popular control of government depends on issue voting. In these assumptions is found the basis for the protracted controversy over voting rationality.

The misleading linkage in that dispute was (and, unfortunately, still is) the identification of rationality with interest voting. Without question, rationality is a crucial component of electoral choice. The distinguishing characteristic of democracies, as Harold Lasswell once observed, is the "open interplay of opinion and policy."[29] If people are not capable of expressing their choices through the electoral process, then elections become a methodology for concealing power rather than for sharing it. Where the controversy over voter rationality has been consistently wrong, then, is not in its emphasis on rationality but in its identification of voter rationality with issue voting. Issues were assumed to mean individual representations of self-interest, as if this were the only component of electoral politics.

But the changes made in the constitutional ideal by the electoral process ensure that the voters have a wider latitude. There is a broad range of choices open to the electorate for distinctive types of political issues—issues which have different characteristics and which perform different functions for the system as a whole. However, the general nature of electoral choice must be understood first, as must the ways in which such choices differ from the notion of popular control of government.

Elections present voters with a range of possibilities. In part these are individual self-interests. But elections also involve people and parties competing for power. This competition cannot be reduced to differences on issues of self-interest in most cases. To the contrary, the structure of campaigns and parties can affect the ability of people to vote their interests. For example, a voter can be terribly unhappy with the performance of the economy and, indeed, have suffered significant economic hardship because of the incumbent administration's policies. But the opposition candidates can make it impossible for this voter to support them by predicating their campaigns on an approach to government that this voter finds anathema.[30]

The choices presented to voters, then, are not one dimensional. Each election contains a range of possibilities—possibilities established in part by the individual preferences and in part by the system of electoral competition. Popular control of government is feasible only when all the differing strands of electoral choice have the same political meaning. Such a convergence can occur in electoral politics. But it is a limiting case. When a single issue comes to dominate the thinking of most voters, and when that issue becomes the basis for electoral competition, and when the various candidates involved in that competition align themselves so as to present clear and dissimilar alternatives, then the concept of popular control is a meaningful category of analysis. This is the politics of crisis. It requires an "issue" on the order of the Great Depression to align choices so that every component of the electorate's decision has the same political meaning.[31] Political crises do not provide a good standard for analysis of the electoral process, however. It is much more fruitful to identify each distinctive strand of electoral choice and to consider the functions that each performs.

226

Political Issues in the Electoral Process

At the heart of my argument is my belief that electoral choices are not unitary, that for each voter and certainly for the electorate as a whole there are distinctive types of issues at play, that these serve manifestly different functions both for the voter and for government, and that the significance of each type of issue is established not by voters themselves but by the nature of constitutionalism as it has been modified by the electoral process. At a minimum, I think that there are five distinctive issue forms that can be identified.

Issues of Self-interest—Opinion Groups, Issue Publics, and Position Issues

This type of political issue has been recognized from the outset. It served as the basis for most of the fears expressed by constitutionalists about the electoral process; it figured prominently in contemporary theories of politics; and, unfortunately, it has been the only type issue to be included in the voting studies on a regular basis. The most distinctive feature of issues of self-interest is their intrinsically subjective character. These issues represent the definitions that people give to their political interests.

From the perspective of the electorate as a whole, the multiplicity of interests must be stressed. One measure of the diversity of self-interests in the system is the enormous number of categories needed to classify them. When the Center for Political Studies (formerly called the Survey Research Center) asks people what they consider to be "the most important problem," several hundred distinct codes are required, and often even this large array is not precise enough for analytical purposes.[32]

Self-interest functions about as one might expect, both for the voter and for the political system. Voters are seeking the realization of their most pressing desires through the use of political power. The public good is molded by highly particularistic causes. And in

227

an important sense political power is meant to be used in this way. The composition of the public good should include the most pressing and popular demands of its citizens. It is easy to see why group theorists were unusually sensitive to opinions of this type, for expressions of self-interest in electoral politics can be seen as a process of free-forming opinion groups. The group is held together by nothing more than shared interests; there are no fixed boundaries; the political landscape can be seen as a series of limitless potential interests and hence potential groups awaiting political definition.[33]

While group theory provides an incomplete description of issues in the electoral process, it does emphasize one very important characteristic of issues of self-interest. Such issues are highly bounded and quite sharply focused. They represent an individual's self-interest, after all. People need not be interested in every public concern, or even in matters that are quite controversial. Thus while the entire electorate may share some particular concern, it is not very likely. Rather, the expectation is to find more discrete clusters of opinion in the population. The political meaning of individual self-interest, then, can be analyzed only after the appropriate population has been defined. This was Philip Converse's conclusion too, only his description of "issue publics" was written after an exhaustive and disappointing search for broader representations of public opinions.

The substantive conclusion . . . is simply that large portions of an electorate do not have meaningful beliefs, even on issues that have formed the basis of intense political controversy among elites for substantial periods of time. . . . Our data argue that, where any single dimension is concerned, very substantial portions of the public simply do not belong on the dimension at all. This should be set aside as not normally any part of that particular *issue public*. And since it is only among "members" of any given issue public that the political effects of a controversy are felt (where "effects" include activated public opinion expressed in the writing of letters to the editor, the changing of votes, and the like), we come a step closer to reality when we recognize the fragmentation of the mass public into a plethora of narrower issue publics.[34]

That is it precisely. Issue publics are highly idiosyncratic and tightly bounded in character. They come in all sizes, shapes, and forms, there being absolutely no expectation of congruence or "constraint" among them. To the contrary, individuals express a multiplicity of interests. There is no requirement in democratic theory that people must be logical and consistent in their demands. Thus many people desire both an expansion of governmental services and a reduction in personal taxes. Combining these positions can be extremely hard on a government, but from the voters' perspective there is nothing prohibitive in such an inconsistancy. Similarly, it is not required in democratic theory that every voter have an interest in every political controversy, even those that have formed the substance of political competition for a number of years.

Individual self-interest in politics functions as a vehicle of personal expression. Self-interest ensures that the voter's definitions of the politically relevant are always kept in view. Or from the perspective of the electoral system as a whole, individual self-interest functions to keep the system open. Self-interest guarantees that the agenda of politics is never a closed list.

Issues of Policy and Performance

This type of issue was described initially by V. O. Key in *The Responsible Electorate.* The burden of that book, however, was the dispute over voter rationality, as we saw in chapter 7. Lost in that controversy was Key's use of questions of different sorts from those usually asked by the Center for Political Studies. This followed from his belief that voters were motivated by their evaluations of governmental policy and performance as they had experienced them in the last election period. This is an emphasis that is decidedly different from expressions of individual self-interest in politics.

Issues of self-interest are identifiable as "the most important problem" people feel is facing them. Issues of policy and performance, by contrast, ask voters whether they think some particular policy is good or bad, whether it has made things better or worse, whether it has helped or hurt. Issues of policy and performance remove an important element of subjectivity from individual expressions. To be sure, it is still the voter who evaluates the policies and performance of government. It continues to be true that people need not to have an opinion one way or another, that they may not feel they have been affected by actions (or inactions) of government, or they simply may not be interested in this aspect of politics. The policies of government are quite real, irrespective of the opinions that people have about them. As opposed to the unfettered subjectivity of individual self-interest, the relevance of policy and performance issues is established for the electorate as a whole.

Expressed in empirical terms, this means that questions of policy and performance extend over a different population than do issues of self-interest. The most important consideration in locating issue publics is defining the relevant population, locating that segment of the electorate truly interested in some particular matter. With issues of policy and performance, the entire electorate is the appropriate focus of analysis. It is what people have experienced (or think they have experienced) that is important. This retrospective focus is the distinguishing characteristic of policy and performance issues, as V. O. Key observed.

> The patterns of flow of the major streams of shifting voters graphically reflect the electorate in its great, and perhaps principle, role as an appraiser of past events, past performances, and past actions. It judges retrospectively; it commands prospectively only insofar as it expresses either approval or disapproval of that which has happened before.[35]

Undoubtedly, issues of policy and performance have become an increasingly important dimension of electoral competition. The very complexity of national and international economies, and of urban life, require higher levels of governmental involvement. Similarly, the technical capacity of government to intervene in the economy has increased. So there is little doubt that policy and performance issues are increasing in significance. But it should be noted that even when governments lack the capacity to formulate national economic policy and when the level of governmental activity is at a minimum, people still vote on a performance basis, particularly on economic matters.[36]

Issues of policy and performance function to hold governments accountable for their actions; they provide voters with an ongoing measure of political responsibility. Thus these issues cut both ways. Governments must pursue policies that maintain the support of voters, or at least do not provoke their disapproval. But in turn, voters, by their acquiescence, become responsible for the policies of government. This clearly is a double-edged sword. It is difficult to argue in electoral politics that government has been acting against the interests of the people.[37]

Candidate Issues

Issues of self-interest and of policy and performance seem to fit easily into democratic theory. Once their distinguishing characteristics are presented clearly, there is little quarrel over the valuable functions they perform. Not so with candidate-centered issues. Such issues have the unpleasant texture of the media and of manipulation. Such feelings of unease are probably warranted, but whatever the discomforts involved, it is essential to observe their distinctive characteristics and to recognize that they serve unique functions in electoral politics.

The personal attributes of the candidates provide the text for these issues, of course. At best they concern matters of governmental ability, competence, and political talent. Less satisfactorily, they include matters of life style, appearance, and charm. The point is that these are issues controlled by candidates. Candidate issues permit politicians to establish issues that are uniquely their own—without respect to party or performance or the interests of constituents. This is their primary function in the electoral process. Candidate issues promote political independence: they provide an avenue of entry for new leaders. For voters, candidate issues help to personalize government, to give complex issues and abstract concerns character and personality; they give expression to vague sentiments and help crystallize feelings.

One of the most devastating examples of the effectiveness of candidate-centered issues in a political campaign occurred in the 1964 presidential race between Lyndon Johnson and Barry Goldwater. In a television spot prepared by Johnson's media people, a little girl is pictured in a field, playing and picking petals off a daisy. Superimposed over this image is first a voice that begins an ominous countdown, then the picture of a nuclear device exploding. Then President Johnson speaks: "These are the stakes, to make a world in which all God's children can live, or to go into the darkness. Either we must love each other or we must die"[38] Barry Goldwater is never mentioned by name. But the personalization of his "irresponsibility," the portrayal of his "unreliability" in a situation where the stakes are enormous, had a devastating effect on his campaign.

It is precisely the manipulative capacity of candidate issues that raises questions about them. Students of electoral behavior have assigned them to the category of images and hence deemed them unworthy of further study. But neither aspect of this approach is correct. Merely because these issues are controlled by candidates does not render them contentless. The example cited was devastating because it articulated a quality in the Goldwater candidacy that was unsound. Whether it was "real" in the sense that it described an attribute of Goldwater's character or whether it was "fictitious" in that Goldwater only appeared "unreliable" is quite beside the point. For the electorate, those images spoke to a very real sentiment. It would have made a nicer story had Goldwater's people found a similar chink in Lyndon Johnson's armor (they certainly did not lack for possibilities). This business of candidate issues takes place in a highly competitive context. But to consider these vacuous images is not quite the right designation. Or if they are to be called images, then their political content should be systematically studied.

The terms of analysis are reasonably clear. These are issues centered upon the personal characteristics of candidates. Voter responses are measured in terms of like or dislike, favorable or unfavorable, approval or disapproval. Incumbents are sharply differentiated from challengers in that issues, for them, are always infused with the attributes of policy. But from the voter's perspective it is whether people approve or disapprove of the way a president has managed the economy or conducted foreign policy. Highly complicated policies become personalized for voters in a way they can comprehend and manage. For politicians, these issues provide a continuing source of independence. Those who seek to lead are not chained to party or the performance of others. They can rise or fall on their own merits, or, rather, they can present the merits of the candidacy in the most favorable light and concentrate on the defects of the opposition as they think best, without the complications of party or the burden of complicated issue representations. Little wonder, then, that electoral systems everywhere have seen a dramatic increase in candidate-centered issues.[39]

Party Issues

Just as candidate issues follow from the independence of a self-recruiting political elite, party issues bespeak the collective nature of alternative visions of the public good. They represent distinctive public philosophies. In principle, such issues are created by the structure of constitutional governments—by the separation of institutions and institutional powers, and by the nature of multiple and independent constituencies. If this design of government promotes the independence of each elected official, and hence the development of candidate issues, it also requires party organization —shared fundamental assumptions among the political elite—in order to produce results and to effect changes. Those shared assumptions, as they exist in the public's mind, are party issues.

The principles of party organizations are nothing more than the desire to control the application of political power, to direct it systematically toward particular ends. It is the definition of the public good in the midst of electoral competition. But unlike the notion of the public good in constitutional theory, these definitions have meaning and immediacy. The public good is formulated in the beliefs that bind politicians together and in the common representations that they make to the mass public. Or looked at from the electoral side of the equation, the competition between alternative visions of the public good can be measured in terms of the distinctive issues associated with each party.

Party issues function to systemize political conflict for voters. They help to arrange the welter of competing candidates in a simpler and more comprehensible order. Familiar symbols and old identifications can be relied upon as guides for current decisions and as criteria for evaluating new political information. But party issues also function to give the political system a degree of coherence. These issues ensure that the past is continued into the present, that the political system does not slide aimlessly about from election to election, that candidates and issues of self-interest cannot remake the political process to suit their immediate purposes.[40] The past is not brought forward by the abstractions of history as it is presented with varying degrees of accuracy in civics textbooks. The past obtains current meaning in the issues and beliefs that people associate with a party. "The past is not over," observed William Faulkner in *Absalom! Absalom!*, "it is not even past." In the electoral process old assumptions and conflicts that appeared over long ago can be quite alive. They are continued in the particular issues that people identify with each party and in the different perceptions partisans have of politics.

Value Choices and Inarticulate Major Premises

The specification of distinctive issue types has been fairly straightforward thus far, in the sense that the issues that have been identified have a meaning that is manifestly political. The reader may wish to quarrel with the categories I have established, and I certainly would expend considerable effort justifying the validity and the analytic power of the distinctions I have drawn. But there can

234

be little doubt that each of these types of issues exists, irrespective of the question of its distinctiveness.

From a theoretical viewpoint the same conclusion can be reached. It is easy to see how the addition of voting and elections to constitutional theory legitimizes issues of self-interest and also how citizens have extended their sovereignty to include the policies and performance of government. And, in turn, it is not difficult to appreciate how the structure of constitutional politics creates opportunities for candidates to develop independent issues for their own candidacy, just as the design of government simultaneously creates the necessity for organized conflicts over the public good in terms of parties and party issues.

Matters are not nearly so precise, however, with values and the issues that derive from them. To begin with, such values rarely enter into electoral decisions as issues, that is, as conscious concerns. More often they remain in people's minds as "major inarticulate assumptions," to borrow Oliver Wendell Holmes's descriptive phrase. But values do enter into political competition in several very important ways, and their presence is a reasonable expectation from theory that I will present in the last section of this chapter.

This expectation derives from the small, but very real, grant of power acquired by voters by virtue of the electoral process. In constitutional theory power is obtained without corresponding responsibilities for the character and the integrity of the political order itself. Unfortunately, constitutionalists tended to be quite vague about the specific composition of these obligations, but the importance of such political principles to their theory of government is quite apparent. With the emergence of the electoral process, voters must certainly gain a portion of these responsibilities. But which values must be maintained in good order by mass publics remains a very unsettled proposition.

The value orientations maintained by people have an importance beyond the question of the integrity of the political order. Values also shape the assumptions of political competition, not only in the conflicts they create, but in the beliefs that are shared. Perhaps the best description of the point I am trying to make here can be found in Samuel Beer's description of British politics.[41] In analyzing five distinct theories of representation that at different times controlled the organized parties, directed public policies, and defined pressure groups, Beer observes that each period was distinguished not so much by the political issues in dispute, although these were surely hotly contested, but by the moral assumptions that all parties to those controversies shared—"the political culture" of the period, to use his term for it.

Part of any definition of political culture in an electoral system is its capacity to sustain the moral assumptions of democratic politics. There are additionally a series of shared beliefs that characterize every political era. These are not usually political issues in an active sense, as I have said. But this does not mean that they go "unrepresented" in either the electoral process or public policy. To the contrary, values function to establish the context of policy decisions by limiting the range of decisions and by giving emphasis and meaning to particular alternatives. And occasionally, values may surface directly in electoral politics as a highly generalized concern distinct from partisanship or interest (as, for example, in a general sentiment against hunger and poverty without carrying with it programmatic intention and perhaps contrary to other issue interests). More systematically, value patterns in the mass public function as a screening process for those who aspire to public office. Aspiration is not the only personal characteristic necessary to gain entry into the electoral process. If their campaign is to be at all viable, candidates also must not contest any of the fundamental assumptions of the mass public. These value assumptions are established by the mass public and are crucial in determining the quality of electoral competition.

Values function, then, by giving shape and texture to the electoral arena, while the other types of issues usually determine the substance of electoral competition. But overall, the point to be stressed is that each type of political issue serves distinctive functions both for voters and for the political system as a whole. If it can be said that the essence of the electoral process is to create choices for voters, it can be observed also that the choices themselves are distinctive, that the possibilities before voters vary themselves both in form and in function.

The Principle of Simultaneous Issue Effects

Usually political issues in any specific election are thought of as if they had a single definition. It is assumed further among the cognoscenti that any student of politics knows what the issues are. For politicians, everything else is a matter of resources, strategy, and tactics. For the more analytically oriented, everything else is a measurement problem. If only the perfect measurement techniques were available—a scaling device with the right calibrations, or perhaps the right sort of open-ended probe—then political opinions could be analyzed without ambiguity. This view, I believe, is terribly inaccurate.

Just as it is wrong to assume that political issues are all of one type, it is equally misleading to assume that issue types are mutually exclusive. The mistake is in the assumption that political issues enter the political process as one distinct form. Rather, *any political concern can find expression simultaneously in several different types of issues.* The propensity of political concerns to appear in multiple forms in the electorate increases directly with the importance of the matter in question. As a problem grows in importance—for example, the economy, racial conflict, foreign policy—the more likely it is that it will be manifest in each of the five characteristic forms that political issues can take. Thus analyzing the effects of political issues in the electoral process is complicated by the simultaneous appearance of the "same" issue in different forms.

From an analytical perspective, the principle of simultaneous effects operates in two ways—in terms of the electorate as a whole *and* in terms of individual voters. For the electorate as a whole, this means that no analysis of the issue effects is complete unless all of the forms that some political concern has taken have been surveyed. This is due to the fact that different segments of the electorate can be responding to different manifestations of the issue. For example, some voters may feel that they have suffered as a result of the incumbent administration's economic policy, while others may personalize their grievances by disapproving strongly of the president's handling of the economy, while still others may view the economy in partisan terms or in terms of immediate self-interest as expressed in their position on inflation or unemployment. Each type of issue, and correspondingly each type of survey question, elicits a different distribution of responses, all of which are relevant to answering the question of how the electorate has responded to the economic problem.

Equally, it is true that individual voters can have opinions on all the distinctive forms that a political issue takes. That is, people are not restricted in the structure of their issue opinions. Each issue type exists for every voter as a distinct possibility. Nor do these preferences have to be consistent. A voter may be unemployed and may hold the incumbent administration and, say, President Carter, responsible. But that person may also feel that economic policy is best made by Democrats and may cast a vote on this basis, despite disliking some Democratic policies. Discovering which issues actually motivate voters is a totally empirical proposition.

The principle of simultaneous effects has an importance in electoral behavior that is not captured simply by stating it. It means at the very least that the number of issues in elections has been seriously understated. Or to put this in terms of the controversy over voter rationality, it means that this dispute has raged for more than twenty-five years on the basis of evidence that was at best fragmentary. But the most significant implications of this principle are not analytical in nature; they are political. Elections always contain more possibilities than their outcome would suggest. History is written with intimations of inevitability. After all, the result is there, and there to be explained. Similarly with the analysis of data: relationships are established and the variance is explained.

But elections, before votes are cast, contain a variety of outcomes. Different choices are possible, not in hypothetical wistful glances at the electorate but empirically, in the diversity of issues and in the different distributions of opinion on them.

The issue of war in Vietnam as it entered into the 1968 election provides a good illustration. Because of the manifest importance of the war, it appeared in at least four distinct types of issues and probably in the fifth as well (although there are no data on that dimension). Certainly it was an issue of self-interest. People took positions—hawk, dove, administration supporter—as they, by their own standards, thought best. The policy and performance issue was the conduct of the war to date, a deeply felt issue between voters. The image of Hubert Humphrey as a willing participant in Johnson's war policies was a crucial negative factor for the Democrat. And, finally, there were those in 1968, as today, whose views of political party platforms are as simple as identifying the Democrats as "The War Party" and the Republicans as "The Peace Party." Every campaign is a theory about public opinion—about how issues are organized and about which issues will actually motivate votes. Elections provide the solution to that puzzle, given the candidates who ran and the campaigns that were conducted. But there are always possibilities that were not seen and motivations that were not touched. The next election creates a new conundrum, one that is only partially understood by the election that preceded it. There are always more issues and issue motivations than there are election outcomes.

Assuming Reasonable Voters

As V. O. Key isolates the characteristics of policy and performance issues and charts their behavior, he establishes an important presumption. "What kinds of relations would be found," Key wonders, "if we assumed that the voter was a fairly reasonable fellow who voted to promote or to discourage public policies he approved or disapproved, insofar as he could perceive the consequences of his vote?"[42] Expanding the number of types of issues that can motivate voters increases the need to have a firm standard of electoral conduct in mind.

The test of reasonableness is the appropriate one, I believe. As it is used here, the "reasonable voter" is meant to describe a person whose voting behavior is intentional, but where what is intended is left to the voter to decide. Voting is conceived of as a conscious act, but one where the definition of intentions is up to the voter. This is a very limited definition of political consciousness, indeed —a procedural definition, if you will. The test for voters—given their political preferences and the relative importance that they assign to each—is whether they use the electoral machinery to their advantage, so that it expresses their preferences.

This is not the loftiest standard that one can imagine. A good deal of electoral behavior is accepted as valid for no other reason than individuals have inherited it from their parents or have acquired it by means of early socialization processes. The focus of the test is quite narrow, on the content of voting decisions. I think that there are good theoretic reasons for this. As we have seen, voting and elections are the political manifestations of individualism, root and branch. To select a standard for electoral behavior that quarrels with individual perceptions and preferences cuts against the grain of this building block of democratic theory.

Nothing in this test of reasonableness requires an uncritical acceptance of whatever voters say. Systematic criticism of the content of voter decisions is necessary from at least two perspectives. First, the public's demands, interests, evaluations, and selections are matters that, although they have acquired face validity as a matter of theory, can be both terribly wrong and quite inappropriate. Demonstrating the inadequacies of particular strands of public sentiment is an essential feature of electoral politics, even though such demonstrations are likely both to be technical in nature and to appear in thinly populated corners of the electoral universe.

240

Nevertheless, the sovereignty of the citizen presumes criticism just as it presumes the capacity of people to change. But the standards appropriate to critical evaluations of individual preferences provide inappropriate measures of the integrity of those opinions in electoral politics. Here people must speak for themselves.

There is a second, and equally important sense, in which a critical perspective is not only appropriate but necessary. This concerns the values that the mass public builds into the system of electoral competition, particularly those values that are related to the maintenance of democratic government. In this area the latitude granted the citizen is not quite so broad. The subjective, self-selecting quality of beliefs remains. But the standards of criticism are higher. Democracy requires certain civic responsibilities; certain values should be a part of an individual's belief system. The quality of political participation establishes the context in which electoral competition takes place. Simply from a critical view, political participation requires constant attention.

Notes

Introduction

1. Peter Natchez, herein, 21.
2. Ibid., 23.
3. Ibid., 23.
4. A. Campbell, "The Classification of Presidential Elections," in *Elections and Political Order,* ed. A. Campbell (New York: John Wiley, 1966), 63–67.
5. This position is lucidly argued in C. West Churchman, *Prediction and Optimal Decision* (Englewood Cliffs, NJ: Prentice-Hall, 1961).
6. V. O. Key Jr., "The State of Discipline," *American Political Science Review* 52 (December, 1958): 961–71.
7. V. O. Key Jr., "The Politically Relevant in Surveys," *Public Opinion Quarterly* 24 (Spring, 1960): 54–61.
8. Morris Fiorina, *Retrospective Voting in American National Elections* (New Haven: Yale University Press, 1981).

Chapter 1

1. For A. Lawrence Lowell, compare *Public Opinion and Popular Government* (New York: Longmans, Green, 1930), a work that is taken as the best of its time, with *Public Opinion in War and Peace* (Cambridge, Mass.: Harvard University Press, 1923), which is in many ways a sharper and more probing analysis of public opinion. And in contrast to both of these, see a curious little volume Lowell published at the outset of the depression, *Conflicts in Principle* (Cambridge, Mass.: Harvard University Press, 1932). Walter Lippmann shifted his view of the mass public and popular participation shamelessly throughout his career. Four of his early books are remarkable not only for this quality, but more so for the powerful insights that each contains: *A Preface to Politics* (Ann Arbor: University of Michigan Press, 1962; orig. pub. 1914); *Public Opinion* (New York: Harcourt, Brace,

1922); *The Phantom Public* (New York: Harcourt, Brace, 1925); and *The Good Society* (Boston: Little, Brown, 1943). A fine review of Lippmann's theories of public opinion and political leadership has been written by Benjamin Wright, *Five Public Philosophies of Walter Lippmann* (Austin: University of Texas Press, 1973), and an excellent biography of Lippmann has been published recently by Ronald Steel, *Walter Lippmann and the American Century* (Boston: Little, Brown, 1980).

2. Philip E. Converse, "Public Opinion and Voting Behavior," in *Handbook of Political Science*, vol. 4: *Non-governmental Politics*, ed. Fred I. Greenstein and Nelson W. Polsby (New York: Addison-Wesley, 1975), esp. 89–111.

3. Robert K. Merton, *Social Theory and Social Structure* (Glencoe, Ill.: Free Press, 1957), 85ff.

4. "Value-free" research has had a very curious meaning throughout the period covered in this book. For the most part, it has been used to justify narrow empiricism and ruthless data keeping, research conducted without articulate theory. As we shall see, this is a pecularity of the period and not at all what Max Weber meant to imply when he coined this term. See Max Weber, *The Methodology of the Social Sciences* (Glencoe, Ill.: The Free Press, 1949).

5. Harry Eckstein, "Critical Case Study and Theory in Political Science," in Fred Greenstein and Nelson Polsby, eds. *Handbook of Political Science*, vol. 7, *Strategies of Inquiry* (Reading, Mass.: Addison-Wesley Press, 1975), chap. 3.

6. Barrington Moore, Jr., *Social Origins of Dictatorship and Democracy: Lord and Peasant in the Making of the Modern World* (Boston: Beacon Press, 1966); Reinhard Bendix, *Nation-Building and Citizenship: Studies of Our Changing Social Order* (New York: John Wiley, 1964); T. H. Marshall, *Class, Citizenship, and Social Development* (Garden City, N.Y.: Doubleday, 1965); Crane Brinton, *A History of Western Morals* (New York: Harcourt, Brace, 1959), chaps. 6, 9–13.

7. A fine description of the feudal tradition has been written by Peter Laslett, *The World We Have Lost* (London: Methuen, 1965).

8. The emergence of both the individual and the nation-state can be looked at a number of different ways. Compare, for example, the following four highly regarded synthetic treatments: Sheldon S. Wolin, *Politics and Vision: Continuity and Innovation in Western Political Thought* (Boston: Little, Brown, 1960), particularly chaps. 5–7; John Plamenatz, *Man and Society*, vols. 1 and 2, (New York: McGraw-Hill, 1963); Ernst Cassirer, *The Philosophy of the Enlightenment* (Boston: Beacon Press, 1955); and Leo Strauss, *Natural Right and History* (Chicago: University of Chicago Press, 1953), chaps. 5 and 6. It is not at all uncommon for contemporary students of political thought to regard the emergence of individualism and nationalism as flawed concepts in that they limit the scope of modern political philosophy and with it the human political potential. Sheldon Wolin captures the spirit of this argument when he writes in *Politics and Vision:*

> The decline of political categories and the ascendancy of social ones are the distinguishing marks of our contemporary situation where political philosophy has been eclipsed by other forms of knowledge. . . . We can gain a firmer purchase on the problem if we recognize that this impoverishment is common also to the wider enterprise of which political theory is a party, namely philosophy. . . . This raises the provocative question of whether some interconnection exists between the state of philosophy and political theory on the one hand, and on the character of the liberal tradition on the other. The clue to the answer lies with the pivotal figure of John Locke, for insofar as modern philosophy is oriented towards empiricism and the anaysis of language, Locke is admittedly one of its founders. And to the extent that modern liberalism can be said

Notes

to be inspired by any one writer, Locke is undoubtedly the leading candidate. (Pp. 292–293)

The same theme is worked for different purposes by C. B. MacPherson, *The Political Theory of Possessive Individualism: Hobbes to Locke* (London: Oxford University Press, 1962).

9. The appropriateness of Rousseau's epigram in this context was suggested to me some years ago by William Schneider.

10. E. P. Thompson, *The Making of the English Working Class* (New York: Random House, 1963), 414.

11. T. H. Marshall, *Citizenship and Social Class* (Cambridge: Cambridge University Press, 1950), 81.

12. Ibid., 10–11.

13. See especially J.G.A. Pocock, "Machiavelli, Harrington and English Political Ideologies in the Eighteenth Century," *William and Mary Quarterly,* 3rd series, 22 (1965), 549–583; Stanley N. Katz, "The Origins of American Constitutional Thought," *Perspectives in American History* 3 (1969), 474–490; and more generally M.J.C. Vile, *Constitutionalism and the Separation of Powers* (Oxford: Claredon Press, 1967); and W. B. Gwyn, *The Meaning of the Separation of Powers* (New Orleans: Tulane University Press, 1965).

14. On the development of constitutionalism in general and the values that it implies, see: Vile, *Constitutionalism and the Separation of Powers;* Gwyn, *The Meaning of the Separation of Powers;* Hannah Fenichel Pitkin, *The Concept of Representation* (Berkeley: University of California Press, 1967); Bernard Bailyn, *The Origins of American Politics* (New York: Knopf, 1965), and *The Ideological Origins of the American Revolution* (Cambridge, Mass.: Harvard University Press, 1967); Betty Kemp, *King and Commons, 1160–1832* (London: Macmillan, 1959), and *Sir Francis Dashwood: An Eighteenth-Century Independent* (New York: St. Martin's Press, 1967); Carinne C. Weston, *English Constitutional Theory and the House of Lords, 1556–1832* (London: Oxford University Press, 1965); J. R. Pole, *Political Representation in England and the Origins of the American Republic* (Berkeley: University of California Press, 1971); J. H. Plumb, *The Origins of Political Stability: England, 1675–1725* (Boston: Houghton Mifflin, 1967); Isaac Kramnick, *Bolingbroke and His Circle* (Cambridge, Mass.: Harvard University Press, 1965); Carole Pateman, *Participation and Democratic Theory* (Cambridge: Cambridge University Press, 1970); Carl J. Friedrich, *Constitutional Government and Democracy* (Boston: Little, Brown, 1941), and an excellent piece by William Holdsworth, "The Conventions of the Eighteenth Century Constitutions," 17 *Iowa Law Review* (1931–32): 160–180.

15. The passage that is often cited as justifying this attribution begins by arguing that men are "independent and equal one amongst another . . . so that the governing Body should move that way whither the greater force carries it, which is the *consent* of the majority; or else it is impossible it should act or continue one Body, one community . . ." Locke, *The Second Treatise on Government,* in *Two Treatises on Government,* ed. Peter Laslett (Cambridge: Cambridge University Press, 1963), 350–351. Laslett takes the "major theme" for Locke's treatises to be the development of the implications of the idea of natural law; see his introduction to Locke, 116; see also Richard Ashcraft, "Locke's State of Nature: Historical Fact or Moral Fiction?" 62 *American Political Science Review* (September 1968): 889–897. But none of this makes Locke into a majoritarian.

16. S. M. Lipset and S. Rokkan, *Party Systems and Voter Alignments* (New York: Free Press, 1967). In their introduction, the authors suggest a two-dimensional,

four-component pattern that is extremely useful; see their ensuing discussion. See also S. Rokkan, *Citizens, Elections and Parties;* Samuel H. Beer, *British Politics in the Collectivist Age* (New York: Knopf, 1965); Mack Walker, *German Home Towns: Community, State, and General Estates, 1648–1871* (Ithaca, N.Y.: Cornell University Press, 1971); William Chambers, *Parties in a New Nation* (New York: Oxford University Press, 1967); Richard Hofstadter, *The Idea of Party* (Berkeley: University of California Press, 1969); Roy C. Nichols, *The Invention of Political Parties* (New York: Macmillan, 1967); Joseph Charles, *The Origins of the American Party System* (New York: Harper, 1961); Caroline Robbins, " 'Discordant Parties': A Study of the Acceptance of Party by Englishmen," 73 *Political Science Quarterly* (1958): 505–529; Roy C. Macridis and Bernard E. Brown, eds., *Comparative Politics: Notes and Readings* (Homewood, Ill.: Dorsey Press, 1964), chaps. 6–8; Harry Eckstein and David E. Apter, eds., *Comparative Politics* (New York: Free Press, 1963), parts 4 and 5; and Maurice Duverger, *Political Parties* (London: Methuen, 1954).

17. The central political fact in a free society is the tremendous contagiousness of conflict. . . .

At the nub of politics are, first, the way in which the public participates and, second, the process by which the unstable relation of the public to the conflict is controlled. . . . The logical consequence of the foregoing analysis of conflict is that the balance of forces in any conflict is not a fixed equation until everyone is involved. (E. E. Schattschneider, *The Semi-Sovereign People: A Realist's View of Democracy in America* [New York: Holt, Rinehart and Winston, 1960], 2–4).

Italics in original omitted. See also David Adamay, "The Political Science of E. E. Schattschneider: A Review Essay," 66 *American Political Science Review* (December 1972): 1321–1340.

18. Compare William Gillette, *The Right to Vote: Politics and Passage of the Fifteenth Amendment* (Baltimore: Johns Hopkins Press, 1965); Fawn Brodie, *Thaddeus Stevens: Scourge of the South* (New York: Norton, 1966); and David Donald, *The Politics of Reconstruction, 1863–1867* (Baton Rouge: Louisiana State University Press, 1965).

19. Stein Rokkan, "The Structuring of Mass Politics in the Smaller European Democracies." Paper presented at the Seventh World Congress of Political Science, Brussels, September 1967; reprinted in part as chap. 3 of Rokkan, *Citizens, Elections, Parties.* Lipset and Rokkan, eds., *Party Systems and Voter Alignments,* parts 2 and 3 especially; and Samuel P. Huntington, *Political Order and Changing Societies* (Buenos Aires: Paidos, 1972), chaps. 5 and 7.

20. Seymour M. Lipset and Stein Rokkan, "Cleavage Structures, Party Systems and Voter Alignments," in *Party Systems and Voter Alignments,* 15. Unquestionably this typology captures the major cleavages in which the party systems are rooted. However, these are not the only forces at work. Some political movements, such as the American Progressives, reflect the disproportionate influence of ideas and politics; others are the consequence of foreign intervention in another nation's affairs.

21. Lipset and Rokkan, "Cleavage Structures, Party Systems and Voter Alignments," 33–34. See also Bendix, *Nation-Building and Citizenship,* chap. 3.

22. Lipset and Rokkan, "Cleavage Structures, Party Systems and Voter Alignments," 34.

23. T. H. Marshall, *Citizenship and Social Class and Other Essays* (Cambridge: Cambridge University Press, 1950), 81.

24. Lipset and Rokkan, "Cleavage Structures, Party Systems and Voter Align-ments," 50–51. Italics in original.

Chapter 2

1. Compare Charles E. Merriam and Harold Gosnell, *The American Party System* (New York: Macmillan, 1940); Charles Merriam and Harold Gosnell, *Non-Voting: Causes and Methods of Control* (Chicago: University of Chicago Press, 1924); Peter H. Odegard and Allen Helms, *American Politics: A Study in Political Dynamics* (New York: Harper and Brothers, 1938); Peter Odegard, *The American Public Mind* (New York: Columbia University Press, 1930); Edward M. Sait, *American Parties and Elections* (New York: The Century Co., 1927); V. O. Key, Jr., *Parties, Politics and Pressure Groups* (New York: T. Y. Crowell, 1942).

2. Lazarsfeld was fascinated by the potential of radio and in particular the question of whether its effect differed from newspapers. See Paul F. Lazarsfeld, *Radio and the Printed Page: An Introduction to the Study of Radio and Its Role in the Communication of Ideas* (New York: Duell, Sloan and Pearce, 1940); Harry Field and Paul Lazarsfeld, *The People Look at Radio* (Chapel Hill: University of North Carolina Press, 1946); and Paul Lazarsfeld and Patricia L. Kendall, *Radio Listening in America: The People Look at Radio—Again* (New York: Prentice-Hall, 1948). However, Lazarsfeld was equally interested in the consumer process and in advertising; for example, see Arthur Kornhauser and Paul Lazarsfeld, "The Analysis of Consumer Actions," and Paul Lazarsfeld, "Evaluating the Effectiveness of Advertising," 5 *Journal of Consulting Psychology* (1941), 170–178. Additionally, Lazarsfeld was interested in purely methodological questions; see Paul F. Lazars-feld and Morris Rosenberg, eds., *The Language of Social Research* (Glencoe, Ill.: Free Press, 1955); Robert K. Merton and Paul F. Lazarsfeld, *Continuities in Social Research: Studies in the Scope and Method of the American Soldier* (Glencoe, Ill.: Free Press, 1950).

3. The business of attracting people who were willing to pay for a national survey (which was not cheap even in the old days) accounts for the pollsters' interest in politics. Newspapers and magazines had been intrigued by the idea of polling opinions well before the concept of the sample survey was perfected; see Claude Robinson, *Straw Votes: A Study of Political Prediction* (New York: Columbia University Press, 1932). Thus the idea of commissioning political surveys had an established appeal. Elmo Roper worked for *Fortune Magazine* (which conducted quarterly surveys of national opinion beginning in 1935). Archibald Crossley sur-veyed opinion for the Hearst papers, while George Gallup sold the idea of monthly surveys to both the United Press *and* the Associated Press (a maneuver that was to establish his firm as preeminent). Of course, the relationship between the papers and the pollsters provided additional dividends in terms of establishing the validity of survey research in the public mind, not to mention the minds of industrialists and politicians. The data collected in these efforts, although not of the highest quality, were extremely useful, particularly for the New Deal years. However, the quality of the publications that the pollsters produced is weak. Perhaps their great-est collective value is in the overidentification between public opinion and democ-racy that marks each of these publications. See, for example, George Gallup and Saul Rae, *The Pulse of Democracy* (New York: Greenwood Press, 1960); John M. Fenton, *In Your Opinion* (Boston: Little, Brown, 1960); William A. Lyngate, *What*

Our People Think (New York: T. Y. Crowell, 1944); a somewhat better work is Jerome S. Bruner, *Mandate from the People* (New York: Duell, Sloan and Pearce, 1944).

4. Apparently the application of survey research to public opinion was conceived of by Paul T. Cherington, a professor in marketing research at the Harvard Business School. He had observed that quality control in manufacturing involved taking a sample of units and inferring from the sample the characteristics of the population of units—the intellectual foundations of statistical inference having been already well established. From this evolved the idea of the opinion survey in its modern form; see *Fortune Magazine* (July 1935), 342. Fittingly, Cherington's own concerns were a perfect blend of Lazarsfeld's interest in social science and the pollsters' interest in advertising; see Paul T. Cherington, *The Elements of Marketing* (New York: Macmillan, 1920), and "Our Freedoms and Our Opinions," *Public Opinion Quarterly* 6 (Winter 1942), 617–621.

5. Arthur Kornhauser and Paul Lazarsfeld, "The Analysis of Consumer Actions," in *The Language of Social Research,* 393. Italics in original.

6. Paul F. Lazarsfeld, Bernard Berelson, and Hazel Gaudet, *The People's Choice: How the Voter Makes Up His Mind in a Presidential Campaign* (New York: Columbia University Press, 1948, 2nd ed.), 1. Erie County was selected for this study because it contained a balance of social conditions. It had an industrial core (the city of Sandusky) but was surrounded by a rural, farm area. No one industry was predominant in the county's economy; and there was a fairly diverse array of social and economic groups (farm organizations, labor unions, church groups). It was also a midwestern county, which made it seem to be the heartland of the United States. This aspect of the study's design appears to have been prompted by *Life Magazine,* which was partly responsible for funding the project and received in return two articles on the election.

7. Peter H. Rossi, "Four Landmarks in Voting Research," in *American Voting Behavior,* ed. Eugene Burdick and Arthur Brodbeck (Glencoe, Ill.: Free Press, 1959), 16; see also Peter H. Rossi, "Trends in Voting Behavior Research, 1933–1963," Paper presented before the American Political Science Association, New York City, September 1963.

8. Bernard Berelson, Paul F. Lazarsfeld and William McPhee, *Voting* (Chicago: University of Chicago Press, 1954).

9. Most important, see Elihu Katz and Paul F. Lazarsfeld, *Personal Influence: The Part Played by People in the Flow of Mass Communications* (Glencoe, Ill.: Free Press; 1955); William N. McPhee and William Glaser, eds., *Public Opinion and Congressional Elections* (Glencoe, Ill.: Free Press; 1962); and Herbert Hyman, *Political Socialization* (Glencoe, Ill.: Free Press; 1959). A remarkable group of young scholars was associated with the Bureau of Applied Social Research during these years: in one way or another, Seymour Martin Lipset, Herbert Hyman, James S. Coleman, and Hazel Gaudet also were associated with the Bureau, and this is a most casually drawn list. An interesting question is why the Bureau of Applied Social Research did not fare better as an institution. Certainly the people and the ideas were there.

10. Lazarsfeld, Berelson, and Gaudet, *The People's Choice,* 74.

11. Ibid., 137; see also pages 16–28 and 62–76. "Whatever the psychological mechanisms, the social and political consequence is very much the same: the development of homogeneous political preferences within small groups and along lines of close social ties connecting them. During a campaign political preferences

Notes

are 'contagious' over the range of personal contracts." Bernard Berelson, Paul F. Lazarsfeld, and William McPhee, *Voting*, 122.

12. Berelson, Lazarsfeld, and McPhee, *Voting*, 94.

13. Lazarsfeld, Berelson and Gaudet, *The People's Choice*, 148–149; see also 153.

14. Berelson, Lazarsfeld, and McPhee, *Voting*, 97; Lazarsfeld, Berelson, and Gaudet, *The People's Choice*, 113–114.

15. Lazarsfeld, Berelson, and Gaudet, *The People's Choice*, 141.

16. Ibid., 90–91. In recent years, there has been a good deal of talk by men of goodwill about the desirability and necessity of guaranteeing the free exchange of ideas in the marketplace of public opinion. Such talk has centered upon the problem of keeping free the channels of expression and communication. Now we find that the consumers of ideas, if they have made a decision on the issue, themselves erect high tariff walls against alien notions.

17. Ibid., 69. Also see Berelson, Lazarsfeld, and McPhee, *Voting*, esp. chapter 10, pp. 12–14. It is noted in the latter volume that only "about one-third of the voters are highly accurate in their perception of where candidates stand on issues" (233), and not surprisingly, these people turn out to be the best educated, the most well informed, and to care most about the election (288 and chart 107).

18. Lazarsfeld, Berelson, and Gaudet, *The People's Choice*, 62; and more succinctly, Berelson, Lazarsfeld, and McPhee, *Voting*, 347, proposition 202.

19. Lazarsfeld, Berelson, and Gaudet, *The People's Choice*, 158.

20. Ibid., 152–153; Berelson, Lazarsfeld, and McPhee, *Voting*, 109, 128–149, 230–231.

21. As Lazarsfeld wrote later:

> The importance of this kind of leadership was discovered almost accidentally. . . . During the course of studying the presidential campaign of 1940, it became clear that certain people in every stratum of the community serve relay roles in the mass communication of electoral information.
>
> This "discovery" began with the finding that radio and the printed page seemed to have only neglible effects on actual voting decisions. . . . [The authors of the study] were interested in how people make up their minds, and why they change them, and in effect, they asked, if the mass media are not the major determinants of an individual's vote decision, then what is?
>
> To investigate this problem, particular attention was paid to those people who changed their vote intention during the course of the campaign. When these people were asked what had contributed to their decision, their answer was: other people. (Katz and Lazarsfeld, *Personal Influence*, 3, 31–32)

22. Ibid., 327.

23. Ibid., 309–310.

24. Ibid., 294–295.

25. The data from the Elmira study showed that secondary group influence was made much stronger to the degree people identified with a particular group. Edward A. Suchman and Herbert Menzel, "The Interplay of Demographic and Psychological Variables in the Analysis of Voting Decisions," in *The Language of Social Research*, 148–154.

26. These propositions are summarized in Berelson, Lazarsfeld, and McPhee, *Voting*, 333–347.

27. In interviews I had with him in 1969 and 1970, Paul Lazarsfeld stated that he felt the index of political predisposition had been very much misunderstood at

the time of its publication. See also Berelson, Lazarsfeld, and McPhee, *Voting*, 120–149.

28. Lazarsfeld, Berelson, and Gaudet, *The People's Choice*, 27.

29. Paul F. Lazarsfeld, "From Vienna to Columbia," 2:2 *Columbia Forum* (Summer 1969), 31–36. Paul F. Lazarsfeld and Anthony R. Oberschall, "Max Weber and Empirical Social Research," Manuscript, 1969; and, more generally, see Anthony R. Oberschall, *Empirical Social Research in Germany, 1848–1914* (Amsterdam: Mouton, 1965).

30. Lazarsfeld made these comments during the course of interviews I had with him in January 1968 and May 1969.

31. Berelson, Lazarsfeld, and McPhee, *Voting*, 306.

32. Ibid., 306–311; and, more generally, Bernard Berelson, "Democratic Theory and Public Opinion," 16 *Public Opinion Quarterly* (Fall 1952), 313–330.

33. One of the finest guides to the influence of the progressives in this regard is Richard Hofstadter, *The Progressive Historians: Turner, Beard, Parrington* (New York: Knopf, 1968); also extremely useful is Justin Kaplan, *Lincoln Steffens: A Biography* (New York: Simon and Schuster, 1974); a fine selection of Progressive writings can be found in Otis Pease, *The Progressive Years* (New York: George Braziller, 1962). Finally, I can not resist recommending, as a fascinating case study of a Progressive in power, Robert Caro, *The Power Broker* (New York: Knopf, 1974).

34. Compare M.J.C. Vile, *Constitutionalism and the Separation of Powers* (London: Oxford University Press; 1967); W. B. Gwyn, *The Meaning of Separation of Powers* (New Orleans: Tulane University Press, 1965); Hannah Fenichel Pitkin, *The Concept of Representation* (Berkeley: University of California Press, 1967); Carinne C. Weston, *English Constitutional Theory and the House of Lords, 1556–1832* (Oxford: Clarendon Press, 1967); and William Holdsworth, "The Conventions of the English Century Constitutions," 17 *Iowa Law Review* (1931–32), 160–180.

35. Berelson, Lazarsfeld, and McPhee, *Voting*, 312.

36. Ibid., 321.

. . . The individual casts his own personal ballot. But . . . that is perhaps the most individualized action he takes in an election. His vote is formed in the midst of his fellows in a sort of group decision—if, indeed, it may be called a decision at all—and the total information and knowledge possessed in the group's present and past generations can be made available for the group's choice. Here is where opinion-leading relationships, for example, play an active role.

37. A consensus on "the rules of the game is" an enduring longing for students of American politics. It is a theme that appears over and over again in a multitude of different theoretical contexts. However, its appearance here is somewhat surprising, for there is nothing in the design of the Erie and Elmira studies to suggest that this notion actually was put to the test, although it is certainly needed in theory. See Berelson, Lazarsfeld, and McPhee, *Voting*, 192, 318.

38. Ibid., 323.

39. Gabriel Almond and Sidney Verba, *The Civic Culture: Political Attitudes and Democracy in Five Nations* (Princeton: N.J.: Princeton University Press, 1963).

40. See, for example, C. George Benello and Dimitrios Roussopoulos, eds., *The Case for Participatory Democracy* (New York: Viking Press; 1971), and Charles A. McCoy and John Playford, *Apolitical Politics: A Critique of Behavioralism* (New York: T. Y. Crowell, 1967).

41. That is, the point was never made except by implication. In a handful of

essays, reference appears to the conservative nature of constitutional theory, particularly on the issue of power, but the point is never generalized and made the basis of criticism of the voting studies.

42. Leo Strauss, "An Epilogue," in *Essays on the Scientific Study of Politics,* ed. Herbert J. Storing (New York: Holt, Reinhardt & Winston, 1962), 327.

43. Walter Berns, "Voting Studies", in *Essays on the Scientific Study of Politics,* ed. Herbert J. Storing (New York: Holt, Reinhardt & Winston, 1962), 57.

44. Letter from V. O. Key, Jr., to Bernard Berelson, 17 July 1952.

45. Isaiah Berlin, "Does Political Theory Still Exist?" reprinted in Isaiah Berlin, *Concepts and Categories* (New York: Viking Press, 1978), 143–172.

Chapter 3

1. This is hardly a new thought. Among other places, it appears in R. R. Palmer, *The Age of the Democratic Revolution,* vol. 1: *The Challenge* (Princeton, N.J.: Princeton University Press, 1959), 239ff.; Louis Hartz, *The Liberal Tradition in America* (New York: Harcourt, Brace, 1955); and F.S.C. Northrop, *The Meeting of East and West* (New York: Macmillan, 1946).

2. Hartz, *The Liberal Tradition in America,* 50.

3. Compare Ray Billington, *Westward Expansion* (New York: Macmillan, 1967); George Orwell catches the expansiveness of this spirit in a short essay on Mark Twain: ". . . he had had his youth and early manhood in the golden age of America, the period when the great plains were opened up, when wealth and opportunity seemed limitless, and human beings felt free, indeed were free, as they had never been before and may not be again for centuries." Sonia Orwell and Ian Angus, eds. *The Collected Essays, Journalism and Letters of George Orwell,* (New York: Harcourt, Brace & World, 1908), 325.

4. Hartz, *The Liberal Tradition in America;* Daniel J. Boorstin, *The Americans* (New York: Random House, 1965); David M. Potter, *People of Plenty* (Chicago: University of Chicago Press, 1954); and Seymour M. Lipset, *Revolution and Counterrevolution: Change and Persistence in Social Structures* (New York: Basic Books, 1968).

5. V. O. Key, Jr., and Frank Munger, "Social Determinism and Electoral Decision: The Case of Indiana," in *American Voting Behavior,* ed. Eugene Burdick and Arthur J. Brodbeck (Glencoe, Ill.: Free Press, 1959), 281.

6. Ibid., 291.

7. Morris Janowitz and Warren E. Miller, "The Index of Political Predisposition in the 1948 Election," 14 *Journal of Politics* (November 1952), 710–727. The ability of Janowitz and Miller to show that the IPP did not generalize to a national sample was among the many reasons why the SRC would predominate over the BASR.

8. Ibid.

9. Morris Janowitz and Dwaine Marvick, *Competitive Pressure and Democratic Consent* (Ann Arbor: University of Michigan Institute of Public Administration, 1956), 91.

10. Ibid.

11. M. Brewster Smith, Jerome S. Bruner, and Robert W. White, *Opinions and Personality* (New York: John Wiley, 1956), 11ff. Paul F. Lazarsfeld, Bernard Berelson, and Hazel Gaudet (*The People's Choice: How the Voter Makes Up His Mind in a Presidential Campaign* [New York: Columbia University Press, 1948, 2nd ed.])

had accounted for the low predictive power of the IPP in these middle categories with the notion of "cross pressures," a concept to be discussed later. Smith, Bruner, and White responded that this concept was both unsubstantiated in the data and of doubtful standing in (psychological) theory.

12. Herbert McClosky and Harold E. Dahlgren, "Primary Group Influence on Party Loyalty," 53 *American Political Science Review* (September 1959), 757–776. Or, more generally, see S. M. Lipset, et al., "The Psychology of Voting," in *Handbook of Social Psychology,* ed. Gardner Lindzey (Reading, Mass.: Addison-Wesley, 1954), 1134–1174; David O. Sears, "Political Behavior," in *Handbook of Social Psychology,* 2nd ed., ed. Gardner Lindzey and Aronson, (1968), 315–458; Sidney Verba, *Small Groups and Political Behavior* (Princeton, N.J.: Princeton University Press, 1961).

13. The singular influence exerted by primary groups on the behavior of their members arises from a number of attributes that distinguish them from other types of groups. Compared with larger and more impersonal associations whose direct impact is only occasionally or sporadically felt, the members of a primary group enjoy unparalleled opportunity to make their attitudes known, to check, modify, or correct each other's views, and to bring dissenters into line. (McClosky and Dahlgren, "Primary Group Influence on Party Loyalty," 758–759)

Lazarsfeld believed that social characteristics were merely a general and indirect way of observing the influence of primary group associations; see Lazarsfeld, Berelson, and Gaudet, *The People's Choice,* 137–138. Lazarsfeld's approach presumes that there is a fairly close correspondence between social and economic cleavages and the structure of primary groups, an assumption that is much more suited to European politics than to politics in the United States. See Robert Alford, *Party and Society* (Chicago: Rand McNally, 1963), 79–123.

14. McClosky and Dahlgren, "Primary Group Influence in Party Loyalty," 775.

15. Ibid., 761–766.

16. Ibid., 773. Sixty-four percent of all group affiliations were found to be reinforcing while 24 percent were discordant. The remaining 12 percent were neutral.

17. Arthur S. Goldberg, "Social Determinism and Rationality as Bases of Party Identification," 63 *American Political Science Review* (March 1969), 5–25.

18. Political socialization is rapidly becoming its own subdiscipline. A nicely organized summary has been written by Richad E. Dawson and Kenneth Prewitt, *Political Socialization* (Boston: Little, Brown, 1969). Virtually all the studies of the socialization process agree that school effects are secondary to those of family and peer group. Almond and Verba, for example, conclude that "in general, as with family participation and political competence, there does appear to be some relationship between school experiences and political attitudes, but the relationship is not a strong one." Gabriel Almond and Sidney Verba, *The Civic Culture: Political Attitudes and Democracy in Five Nations,* (Princeton, N.J.: Princeton University Press, 1963), 355, and in general 323–377. See also James C. Davies, "The Family's Role in Political Socialization," *Annals of the American Academy of Political and Social Science* 361 (September 1965): 10–19; Edgar Litt, "Civic Education, Community Norms, and Political Indoctrination," 28 *American Sociological Review* (1963), 69–75; Kenneth P. Langton, "Peer Group and School and the Political Socialization Process," 61 *American Political Science Review* (September 1967), 751–762; Robert D. Hess and Judith U. Torney, *The Development of Political Attitudes in Children* (Chicago: Aldine, 1967); Fred Greenstein, *Children and Politics* (New Haven: Yale University Press, 1965).

Notes

19. Donald O. Sears, "Political Socialization," in *The Handbook of Political Science,* ed. Fred I. Greenstein and Nelson W. Palsby, vol. 2, *Theoretical Aspects of Micropolitics* (Reading, Mass.: Addison-Wesley, 1975), 93–154; Herbert H. Hyman and Paul B. Sheatsley, "Attitudes on Integration," *Scientific American* (December 1956): 35–39.

20. A. R. Radcliffe Brown, "On Social Structure," 70 *Journal of The Royal Anthropological Institute of Great Britain and Ireland,* (1940), 9–10, and "On the Concept of Function in Social Science," *American Anthropologist* (1935), 37. As applied to the study of politics, see Robert K. Merton, *Social Theory and Social Structure* (Glencoe, Ill.: Free Press, 1957), chap. 1.

21. Dean Jaros, Herbert Hirsch, and Frederic Fleun, Jr., "The Malevolent Leader: Political Socialization in the American Sub-Culture," 62 *American Political Science Review* (1968), 564–575.

22. Angus Campbell et al., *The American Voter,* (New York: John Wiley, 1960), esp. chap. 6.

23. Gerhard E. Lenski, *The Religious Factor* (New York: Doubleday, 1963); Lipset, *Revolution and Counterrevolution;* Lawrence Fuchs, *The Political Behavior of American Jews* (Glencoe, Ill.: Free Press, 1956).

24. Andrew M. Greeley and William C. McCready, *Ethnicity in the United States: A Preliminary Reconnaissance* (New York: John Wiley, 1974); Andrew M. Greely, *Ethnicity Denomination and Inequality* (Beverly Hills, Calif.: Sage, 1976); Michael Parenti, "Ethnic Politics and the Persistence of Ethnic Identification," 61 *American Political Science Review* (1967), 717–726.

25. Philip E. Converse, "Religion and Politics: The 1960 Election", in *Elections and the Political Order,* ed. Angus Campbell, et al. (New York: John Wiley, 1966), chap. 6; Angus Campbell and H. C. Cooper, *Group Differences in Attitudes and Votes: A Study of the 1954 Congressional Election* (Ann Arbor, Mich.: Burney Research Center, 1954), 90; Edward A. Suchman and Herbert Menzel, "The Interplay of Demographic and Psychological Variables in the Analysis of Voting Decisions," in *The Language of Social Research,* ed. Paul F. Lazarsfeld and Morris Rosenberg (Glencoe, Ill.: Free Press, 1955), 148–154.

26. Almond and Verba, *The Civic Culture,* esp. chap. 11.

27. Sidney Verba and Norman Nie, *Participation in America* (New York: Harper & Row, 1972), 184.

28. See, in particular, S. E. Asch, "Effects of Group Pressure Upon the Modification and Distortion of Judgment," in *Groups, Leadership and Man,* ed. Harold Guetzkow (Pittsburgh: Carnegie Press, 1951), 177–205; J.R.P. French and G. Levinger, "Coercive Power and Forces Affecting Conformity," 61 *Journal of Abnormal Social Psychology* (1960), 93–101; Stanley Milgram, *Obedience to Authority* (New York: Harper & Row, 1974); and Paul M. Sniderman, *Personality and Democratic Policies* (Berkeley: University of California Press, 1975), esp. chap. 4.

29. Verba and Nie, *Participation in America,* 200–205.

30. Sidney Verba, Norman H. Nie, and Jae-on Kim, *Participation and Political Equality* (New York: Cambridge University Press, 1978), 200–205.

31. This is hardly an original finding. See V. O. Key, Jr., *Public Opinion and American Democracy* (New York: Knopf, 1961), chap. 8. Also, Verba and Nie, *Participation in America,* chap. 7, and Verba, Nie, and Kim, *Participation and Political Equality,* 307–308.

32. David Truman, *The Governmental Process* (New York: Knopf, 1951). This book had been through eight printings by 1962.

33. Arthur F. Bentley, *The Process of Government,* ed. Peter H. Odegard (Cam-

bridge, Mass.: Harvard University Press, 1967), chaps. 7, 8, and 20; Truman, *The Governmental Process,* see chaps. 8, 9, and 16 in particular; Earl Latham, "The Group Basis of Politics: Notes for a Theory," *American Political Science Review* 45 (June 1952), 376–397; certainly the best general review of the emergence of group theory has been written by G. David Garson, "On the Origins of Interest-Group Theory: A Critique of a Process," 68 *American Political Science Review* (December 1974): 1505–1519.

34. Myron C. Hale, "The Cosmology of Arthur F. Bentley," 54 *American Political Science Review* (December 1960): 955–961; Oliver Garceau, "Research in the Political Process," 45 *American Political Science Review* (March 1951): 69–85; Peter H. Odegard, Introduction, to the 1967 edition of Arthur F. Bentley, *The Process of Government* (Cambridge, Mass.: Harvard University Press), vii–xxviii; Richard W. Taylor, ed., *Life, Language, Law: Essays in Honor of Arthur F. Bentley* (Yellow Springs, Ohio: Ohio State University Press, 1957); perhaps the most succinct presentation of Bentley's philosophy has been written by Sidney Ratner, "Arthur F. Bentley's Inquiries into the Behavioural Sciences and the Theory of Scientific Inquiry," 8 *British Journal of Sociology* (March 1957): 40–58.

35. A penetrating presentation of this orientation can be found in Harry Eckstein, *Pressure Group Politics: The Case of the British Medical Association* (Stanford, Calif.: Stanford University Press, 1960), 15–39; see also Charles B. Hagan, "The Group in Political Science," in *Approaches to the Study of Politics,* ed. Roland Young (Evanston, Ill.: Northwestern University Press, 1958).

36. See G. David Garson, "On the Origins of Interest-Group Theory: A Critique of a Process," 68 *American Political Science Review* (December 1974): 1505–1519. See also Robert J. Golembiewski, "The Group Basis of Politics: Notes on Analysis and Development," 54 *American Political Science Review* (December 1960): 962–971; L. Harmon Zeigler and G. Wayne Peak, *Interest Groups in American Society* (Englewood Cliffs, N.J.: Prentice-Hall, 1972); and Stanley Rothman, "Systematic Political Theory: Observations on the Group Approach," *American Political Science Review* 54 (March 1960): 15–33.

37. Bentley, *The Process of Government,* uses this phrase—"This book is an attempt to fashion a tool"—as the dedication for the volume; David Truman transmutes this to the study of "Political Interest and Public Opinion" in the subtitle of *The Governmental Process.* Bentley himself drifted away from the study of government after the publication of *The Process of Government* into more explicitly philosophical matters. Compare John Dewey and Arthur F. Bentley, *A Philosophical Correspondence, 1932–1951,* ed. Sidney Ratner and Jules Altman (New Brunswick, N.J.: Rutgers University Press, 1964); Sidney Ratner, ed., *Inquiry into Inquiries: Essays in Social Theory* (Boston: Little, Brown, 1954). "One of the questions that has most frequently been asked me," Bentley commented during a dinner in his honor in 1953,

> is why, after having made something of a start in the study of government, I did not continue it. My answer has regularly been that I did continue. . . . The point lies in what we are to understand by "government," and indeed by "process" as well. I saw before me a study of human behavior, taking government as immediate materials. . . . Government was just the locus of my descriptions and interpretations for the moment. (Cited by Peter Odegard in the Introduction to the 1967 edition of Bentley, *The Process of Government,* xiii).

38. These studies began to gain predominance in the late 1920s and continued to build up steam in the 1930s and 1940s. Perhaps the best general guide to their

Notes

influence can be found in the first edition of V. O. Key's *Politics, Parties and Pressure Groups* (New York: T. Y. Crowell, 1942). Among the most influential studies were: Peter H. Odegard, *Pressure Politics: The Story of the Anti-Saloon League* (New York: Columbia University Press, 1928); E. E. Schattschneider, *Politics, Pressures and the Tariff* (New York: Prentice-Hall, 1935); Pendleton Herring, *Group Representation Before Congress* (Baltimore: Johns Hopkins Press, 1929), and *Public Administration and the Public Interest* (New York: McGraw-Hill, 1936); C. V. Gregory, "The American Farm Bureau Federation and the AAA," 179 *Annals of the American Academy of Political and Social Sciences* (1935): 152–157; Belle Zeller, *Pressure Politics in New York* (New York: Prentice-Hall, 1937), and "The Federal Regulation of the Lobbying Act," 42 *American Political Science Review* (April 1948): 239–272; Dayton D. McKean, *Pressures on the Legislature of New Jersey* (New York: Columbia University Press, 1938); Harwood Childs, *Labor and Capital in National Politics* (Columbus: Ohio State University Press, 1930); Peter Odegard and E. Allen Helms, *American Politics: A Study in Political Dynamics* (New York: Harper and Brothers, 1938); and Oliver Garceau, *The Political Life of the American Medical Association* (Cambridge, Mass.: Harvard University Press, 1944).

39. It is of no small significance that the starting place for group theory is in anthropology rather than in sociology. Groups as the unit of analysis are "primary" in both fields. In anthropology, however, the group concept was not associated with any of the Marxian implications that were often present in its sociological rendering. Thus, with an anthropological emphasis, the group approach tended to use the idea of groups without any of its class implications. As we have seen, when Lazarsfeld, drawing upon the sociological definition of groups, used the same idea, it had a much different emphasis.

40. The term "group" is used throughout this work in a technical sense. It means a certain portion of the men of a society, taken, however, not as a physical mass cut off from other masses of men, but as a mass activity, which does not preclude the men who participate in it from participating likewise in many other group activities. It is always so many men with all their human quality. It is always so many men, acting or tending toward action—that is, in various stages of action. Group and group activity are equivalent terms with just a little difference of emphasis useful only for clearness of expression in different contexts . . . There is no group without its interest. An interest . . . is the equivalent of a "group." Bentley, *The Process of Government,* 211.

41. Ibid., 210.

42. Truman, *The Governmental Process,* 228, 230.

43. Ibid.

44. The notion that groups and group competition provide the essential ingredients for electoral democracies was (and is) an important theme. But between 1950 and 1960, the idea, which was often mistaken for the essence of democratic politics, appeared to hold a particular fascination for scholars in the United States, See, for example, John Kenneth Galbraith, *American Capitalism: The Concept of Countervailing Power* (London: Hamish Hamilton, 1952). Truman, *The Governmental Process,* chap. 16, is very articulate in this regard:

The group process will proceed in the usual fashion. Whether it eventuates in disaster will depend in the future as in the past basically upon the effects of overlapping membership, particularly the vitality of membership in those potential groups based upon interests held widely throughout the society. These memberships are the means both of stability and of peaceful change. In the future as in the past, they will provide the answer to the ancient question: quis custodiet ipsos custodes? Guardianship will emerge out of the affiliations of the guardians. (P. 535)

See also the argument for the group basis of democratic politics in William Kornhauser, *The Politics of Mass Society* (New York: Free Press, 1959); and on the dimension of leadership in particular, see Sidney Verba, *Small Groups and Political Behavior: A Study of Leadership* (Princeton, N.J.: Princeton University Press, 1961).

45. Seymour Martin Lipset, *Political Man: The Social Bases of Politics* (Garden City, N.Y.: Doubleday, 1960); Hyman, *Political Socialization* (Glencoe, Ill.: The Free Press, 1959); Robert K. Merton, *Mass Persuasion: The Social Psychology of a War Bond Drive* (New York: Harper, 1946); Robert Merton and Paul Lazarsfeld, eds., *Studies in the Scope and Method of "The American Soldier"* (Glencoe, Ill.: Free Press, 1951).

46. In the preface to Angus Campbell et al., eds., *The Voter Decides* (Evanston, Ill.: Row, Peterson & Co., 1954), the 1952 SRC election study, Campbell, Gurin, and Miller write,

> This project is an outgrowth of a series of meetings of the Social Science Research Committee on Political Behavior. While this committee has not taken direct responsibility for any specific research project, it has given considerable attention to the present study in both its planning phase and during the preparation of this report. (P. v).

David Truman and V. O. Key were particularly involved with this study. See The Papers and Correspondence of V. O. Key, at the Widner Library, Harvard University, for 1951 in particular.

47. Donald E. Stokes, "Analytic Reduction in the Study of Institutions," Paper delivered at the 1966 meetings of the American Political Science Association, New York, 1966.

48. Campbell et al., *The American Voter*, 147.

Chapter 4

1. T. W. Adorno, et al., *The Authoritarian Personality* (New York: Norton, 1969; orig. pub. by Harper & Row, 1950).

2. World War I did not produce Freud's focus on aggression any more than his cancer was later directly responsible for his theory of a death instinct. . . . Before his first essay on war, we have encountered aggression in Freud's social applications of psychoanalysis in the early essay relating religion to guilt feelings over death wishes. The tale of the primal crime also illustrates his preoccupation with human barbarousness.

> Instead of the disillusionment a civilized man might feel at the horrors of war, or at the credulous mass belief in atrocity stories, Freud thought his general view of man had been confirmed. (Paul Roazen, *Freud: Political and Social Thought* [New York: Knopf, 1968], 194–195).

See also Paul Roazen, *Freud and His Followers* (New York: Knopf, 1974); and Fred I. Greenstein, "The Impact of Personality on Politics: An Attempt to Clear Away Underbrush," 61 *American Political Science Review* (September 1967), 629–641;

3. Adorno et al., *The Authoritarian Personality*, 1.

4. The emphasis throughout was upon obtaining different *kinds* of subjects to ensure wide variability of opinion and attitude and adequate coverage of the

factors supposed to influence ideology. The subjects are in no sense a random sample of the noncollege population nor, since there was no attempt to make a sociological analysis of the community in which they lived, can they be regarded as a representative sample. The progress of the study was not in the direction of broadening the basis for generalization about larger populations, but rather toward the more intensive investigation of "key groups," that is, groups having the characteristics that were most crucial to the problem at hand. Some groups were chosen because their sociological status was such that they could be expected to play a vital role in the struggle centering around social discrimination. . . . Other groups were chosen for intensive study because they presented extreme manifestations of the personality variables deemed most crucial for the potentially anti-democratic individual. (Adorno et al., *The Authoritarian Personality,* 20–22).

In methodological terms, this explanation is nonsense. It amounts to a reason for introducing systematic biases into the analysis, which is precisely what happened. See Herbert H. Hyman and Paul B. Sheatsley, " *'The Authoritarian Personality':* A Methodological Critique," in *Studies in the Scope and Method of "The Authoritarian Personality,"* ed. Richard Christie and Marie Jahoda (Glencoe, Ill.: Free Press, 1954), 123–197.

5. Most of the items of the A-S scale have been formulated as pseudodemocratically as possible. This consideration was, in fact, one of the main reasons for the use of negative items only [i.e., items where "no" indicated a democratic, unprejudiced response]. The following rules have been followed in general: Each item should be made appealing and "easy to fall for" by avoiding or soft-pedaling or morally justifying ideas of violence and obvious antidemocracy. . . . Items were worded so that the person can add at the end: "but I am not anti-Semitic." Seeming tentativeness is introduced by qualifications as "it seems that," "probably," and "in most cases." Finally an attempt is made to give each statement a familiar ring, to formulate it as it has been heard many times in everyday discussions. Adorno et al., *The Authoritarian Personality,* 61–62. For a more exacting discussion of the index, see Daniel Levinson and R. Nevitt Sanford, "A Scale for the Measurement of Anti-Semitism," 17 *Journal of Psychology* (1944), 339–370.

6. Adorno et al., *The Authoritarian Personality,* 107.

7. However, it [the data] suggests once again that anti-Semitism, while it is essentially a facet of a broader ethnocentric pattern, may nevertheless have certain independent determinants of its own. . . . While there are probably considerable sectional, class and individual differences regarding which groups are regarded as outgroups, it would appear that an individual who regards a few of these groups as outgroups will tend to reject most of them. (Adorno, et al., *The Authoritarian Personality,* 123, 147).

8. Ibid., 147.

9. Gertrude J. Selznick and Stephen Steinberg, *The Tenacity of Prejudice: Anti-Semitism in Contemporary America* (New York: Harper & Row, 1969), 182; also Seymour Martin Lipset and Earl Raab, *The Politics of Unreason: Right-Wing Extremism in America, 1790–1970* (New York: Harper & Row, 1970).

10. In view of these considerations, and in order to make room for the inclusion of other material, the PEC scale was cut literally to the bone. . . . It appears now that it would have been wiser to have used a 10-item scale form; the short form used did, however, make possible the comparison of groups and the study of the relationships between this scale and the others.

The five questions used in the short form are as follows:
Labor unions should become stronger and have more influence generally.
America may not be perfect, but the American Way has brought us about as close as human beings can get to a perfect society.
Most government controls over business should be continued even though the war is over.
Men like Henry Ford or J.P. Morgan, who overcame all competition on the road to success, are models for all young people to admire and imitate.
In general, full economic security is bad; most men wouldn't work if they didn't need the money for eating and living. (Adorno, et al., *The Authoritarian Personality,* 168, 169.)

11. Ibid., 206.

12. The view expressed in *The Authoritarian Personality*—that personality characteristics can be measured by means of survey research—has prevailed, although the particular theory that work elaborated has not. However, there is every reason to reopen this issue. See Roazen, *Freud: Political and Social Thought,* 59ff.

13. The F-scale is defined as a composite of the following characteristics:
  a. *Conventionalism.* Rigid adherence to conventional, middle-class values.
  b. *Authoritarian submission.* Submissive, uncritical attitude toward ideologized moral authorities of the ingroup.
  c. *Authoritarian aggression.* Tendency to be on the lookout for, and to condemn, reject, and punish people who violate conventional values.
  d. *Anti-intraception.* Opposition to the subjective, the imaginative, the tender-minded.
  e. *Superstition and stereotype.* The belief in mystical determinants of the individual's fate; the disposition to think in rigid categories.
  f. *Power and "toughness."* Preoccupation with the dominance-submission, strong-weak, leader-follower dimension; identification with power figures; overemphasis upon the conventionalized attribute of the ego; exaggerated assertion of strength and toughness.
  g. *Destructiveness and cynicism.* Generalized hostility, vilification of the human.
  h. *Projectivity.* The disposition to believe that wild and dangerous things go on in the world; the projection outwards of unconscious emotional impulses.
  i. *Sex.* Exaggerated concern with sexual "goings-on." (Adorno et al., *The Authoritarian Personality,* 228).

14. Ibid., 259–261, and table 9 particularly.

15. The amount of research generated by *The Authoritarian Personality* is staggering. See Richard Christie and Peggy Cook, "A Guide to Published Literature Relating to *The Authoritarian Personality* through 1956," 45 *Journal of Psychology* (1958), 143–159. Thereafter one must hunt the controversy down oneself. Roger Brown, *Social Psychology,* (New York: The Free Press, 1965), 544–546, carries the discussion of research up through 1965, and most recently Paul M. Sniderman, *Personality and Democratic Politics* (Berkeley: University of California Press, 1975), is a more or less current reading of the state of things.

16. Richard Christie, R. Havel, and B. Seidenberg, "Is the F-scale Reversible?" 56 *Journal of Abnormal and Social Psychology* (1958), 153–161; L. J. Chapman and D. T. Campbell, "Response Set in the F-Scale," *Journal of Abnormal and Social Psychology* (1957), 129–132; T. S. Cohn, "The Relation of the F-Scale to a Response

Notes

Set to Answer Positively," 44 *Journal of Social Psychology* (1956), 129–133; Lee J. Cronback, "Further Evidence on Response Sets and Test Design," 10 *Educational and Psychological Measurement* (1950), 3–31; Donald T. Campbell, Carole R. Siegman, and Matilda B. Rees, "Direction-of-Wording Effects in the Relationships Between Scales," 68 *Psychological Bulletin* (November 1967), 293–303; and Franz Samuelson and Jacques F. Yates, "Acquiescence and the F Scale: Old Assumptions and New Data, 68 *Psychological Bulletin* (August 1967), 91–103.

17. For example, a couple of researchers thought they saw in these data a psychological trait on the part of some people to respond favorably to survey questions while others were predisposed to answer negatively. Arthur Couch and Kenneth Keniston, "Yeasayers and Naysayers: Agreeing Response Set as a Personality Variable," 60 *Journal of Abnormal and Social Psychology* (1960), 151–170; and Arthur Couch and Kenneth Keniston, "Agreeing Response Set and Social Desirability," 62 *Journal of Abnormal and Social Psychology* (1961), 175–179. This finding in turn was later questioned. Leonard G. Rorer, "The Great Response-Style Myth," 63 *Psychological Bulletin* (March 1965), 129–156. Perhaps new evidence will be forthcoming.

18. See, for example, Fawn Brodie, *Thomas Jefferson: An Intimate History* (New York: Norton, 1974); Edmund Morris, *The Rise of Theodore Roosevelt* (New York: Ballantine Books, 1980); or, at the level of the mass public, see Lipset and Raab, *The Politics of Unreason,* 460ff.

19. V. O. Key, Jr., "The Politically Relevant in Surveys," 24 *Public Opinion Quarterly* (Spring 1960), 59–60.

20. Wrote Madison:

[I]t may be concluded, that a pure Democracy, by which I mean a society, consisting of a small number of citizens, who assemble and administer the Government in person, can admit of no cure for the mischiefs of faction. A common passion or interest will, in almost every case, be felt by a majority of the whole; a communication and concert results from the form of Government itself; and there is nothing to check the inducements to sacrifice the weaker party, or an obnoxious individual. Hence it is, that such Democracies have ever been spectacles of turbulence and contention; have ever been found incompatible with personal security, or the rights of property; and have in general been as short in their lives, as they have been violent in their deaths. Theoretic politicans, who have patronized this species of Government, have erroneously supposed, that by reducing mankind to a perfect equality in their political rights, they would at the same time, be perfectly equalized and assimilated in their possessions, their opinions, and their passions." (James Madison, *The Federalist no. 10,* in the Jacob E. Cooke edition (Cleveland: Meridian Books, 1961), 61–62.

At the same time, of course, the framers of the Constitution favored the electoral system, albeit limited, balanced and checked in its influence. The weight of sentiment against the notion of political equality is much better captured in *The Records of the Federal Convention of 1787,* ed. Max Farrand, (New Haven: Yale University Press, 1965) than it is in *The Federalist Papers,* the discourse being freer and the indictment more detailed. An admirable summary of the extension of the franchise can be found in Robert E. Lane, *Political Life* (New York: The Free Press, 1961), chaps. 2 and 3.

21. Most of this is a romantic vision that has little to do with the politics of the Second World War. It would be much closer to the truth to observe that the United

States failed to articulate the fundamental values for which it it was fighting, either in word or in deed. See John Morton Blum, *V Was for Victory: Politics and American Culture During World War II* (New York: Harcourt, Brace, 1976).

22. Carl J. Friedrich, *The New Belief in the Common Man* (Boston: Little, Brown, 1942). In the same vein see Ralph Barton Perry, *Shall Not Perish from the Earth* (New York: Vanguard Press, 1940).

23. Samuel A. Stouffer, *Communism, Conformity and Civil Liberties: A Cross-section of the Nation Speaks Its Mind* (Gloucester, Mass.: Peter Smith, 1963; from the Doubleday edition, 1955). The design of the study involved two national samples, one conducted by the American Institute of Political Opinion (AIPO) and the other by the National Opinion Research Center. It appears that the board of directors for the Fund for the Republic doubted the idea of probability sampling, or at least they were suspicious enough of it to insist that two samples be drawn so that the results could be compared. See the Collected Papers of Samuel Stouffer, Widner Library Archives, Harvard University.

24. Stouffer, *Communism, Conformity and Civil Liberties,* 27.

25. Ibid., 36.

26. Richard T. LaPiere, "Attitude vs. Actions," 12 *Social Forces* (March 1934), 230–237, noted in his studies of social prejudice that people often sound more prejudiced than they really are or, more precisely, make verbal statements of prejudice that they are unwilling to act upon. This finding has generated a small controversy of its own, a controversy that has two dimensions. First, there is the problem of the meaning of attitudes, particularly when they do not form the basis of action. See Philip Converse, "Attitudes and Non-Attitudes: Continuation of a Dialogue," (Survey Research Center, November 1963) in R. R. Tufte, ed., *The Quantitative Analysis of Social Problems* (Reading, Mass: Addison Wesley, 1970), 168–189, and, more recently, John C. Pierce and Douglas D. Rose, "Nonattitudes and American Public Opinion: The Examination of a Thesis," 68 *American Political Science Review* (June 1974), 626–666, with comments and rejoinders following. The other question is how to develop tools of measurement that are sensitive enough to distinguish attitudes that are related to behavior from those that are not. See Irwin Deutscher, "Words and Deeds: Social Science and Social Policy," Presidential address presented to the Society for the Study of Social Problems, 28 August 1965; and, more recently, Howard Schuman, "Attitudes vs. Actions versus Attitudes vs. Attitudes," 36 *Public Opinion Quarterly* (Fall 1972), 343–354; Alan G. Weinstein, "Predicting Behavior from Attitudes," 36 *Public Opinion Quarterly* (Fall 1972), 355–360.

27. See Michael P. Rogin, *The Intellectuals and McCarthy: The Radical Specter* (Cambridge, Mass.: MIT Press; 1967); Lipset and Raab, *The Politics of Unreason,* chap. 6; or, from a somewhat different perspective, Lillian Hellman, *Scoundrel Time* (Boston: Little, Brown, 1976).

28. James W. Prothro and Charles M. Grigg, "Fundamental Principles of Democracy: Bases of Agreement and Disagreement," 22 *Journal of Politics* (1960), 276–293.

29. Herbert McClosky, "Consensus and Ideology in American Politics," 58 *American Political Science Review* (June 1964), 361–382, particularly Tables I–III and the following discussion. This sample is most completely described in a previous publication: Herbert McClosky, Paul J. Hoffman, and Rosemary O'Hara, "Issue Conflict and Consensus Among Party Leaders and Followers," 54 *American Political Science Review* (June 1960), 406–427.

30. McCloskey, "Consensus and Ideology in American Politics," 375.

Notes

31. If the particular traits that comprised the virtuous citizen, and in turn the well-administered government, were vague, the absence of them had a very specific meaning. "Corruption" was the appropriate category of analysis, and this tended to have a very technical usage. See J.G.A. Pocock, "Machiavelli, Harrington, and English Political Ideologies in the Eighteenth Century," *William and Mary Quarterly*, 3rd series, 22 (1965), 549–583; Stanley N. Katz, The Origins of American Constitutional Thought," *Perspectives in American History*, vol. 3 (Cambridge, Mass.: Harvard University Press, Charles Warren Center for Studies in American History, 1969), 474–490; and Gordon S. Wood, *The Creation of the American Republic, 1776–1787* (New York: Norton, 1969), 65–69.

32. Robert Jackman, "Political Elites, Mass Publics, and Support for Democratic Principles, 34 *Journal of Politics* (August 1972), 753–773.

33. Rogin, *The Intellectuals and McCarthy*, chap. 8; and Hellman, *Scoundrel Time*. It would be extremely useful to have the relationship for both mass and elites run on McClosky's data. On the face of it, the elites seem to do better in this data set, but it would be interesting to see just the same.

34. Robert T. Riley and Thomas F. Pettigrew, "Relative Deprivation and Wallace's Northern Support," Paper presented before the American Sociological Association, San Francisco, 1969; Lipset and Raab, *The Politics of Unreason*, chaps. 10 and 11; Harlan Han and Timothy Almy, "Ethnic Politics and Racial Issues: Voting in Los Angeles," 24 *Western Political Quarterly* (December 1971), 719–730; Michael Rogin, "Wallace and the Middle Class: The Wallace Backlash," 30 *Public Opinion Quarterly* (Spring 1966), 98–108; M. Margaret Conway, "The White Backlash Re-examined: Wallace and the 1964 Primaries, 49 *Social Science Quarterly* (December 1968), 710–719; Robert Riley, David O. Sears, and Thomas F. Pettigrew, "Race, Unrest and the Old Angeline: The Bradley Defeat in Los Angeles," *Los Angeles Times*, 8 June 1969,

35. Seymour Martin Lipset, *Political Man* (Garden City, NY: Anchor Books, 1963) 122–123.

36. Ibid., 176–177.

37. William Sheridan Allen, *The Nazi Seizure of Power: The Experience of a Single German Town, 1930–1935* (Chicago: Quadrangle Books, 1965); Rudolf Herberle, *From Democracy to Nazism: Regional Case Study on Political Parties in Germany* (New York: Grosset & Dunlap, 1945); Lucy S. Dawidowicz, *The War Against the Jews, 1933–1945* (Holt, Rinehart and Winston, 1975), esp. chaps. 1–3.

38. See, for example, Ernest S. Griffith, John Plamenatz and J. Roland Pennock, "Cultural Prerequisites to a Successfully Functioning Democracy: A Symposium," 50 *American Political Science Review* (March 1956), 101–137; Peter Bachrach, "Elite Consensus and Democracy," 24 *Journal of Politics* (August 1962), 449–452; Edward Davis, "Cost of Realism: Contemporary Restatement of Democracy," 18 *Western Political Quarterly* (March 1964), 37–46.

39. This literature has too many separate pieces to describe each one of them. A fine summary may be found in Lester W. Milbrath, *Political Participation: How and Why Do People Get Involved in Politics* (Chicago: Rand McNally, 1965), esp. 48–89; and, more recently, Sniderman, *Personality and Democratic Politics*, 64–115. A taste of the findings that began rolling in can be had by glancing at Morris Rosenberg, "Some Determinants of Political Apathy," *Public Opinion Quarterly* (Winter 1955), 349–366; Bernard Hennessey "Political and Apolitics: Some Measurements of Personality Traits," 3 *Midwest Journal of Political Science* (November 1959), 336–355; Murray B. Levin, *The Alienated Voter* (New York: Holt, Rinehart and Winston, 1960).

Notes

40. Angus Campbell, "The Passive Citizen," 6 *Acta Sociologica* (1962), 9–21; and, more generally, Angus Campbell et al., *The American Voter* (New York: John Wiley, 1960) 89ff.
41. Gabriel Almond and Sidney Verba, *The Civic Culture: Political Attitudes and Democracy in Five Nations* (Princeton, N.J.: Princeton University Press, 1963).

Chapter 5

1. Angus Campbell et al., *The American Voter* (New York: John Wiley, 1960). In 1964, an abridged edition of *The American Voter* appeared. Unfortunately, the primary virtue of this edition is that it is only half as long as the original.
2. Gabriel Almond and Sidney Verba, *The Civic Culture: Political Attitudes and Democracy in Five Nations* (Princeton, N.J.: Princeton University Press, 1963).
3. This observation belongs to Lois A. Wasserspring. She notes astutely that prior to *The Civic Culture,* comparative politics belonged to area specialists. Whatever the virtues of specialization, it lay outside the mainstream of political science and the increasing emphasis on methodological rigor and theoretical formality. Almond and Verba demonstrated that the "new" political science could be successful in a comparative perspective. At the same time, their book seemed to confirm the essential truths about the strategy of political development that had emerged under the direction of area specialists.
4. Almond and Verba, *The Civic Culture,* 14.
5. Gabriel A. Almond and Sidney Verba, eds., *The Civic Culture Revisited* (Boston: Little, Brown, 1969); see esp. Almond's opening essay, 1–36.
6. Almond and Verba, *The Civic Culture,* 31.
7. Ibid., 99. Table 14, in particular, summarizes patterns of political cognition.
8. Comparisons on this score are likely to be misleading. There is considerably more distance between the Communist party and the Christian Democratic party in Italy than there is between Republicans and Democrats in the United States. But Almond and Verba could argue that these differences in the *structure* of political competition are themselves a result of aspects of the civic culture. Were the political fabric in Italy more unified, more trusting, and more positive, perhaps differences between parties would moderate.
9. Differences between the United States and Great Britain show up most vividly in the pattern of group memberships. The entire discussion of secondary and nonpolitical groups is one of the high points in *The Civic Culture.* To begin with, it remedies a defect in earlier voting studies where the magnitude of voluntary associations in the United States was systematically underreported. But Almond and Verba also use the data in an interesting way, building an argument that formal and informal groups comprise the "capillary structure of democracy" (see esp. pp. 316–322). Along these lines, see also William Kornhauser, *The Politics of Mass Society* (New York: Free Press, 1959).
10. Almond and Verba, *The Civic Culture,* 371.
11. This rank order in the strength of relationship between the various modes of nonpolitical participation and political attitudes suggests an important specification in the way nonpolitical participation affects political attitudes. The individual's experiences at work and in voluntary associations differ basically from those in the family and school in that they are closer, in time as well as

Notes

structure, to the polity. Job and group memberships are contemporaneous with political participation. (Almond and Verba, *The Civic Culture,* 372).

12. Norman H. Nie, G. Bingham Powell, Jr., and Kenneth Prewitt, "Social Structure and Political Participation: Developmental Relationships, Parts I and II," 63 *American Political Science Review* (June, September), 361–377, 808–832.

13. Ibid., 372. Italics in original.

14. Seymour Martin Lipset, *Political Man: The Social Bases of Politics* (New York: Doubleday, 1960), chap. 2.

15. Joseph La Palombara, "Decline of Ideology: A Dissent and an Interpretation," 60 *American Political Science Review* (March, 1966): 5–16, and in the same issue Seymour M. Lipset, "Some Further Comments on the End of Ideology," 17–18.

16. Nie, Powell, and Prewitt, "Social Structure and Political Participation," 811. Italics in original.

17. The compensatory benefits of political parties in this regard are best described in Sidney Verba and Norman H. Nie, *Participation in America: Political Democracy and Social Equality* (New York: Harper & Row, 1972), chap. 12.

18. Participatory democracy was a utopian idea that began to circulate widely in the nineteenth century. Its force in contemporary politics, however, comes from the Progressives. The idea still lingers in the corners of the political process as a "radical" alternative—during the sixties there was a brief flurry of interest in it. Compare C. George Benello and Dimitrios Roussopoulos, eds., *The Case for Participatory Democracy* (New York: Macmillan, 1971).

19. The Progressives were particularly unrealistic in this regard. They believed that the manifest evils of politics were imposed upon an otherwise virtuous people by the imperfections of the system. They had in mind the real evils of the political machines, of course. But however noxious these creatures, the Progressives vastly overestimated the virtue of the mass public. This was not at all uncommon among people pursuing this line of thought. The Utilitarians and the Democratic Socialists made much the same type of error.

20. Sidney Verba, Norman H. Nie, and Jae-on Kim, *Participation and Political Equality: A Seven-Nation Comparison* (Cambridge: Cambridge University Press, 1978).

21. These factors are described most systematically in a short monograph by Sidney Verba, Norman Nie, and Jae-on Kim, *The Modes of Democratic Participation: A Cross-National Comparison* (Beverly Hills, Calif.: Sage Publications, 1971).

22. The inclusion of Mexico is based upon my own reanalysis of data from *The Civic Culture.* The pattern is not completely stable. Yugoslavia, for example, exhibits some minor variation. See Verba, Nie, and Kim, *Participation and Political Equality,* 75ff.

23. Mexico is perhaps the most difficult country among these to exclude from the democratic rubic. Nonetheless, some scholars have made a powerful case for doing so. See Ron Rogowski and Lois Wasserspring, *Does Political Development Exist?* (Beverly Hills, Calif.: Sage Publications, 1971).

24. Almond and Verba, *The Civic Culture Revisited,* 177–211; also Norman H. Nie et al., *The Changing American Voter* (Cambridge, Mass.: Harvard University Press, 1979), 194–242 and 319–344; Almond and Verba, *The Civic Culture;* Louis Hartz, *The Liberal Tradition in America* (New York: Harcourt, Brace & World, 1963 c.1955); Daniel J. Boorstin, *The Genius of American Politics* (Chicago: University of Chicago Press, c. 1953, 1958); David M. Polter, *People of Plenty* (Chicago: University of Chicago Press, 1954).

25. Two additional points should be made: First, there was the tremendous development of the United States economy following the Second World War. Money seems to make solvent otherwise preposterous beliefs. And second, it should be noted that many of these authors were themselves models of the American dream. From indifferent backgrounds and modest circumstances, they rose through the educational system by virtue of their talent and desire. By the time each paused to write on the United States, they had both earned and enjoyed the fruits of the system.

26. The pressure on the nation's universities and colleges during this period was intense. See Michael Paul Rogin, *The Intellectuals and McCarthy: The Radical Spectre* (Cambridge, Mass.: MIT Press, 1967). What has not been as carefully documented is how these institutions responded. Some inkling of this sorry tale has been told by Seymour Martin Lipset in his essay on Harvard University. "The Sources of the Radical Right—1955" in Daniel Bell, ed., *The Radical Right* (New York: Doubleday, 1955), 259–312.

This material together with the Stouffer data suggest that elites often possess a *verbal consciousness* of democratic norms without there being a corresponding practice.

27. Almond and Verba, *The Civic Culture,* 490.

28. Ibid., 479.

29. Ibid., 480–481.

30. Ibid., 481.

31. Robert Dahl, *Who Governs? Democracy and Power in an American City* (New Haven: Yale University Press, 1961), 316.

32. Compare Lipset, *Political Man,* chap. 4; and, in a more general sense, Seymour Martin Lipset, Martin Trow, and James Coleman, *Union Democracy: What Makes Democracy Work in Labor Unions and Other Organizations?* (Garden City, N.Y.: Doubleday, 1956), chap. 14; Herbert McClosky, "Consensus and Ideology in American Politics," 58 *American Political Science Review* (June 1964), 361–382; Richard Rose, *Influencing Voters: A Study of Campaign Rationality* (New York: St. Martin's Press, 1967), chaps. 10 and 11; Samuel Huntington, *Political Order in Changing Societies,* (Buenas Aires; Paidos, 1972), 86ff. It should be mentioned also that Campbell, Converse, Miller, and Stokes rely on the notion of process in ways that are not fundamentally dissimilar to the usage of the Bureau of Applied Social Research; see *The American Voter,* chaps. 19 and 20; and Warren Miller, "The Political Behavior of the American Electorate," in *American Government Annual, 1960–1961,* ed. Earl Latham (New York: Holt, Rinehart and Winston, 1964), 41–60.

33. Compare the following theoretical insights of Bernard Berelson, Paul F. Lazarsfeld, and William McPhee to those of Almond and Verba.

> That is the paradox. *Individual voters* today seem unable to satisfy the requirements for a democratic system of government outlined by political theorists. But the *system of democracy* does meet certain requirements for a going political organization. The individual members may not meet all the standards, but the whole nevertheless survives and grows. This suggests that where the classical theory is defective is in its concentration on the *individual citizen.* What are undervalued are certain collective properties that reside in the electorate as a whole and in the political and social system in which it functions. (Berelson, Lazarsfeld, and McPhee, *Voting* [Chicago: University of Chicago Press, 1954], 312. Italics in original.)

Our data suggest that in two broad ways the civic culture maintains the

Notes

citizen's active-influential role as well as his more passive role: on the one hand, there is in society a *distribution* of individuals who pursue one or another of the conflicting citizen goals; on the other hand, certain *inconsistencies in the attitudes of individuals* make it possible for him to pursue these seemingly conflicting goals at the same time. (Almond and Verba, *The Civic Culture,* 479. Italics in original.)

34. There is more information available than can be packed comfortably into a note. I mention here only the books that I have found extremely helpful. Hanna Freichel Pitkin, *The Concept of Representation* (Berkeley: University of California Press, 1967); M.J.C. Vile, *Constitutionalism and the Separation of Powers* (Oxford: Clarendon Press, 1967); W. B. Gwyn, *The Meaning of the Separation of Powers* (New Orleans: Tulane University Press, 1965); J.G.A. Pocock "Machiavelli, Harrington, and English Political Ideologies in the Eighteenth Century," 22 *William and Mary Quarterly,* 3rd series, (1965), 549–583; Betty Kemp, *Sir Francis Dashwood: An Eighteenth-Century Independent* (New York: St. Martin's Press, 1967); Isaac Kramnick, *Bolingbroke and His Circle* (Cambridge: Harvard University Press, 1968); Bernard Bailyn, *The Ideological Origins of the American Revolution* (Cambridge, Mass.: Harvard University Press, 1967); Gordon S. Wood, *The Creation of the American Republic, 1776–1787* (New York: Norton, 1972).

35. Just in technical terms quantitative analysis has come a long way in a very short space of time. Through the early sixties large computers were relatively inconvenient for social scientists. They did not process large data arrays, those typical in political surveys, with ease, nor were the analytical packages convenient to use. With the IBM 360 series, all of this changed. The larger models in this series —the 360–50, 360–60, and on up—could handle huge data arrays without any effort and without huge expense. Also, prepackaged statistical routines began to circulate more widely, most notably the SPSS package written by Norman Nie, Dale H. Bent, and C. Hadlai Hull.

Part II

1. Compare M.J.C. Vile, *Constitutionalism and the Separation of Powers* (Oxford: Clarendon Press, 1967); W. B. Gwyn, *The Meaning of Separation of Powers* (New Orleans: Tulane University Press, 1965); Hanna Freichel Pitkin, *The Concept of Representation* (Berkeley: University of California Press, 1967); Bernard Bailyn, *The Origins of American Politics* (New York: Knopf, 1965), and *The Ideological Origins of the American Revolution* (Cambridge, Mass.: Harvard University Press, 1967); Betty Kemp, *King and Commons, 1160–1832* (London: Macmillan, 1959), and *Sir Francis Dashwood: An Eighteenth-Century Independent* (New York: St. Martin's Press, 19670; Carinne C. Weston, *English Constitutional Theory and the House of Lords, 1556–1832* (London: Oxford University Press, 1965); J. R. Pole, *Political Representation in England and the Origins of the American Republic* (Berkeley: University of California Press, 1971); J. H. Plumb, *The Origins of Political Stability: England, 1675–1725* (Boston: Houghton Mifflin, 1967); Isaac Kramnick, *Bolingbroke and His Circle* (Cambridge, Mass.: Harvard University Press, 1968); Carole Pateman, *Participation and Democratic Theory* (Cambridge, London: Cambridge University Press, 1970). It must be stressed that this is a shift of emphasis. This line of interpretation was not entirely absent during previous years; see, for example, Carl J. Friedrich, *Constitutional Government and Democracy* (Boston: Little, Brown, 1941),

and an excellent piece by William Holdworth, "The Conventions of the Eighteenth Century Constitutions," 17 *Iowa Law Review* (1931–32), 160–180.

2. Seymour Martin Lipset and S. Rokkan, *Party Systems and Voter Alignments* (New York: Free Press, 1967), introduction, and S. Rokkan, *Citizens, Elections and Parties* (New York: McKay, 1970).

3. See, for example, Carl J. Friedrich, *The New Belief in the Common Man* (Boston: Little, Brown, 1942), and *Constitutional Government and Democracy* (Boston: Little, Brown, 1950); Thomas Vernor Smith, *Beyond Conscience* (New York: Simon and Schuster, 1934); John Dewey, *The Public and Its Problems* (New York: Halt, 1927); Joseph A. Schumpeter, *Capitalism, Socialism and Democracy* (New York: Harper & Row, 1975). These provide a good illustration of the difficulty that contemporary political philosophers have had with the idea of democracy. The quality of thought in these works is extremely high. But these efforts at theory have not proven to be substantial.

4. John Platt, *Steps To Man* (New York: John Wiley, 1966), 19–36.

Chapter 6

1. This is not to slight the efforts of Angus Campbell. Not only was he the driving force behind the SRC during its first years, he was responsible for pushing that organization into the business of electoral surveys in the first place. His influence can be seen in the work through the 1956 election study and the publication of Angus Campbell et al., *The American Voter* (New York: John Wiley, 1960).

2. This mode of explanation has its intellectual roots in the movement known as "field theory," fostered in the behavior sciences by Kurt Lewin. In essence the field-theoretical approach represents a reaction against a genetic treatment of casuality. . . . In field theory, however, the "field" at the moment is seen as a product of the field in the immediate neighborhood at the time just past. . . . The use of political attitudes to predict voting behavior hinges upon this proximal mode of explanation. (Campbell et al., *The American Voter*, 33, 34).
More specifically, see Kurt Lewin, *Field Theory in Social Science* (New York: Harper & Row, 1951).

3. This phrase is found in almost identical form in Warren Miller, "The Socio-Economic Analysis of Political Behavior," *Midwest Journal of Political Science*, 11 (August 1958), 242; George Belknap and Angus Campbell, "Political Party Identification and Attitudes Toward Foreign Policy," 15 *Public Opinion Quarterly*, (Winter 1951), 601–623; and Warren Miller, "Party Preferences and Attitudes and Political Issues: 1948–51," 46 *American Political Science Review* (March 1953).

4. Miller, "Socio-Economic Analysis of Political Behavior," 241, 242.

5. Things were not quite so opaque. Key wrote Campbell that "the plan does not give, it seems to me, adequate recognition to the political: I hasten to concede that most of your data could be analyzed in those terms, but it may be that you ought to have a more deliberate injection of the political into the planning." Letter from V. O. Key, Jr., to Angus Campbell, 15 April 1951. I am grateful to Luella Key and Merle Fainsod for granting me access to these papers.

6. Warren Miller, "The Study of Electoral Behavior" (Ann Arbor, Mich.: Survey Research Center, 1959). Mimeographed. This article is published as "The Political Behavior of the Electorate," in Earl Latham, ed., *American Government Annual, 1960–61* (New York: Holt, Reinhart and Winston, 1960), 41–60.

Notes

7. Joseph Harris, reviewing Angus Campbell et al., *The Voter Decides* for the 7 *American Political Science Review* (March 1955), 225–229, is particularly critical on this point. See also Robert Lane's review in *Political Science Quarterly* (March 1955), 153, 154.

8. Campbell, et al., *The American Voter*, 18–38.

9. Ibid., 24–32. Figure 6.1 represents my visual interpretation of this metaphor. It is not taken from any of the SRC's work.

10. Campbell and associates explain that their work in 1952 considered only forces at the narrowest part of the funnel.

> The attitudinal approach, exemplified by *The Voter Decides*, represents a strategy that maximizes explanatory power while dealing with a minimum number of variables. The solution to the dilemma is accomplished by concentration on a cross section of measurements at a point close to the dependent behavior. At such a point, the funnel is narrow. (Campbell, et al., *The American Voter*, 33).

11. The quest for theory has been met with such a vengeance that the resulting "master theory" does not ring quite true. An effort is made to order the vast array of factors presumably influencing the voter in a "funnel of causality" (which in turn describes the field of forces operating on the individual at any given time) which it turns out is not a theory generating research hypotheses, but at most a convenient device to establish a hierarchy of influences, some close to and others more remote from the voting act. (Heinz Eulau, 54 *American Political Science Review* [December 1960], 993, 994). See also V. O. Key, Jr., "The Politically Relevant in Surveys," 24 *Public Opinion Quarterly* (Spring 1960), 54–61.

12. "The Concept of the Normal Vote," in Campbell, et al., *Elections and the Political Order*, (New York: John Wiley, 1966), 33, and chap. 6; Warren Miller, "Voting and Foreign Policy," in *Domestic Sources of Foreign Policy*, ed. James N. Rosenau (New York: Free Press, 1967), 213–230.

13. On the importance of "research orientations" in guiding research, see Robert Merton, *Social Theory and Social Structure* (Glencoe, Ill.: Free Press, 1957).

14. Angus Campbell and H. C. Cooper, *Group Differences in Attitudes and Votes: A Study of the 1954 Congressional Election* (Ann Arbor: Survey Research Center, 1956), 95. Campbell et al., *The Voter Decides* (Evanston: Row Peterson, 1954), 90, states the principle more broadly:

> The present analysis of party identification is based on the assumption that the two parties serve as standard-setting groups for a significant proportion of the people of this country. In other words, it is assumed that many people associate themselves psychologically with one or the other of the parties, and that this identification has predictable relationships with their perceptions, evaluations, and actions.

15. Campbell and Cooper, *Group Differences in Attitudes and Votes*, 81.

16. Ibid., 16.

17. Letter from V. O. Key, Jr., to Angus Campbell, 8 April 1952. Warren Miller recalls in a conversation with the author that the SRC hit upon this phrasing of the questions independently of Key's suggestion. In any case, party identification is now measured by questions that read: "Generally speaking, do you think of yourself as a Republican, a Democrat, an Independent, or what?" Those who classified themselves as Democrats or Republicans were asked: "Would you call yourself a strong (Republican, Democrat) or a not very strong (Republican, Democrat)?" Those who classified themselves as Independent were asked: "Do you think of yourself as closer

to the Republican or Democrat Party?" (Angus Campbell et al., *The American Voter,* 122, footnote 1).

18. The decline of party has been described in a number of places, nowhere more succinctly than by Norman Nie, Sidney Verba and John Petrocik, *The Changing American Voter,* (Cambridge, Mass.: Harvard University Press, 1976) 47–94; also see Walter Dean Burnham, *Critical Elections and the Mainsprings of American Politics* (New York: Norton, 1970), 91ff.

19. Campbell, et al., *The American Voter,* 142–143.

20. Ibid., 146–147.

21. M. Kent Jennings and Richard G. Niemi, *The Political Character of Adolescence: The Influence of Families and Schools* (Princeton, N.J.: Princeton University Press, 1974), 61.

22. Campbell, et al., *The American Voter,* 327.

23. Key defines a "critical election" held in a time of national crisis as one in which partisan loyalties are redistributed. In such elections, Key notes enduring shifts in voting behavior, which can be analyzed only retrospectively. This view differs somewhat from Campbell's analysis. Campbell distinguishes a "realigning election" as one in which there are enduring shifts in individual party identification. The two definitions, while conceptually close, are not identical. Compare V. O. Key, Jr., "A Theory of Critical Elections," 18 *Journal of Politics* (February 1955), 3–18, and Angus Campbell, "A Classification of Presidential Elections," in *Elections and the Political Order,* ed. Campbell et al., chap. 4.

Campbell constructs a typology that results from the joint space of party identification and party position (in or out of power):

		Party ID of Majority	
		Unchanged	Changed
Candidate Election Specific Forces	Party in power	maintaining (reinstating)	(reinforcing) (converting)
	Party out of power	deviating	critical or realigning

Only in critical elections does the basic shape of the American political universe change. Compare Campbell, "A Classification of Presidential Elections," and Philip Converse et al., "Stability and Change in 1960: A Reinstating Election," in *Elections and the Political Order,* chap. 5.

The identification of a critical election is first discussed by Samuel Lubell, *The Future of American Politics* (New York: Harper Bros., 1951). See also Seymour M. Lipset, "Religion and Politics in the American Past and Present" in his *Revolution and Counter Revolution: Change and Persistence in Social Structures* (New York: Basic Books, 1968), 246–304, and V. O. Key, Jr., "Secular Realignment and the Party System," *Journal of Politics* 21 (May 1959): 198–210. Also see W. D. Burnham, "American Voting Behavior and the 1964 Election," *Midwest Journal of Political Science,* 12 (February 1968): 1–40; Charles Sellers, "Equilibrium Cycles in Two Party Politics," *Public Opinion Quarterly* 29 (Spring 1965): 535–566; and most completely Walter Dean Burnham, *Critical Elections and The Mainsprings of American Politics* (New York: Norton, 1970). See also Gerald Pomper, *Elections in America: Control and Influence in Democratic Politics* (New York: Dodd, Mead, 1965), 99–125.

Notes

24. Miller, "The Study of Electoral Behavior," 63. Italics added.

25. Norman H. Nie, Sidney Verba, and John R. Petrocik, eds., *The Changing American Voter*, (Cambridge, Mass.: Harvard University Press, 1979). See figure 7.3 p. 115 and table 2.3, p. 21 for the Klingemann "Modes of Conceptualization and the Organization of Issue Beliefs in Mass Publics", a paper presented at The World Congress of the International Political Science Association, Montreal, 1973.

26. Philip Converse, "The Nature of Belief Systems in Mass Publics," in *Ideology and Discontent*, ed. David E. Apter, (New York: Free Press, 1964), 206–261.

27. Ibid.

28. T. H. Jackson and G. E. Marcus, "Political Competence and Ideological Constraint," *Social Science Research* 4:93–111; J. C. Pierce and P. R. Hagner, "Changes in the Public's Political Thinking: The Watershed Years, 1965–1968," in *The Electorate Reconsidered*, ed. J. C. Pierce and J. L. Sullivan (Beverly Hills, Calif.: Sage Publications, 1980), 69–90.

29. Miller, "The Study of Electoral Behavior," 54.

30. Campbell, et al., *The American Voter*, 524–531; see also Warren Miller, "Components of Electoral Decision," 52 *American Political Science Review* (June 1958), 367–387; Donald Stokes, "Some Dynamic Elements of Contests for the Presidency," 60 *American Political Science Review* (March, 1966) 19–28; and Donald Stokes, "Spatial Models of Party Competition," in *Elections and the Political Order*, op. cit. chap. 9. This model seems to be primarily the work of Donald Stokes, just as the normal vote construct is attributed largely to Philip Converse; however, it is fair to view both these models as representative of the SRC's interpretation.

31. Stokes reports that the multiple correlation of his six components of electoral decision with partisan choice "varied in the range of .72 and .75" over the four presidential elections he studied. However, it seems that he was able to estimate the actual majority of the vote quite well.

> Indeed, the correlation of the estimated and actual majorities over these four contests is .98, a figure which increases our confidence that we have faithfully measured many of the immediate dimensions of popular feeling which have been deeply involved in changes of party fortune. (Stokes, "Some Dynamic Elements of Contests for the Presidency," 28).

32. Ibid., p. 27.

33. Stokes cautions against the interpretation of the candidates attitude dimensions strictly in image terms: "It would be a mistake to read into these figures too simple an explanation of the impact of candidate personality on the mass public" (ibid., 23). And he remarks further on the complex interplay between "stimulus object" and individual screens of selective perception. "Nevertheless . . ." he concludes, "the turnover of objects—of personalities, issues, and events of national politics—is the more important source of short-run electoral change. This is the more true since a stimulus object can affect communication and response dispositions themselves" (25, 26). The impression here is that Stokes means to talk about images despite the note of caution he sounds. "The evidence of changing personal impact of the candidates is especially impressive" (26). Although such personal impact may reach "beyond sheer personal appeal," it does so only as it reflects "popular feelings" about issues and group benefits. (Ibid).

34. For example, see Sidney Blumenthal, *The Permanent Campaign: Inside the World of Elite Political Operatives* (Boston: Beacon Press, 1980). Also see Joseph Napolitan, *The Selection Game and How to Win It* (Garden City, N.Y.: Doubleday, 1972), esp. chap. 5; and Malcolm D. MacDougall, *We Almost Made It* (New York: Crown, 1977).

35. Stanley Kelly, Jr., *Professional Public Relations and Political Power* (Baltimore, Md.: Johns Hopkins Press, 1956), 212.

36. Peter B. Natchez, "Images of Voting: The Social Psychologists," 18 *Public Policy* (Summer 1970), 553–588. The astute observer will notice changes in interpretation from that effort to this. (See fig. 4, p. 578.)

37. Warren Miller, "The Study of Election Behavior," 54. "Spared the exigencies of national disaster or unanticipated catastrophe, it would appear that the American party system is a self-perpetuating and self-sufficient vehicle for the articulation of the demands of the electorate."

Chapter 7

1. V. O. Key, Jr., *Politics, Parties and Pressure Groups* (New York: Thomas Y. Crowell, 1948), 601.

2. Letter from V. O. Key to Angus Campbell, 15 April 1951. From the collected papers of V. O. Key, Jr.

3. V. O. Key, Jr., "The State of the Discipline," *American Political Science Review* 52 (December 1958), 966ff.; and especially his "Strategy in Research on Public Affairs," *Items* 10 (1956): 2932. As a member of the Social Science Research Council, Key was of great assistance to the SRC. That body underwrote the SRC's first comprehensive surveys. In his assistance to Angus Campbell, Key clearly was looking for an alternative to the work of the Bureau of Applied Social Research and especially to its emphasis on social determinism, which he found particularly inappropriate. See the correspondence between Key and Angus Campbell between 1951 and 1953, in vols. 2 and 3 of Key's papers.

4. V. O. Key, Jr., "The Politically Relevant in Surveys," 24 *Public Opinion Quarterly* (1960), 54. Here Key is referring to the first fifteen years of the voting studies and not to *The American Voter* specifically.

5. Key, "The Politically Relevant in Surveys," 55–56.

6. This quality is most apparent in *Southern Politics* (New York: Knopf, 1950), a book that is all the more remarkable because Key had to be pressured into writing it, and in *Politics, Parties and Pressure Groups* (New York: T. Y. Crowell, 1942), a book that has gone through numerous editions and still has not been replaced in the field despite its age.

7. Compare Sidney Verba and Norman Nie, *Participation in America,* (New York: Harper & Row, 1972) chaps. 5 and 6 particularly, and William Schneider, "The Origins of Participation: Nation, Class Issues and Party," Ph.D. diss., Harvard University, 1971. The notes in these works provide a good guide to the development of this idea.

8. Key's style was very much a matter of professional preference and conscious choice. In his letters he tends to be surprisingly tough-minded and critical. He was quite capable of firing off withering criticism of draft manuscripts (see, for example, his comments to Bernard Berelson cited in chapter 6); his evaluations of colleagues were devastatingly balanced (see, for example, his response for his estimation of Harold Gosnell, a man who was one of Key's professors in graduate school and who was a considerable scholar in his own right), and his letters of recommendation for his graduate students were quite honest, distant, and candid.

9. It was not until H. Douglas Price reworked the argument that Key's system

Notes

of causal priorities reemerged. See H. Douglas Price, "Rise and Decline of One-Party Systems in Anglo-American Experience," in *Authoritarian Politics in Modern Society: The Dynamics of Established One Party System,* ed. Samuel P. Huntington and Clement H. Moore (New York: Basic Books, 1970), esp. 92–95 and fig. 3.4. The ambiguity with which Key presented these ideas in *Southern Politics* resulted in a narrow and misleading rendering of his idea of the consequences of party competition. Compare Duane Lockard, *New England State Politics* (Princeton, N.J.: Princeton University Press, 1959); Robert T. Golembiewski, "A Taxonomic Approach to State Political Party Strength," 11 *Western Political Quarterly* (1958), 494–513; Richard E. Zody and Norman R. Luttbeg, "An Evaluation of Various Measures of State Party Competition," 21 *Western Political Quarterly* (1968), 723–734; and Donald R. Matthews and James W. Prothro, *Negroes and the New Southern Politics* (New York: Harcourt, Brace, 1966).

10. Key, *Public Opinion and American Democracy,* 454–455.

11. Ibid., 436–437.

12. The definition of public opinion that Key provides is undoubtedly the book's least satisfactory part: "Public opinion . . . may simply be taken to mean those opinions held by private persons which governments find prudent to heed," *Public Opinion and American Democracy,* 14. No effort was made to distinguish public opinions from political issues.

13. Key had mixed feelings about the book. In his correspondence he both liked the effort as a whole and was dissatisfied with the results. See vols. 12 and 13 of the collected papers of V. O. Key, Jr., particularly letters to David Truman and Oliver Garceau.

14. V. O. Key, Jr., *The Responsible Electorate: Rationality in Presidential Voting, 1936–1960* (Cambridge, Mass.: Harvard University Press, 1966), 7–8.

15. This classification of voters is not complete. People who have previously voted but choose to abstain in the subsequent election are not provided for in Key's system of accounting. Also, no provision is made for nonparticipants. Both of these are substantial omissions.

16. Key, *The Responsible Electorate,* 10.

17. Ibid., 55–56.

18. Compare V. O. Key's *Public Opinion and American Democracy* (New York: Knopf, 1961), particularly parts 5 and 6, with Angus Campbell's *Elections and the Political Order* (New York: John Wiley, 1966), particularly parts 2 and 4, or with David Butler and Donald Stokes *Political Change in Britain,* (New York: St. Martins, 1976), part 4.

19. Key, *The Responsible Electorate,* 7–8. See also Philip Converse's discussion of this definition of political issues in "Public Opinion and Voting Behavior," in *Handbook of Political Science,* ed. Fred I. Greenstein and Nelson W. Polsby, vol. 4: *Nongovernmental Politics* (Reading, Mass.: Addison-Wesley, 1975), 113–136. An excellent summary of Key's model of public opinion can be found in Forrest P. Chisman, *Attitude Psychology and the Study of Public Opinion* (University Park, Pa.: Pennsylvania State University Press, 1976), 164–173.

20. Key, *The Responsible Electorate,* 9.

21. Ibid., 40–41.

> Probably the more general rule is that the electorate responds most markedly and most clearly to the events it has experienced and observed, vicariously or directly. . . . The prospects for the future may generally tend less to engage the voter or to govern his actions. Those prospects tend to be hazy, uncertain,

problematic. Voters may respond most assuredly to what they have seen, heard, experienced. Forecasts, promises, predicted disaster, or pie in the sky may be less moving (p. 52).

22. Compare Samuel Stouffer, *Communism, Conformity and Civil Liberties* (Garden City: Doubleday, 1955), 72–88; Michael Rogin, *The Intellectuals and McCarthy* (Cambridge, MA: MIT Press, 1967), chap. 8; Key, *The Responsible Electorate,* chap. 4; and Seymour Martin Lipset and Earl Raab, *The Politics of Unreason* (Chicago: University of Chicago Press, 1978), chap. 6.

23. Key, *The Responsible Electorate,* 61. Key continues:

Voters may reject what they have known, or they may approve what they have known. They are not likely to be attracted in great numbers by promises of the novel or unknown. Once innovation has occurred they may embrace it, even though they would have, earlier, hesitated to venture forth to welcome it.

See also pp. 76–77.

24. John Mueller, "Presidential Popularity from Truman to Johnson, 64 *American Political Science Review* (March 1970), 18–34; and especially Samuel Kernell, "Explaining Presidential Popularity," 72 *American Political Science Review* (June 1978), 506–522.

25. The maintenance of a supportive majority requires governmental actions, policies, and gestures that reinforce the confidence of those who have placed their faith in the Administration. Yet to govern is to antagonize not only opponents but also at least some supporters; as the loyalty of one group is nourished, another group may be repelled. A series of maintaining elections occurs only in consequence of a complex process of interaction between government and populace in which old friends are sustained, old enemies are converted into new friends, old friends become even bitter opponents, and new voters are attracted to the cause—all in proper proportions to produce repeatedly for the dominant party its apparently stable and continuing majority. (Key, *The Responsible Electorate,* 30).

26. Ibid., 77, 78.

27. Peter B. Natchez, *Issues and Voters in the 1972 Election* (Morristown, N.J.: General Learning Press, 1974), 17ff.

28. Key, *The Responsible Electorate,* 76.

29. Key's insensitivity to the course of political history in the modern period can be attributed solely to his struggle to create a theory. There is little doubt in his other writing and correspondence that he knew a great deal more history than he displays here. See, for example, V. O. Key, *American State Politics* (Westport, Conn.: Greenwood Press, 1983), particularly chap. 3.

30. Perhaps the most systematic discussion of this trend has been made with reference to the Congress; see David R. Mayhew, *Congress: The Electoral Connection* (New Haven, Conn.: Yale University Press, 1974).

31. Angus Campbell, review of *The Reasonable Electorate,* by V. O. Key, 60 *American Political Science Review* (December 1966), 1007–1008. At the time of Key's death, Arthur Maass was chairman of the Department of Government at Harvard University. He wrote a sympathetic forward to the *The Responsible Electorate* explaining the circumstances surrounding its publication. Needless to say, Professor Maass's "inference" correctly stated Key's intentions.

32. Maurice Pincard, *Review of Books* (1967), 616. Only Robert Lane reviewed the book favorably, 31 *Public Opinion Quarterly* (Summer 1967), 323–325.

33. Key's manuscript was much more complete than his critics wished to acknowledge. To be sure, marginal notes in the draft indicated places at which

revision was intended. But these notes were truly marginal, and nowhere do they alter the flow of the argument. Milton Cummings wrote the final chapter around a first draft that Key had completed but had not circulated. So careful was Professor Cummings in completing the book that there is no noticeable break in thought or style. Key's notes for the conclusion were published as they stood with no attempt to develop them into a full chapter.

34. Philip E. Converse, et al., "Continuity and Change in American Politics: Parties and Issues in the 1968 Election," Paper delivered before the American Political Science Association, New York, September 1969. This paper was subsequently published in the *American Political Science Review* (December 1969), 1095–1101, without major revision. The notes and discussion here refer to the paper as it was initially presented.

35. Ibid., 16.

36. Ibid., 17. Italics added.

37. Ibid., 20.

38. Ibid., 26ff.

39. Ibid., 20–21.

40. The best guide to the first five years of this controversy can be found in a research note by John Kessel, "Comment: The Issues in Issue Voting," 62 *American Political Science Review* (June 1972), 459–465. And for the second five years, see Norman H. Nie, Sidney Verba, and John R. Petrocik, *The Changing American Voter* (Cambridge, Mass.: Harvard University Press, 1976), chaps. 11 and 18.

41. Converse, "Public Opinion and Voting Behavior," in vol. 4, *Nongovernmental Politics*, 124–125. This article also contains an excellently reasoned review of the controversy over issue voting.

Chapter 8

1. Gerald H. Kramer, "Short-Term Fluctuations in U.S. Voting Behavior, 1896–1964," Paper presented at the Seventh World Congress, International Political Science Association, Brussels, September 1967, and subsequently revised and published in *American Political Science Review* 65 (1971), 131–143; Gerald H. Kramer and Susan Lepper, "Congressional Elections, 1896–1964," Paper presented before the Conference on Applications of Quantitative Methods to Political, Social and Economic History, University of Chicago, 1969; and more recently, Edward R. Tufte, "Determinants of Outcomes of Midterm Congressional Elections," *American Political Science Review* 69 (September 1975), 812–825.

2. George J. Stigler, "Micropolitics and Macroeconomics: General Economic Conditions and National Elections," 63 *American Economic Review* (1973); F. Arcelus and A. H. Meltzer, "The Effect of Aggregate Economic Variables on Congressional Elections," *American Political Science Review* 69 (December 1975), 1232–1239; Howard Bloom and H. Douglas Price, "Voter Response to Short-Run Economic Conditions: The Asymmetric Effect of Prosperity and Recession," *American Political Science Review* 69 (December 1975), 1240–1264; Saul Goodman and Gerald Kramer, "The Effect of Aggregate Conditions on Congressional Elections," *American Political Science Review* 69 (December 1975), 1255–1265.

3. Bloom and Price, "Voter Response," 1251.

4. Ibid., 17. The measure of economic performance that Bloom and Price use is change in real income. This variable results from a combination of influences on

the economy: changes in prices, wage rates, hours worked, unemployment, monetary policy, and the like. Kramer and Lepper looked at the relationship between voting and these other determinants of economic performance and found that they had rather mixed effects. Prices appeared to have little direct influence, and unemployment seemed to appear continually with the wrong sign (and a large standard error). Bloom and Price are undoubtedly correct in their argument that these factors are reflected in short-run changes in real income and thus are not directly related to voting behavior. The one exception may be prices. As they note:

> Strong inflation is historically infrequent and largely associated with the occurrence of wars. High peacetime inflation rates are a recent phenomenon. Unemployment rates correlate with real income changes. For these reasons, it is unlikely that aggregate time series can provide meaningful estimates of the relative impact on voting behavior of inflation and unemployment. However, such information would be quite useful to public officials who must decide upon politics which make tradeoffs between these problems. In our opinion, survey research techniques are the most fruitful potential source of this information (p. 1251).

5. Edward R. Tufte, *Political Control of the Economy* (Princeton, N.J.: Princeton University Press, 1978); David Mayhew, *Congress: The Electoral Connection* (New Haven, Conn.: Yale University Press, 1974); Morris P. Fiorina, *Congress: Keystone of the Washington Establishment* (New Haven, Conn.: Yale University Press, 1977).

6. John E. Jackson, "Some Indirect Evidence of Constituency Pressure on the Senate," 16 *Public Policy* (1967), 253–270; *Constituencies and Leaders in Congress: Their Effects on Senate Voting Behavior* (Cambridge, Mass.: Harvard University Press; 1974), 140; "Statistical Models of Senate Roll-Call Voting," *American Political Science Review* 65 (June 1971), 451–470.

7. David E. RePass, "Issue Salience and Party Choice" *American Political Science Review* 65 (June 1971), 389–400.

8. Peter B. Natchez and I. C. Bupp, "Candidates, Issues and Voters," 18 *Public Policy* (Summer), 409–437; Gerald Pomper, *Elections in America,* (New York: Dodd Mead, 1968), chaps. 4 and 5.

9. Richard W. Boyd, "Popular Control of Public Policy: A Normal Vote Analysis of the 1968 Election," *American Political Science Review* 66 (June 1972), 450–458.

10. Or in the more exacting languages of Converse's original:

> A somewhat less cumbersome method gives a very good approximation of the normal vote where the distribution of partisanship is not extremely skewed to one side or the other. Let V be the expected Democratic proportion of the vote; let M be a "mean party identification" for the distribution, where the scale scores $(+2, +1, 0, -1, -2)$ have been assigned to the first classes from Strong Democrats to Strong Republicans, respectively. Then $V = -0.268M + 0.483$, the approximation being good to roughly 1 percent, where $M < 10.81$." (Philip Converse, "The Concept of the Normal Vote," in Angus Campbell, et al, *Elections and the Political Order* [New York: Wiley, 1966], 36).

All of this demonstrates that technical appendixes can be very useful for subsequent research.

11. Arthur H. Miller, et al., "A Majority Party in Disarray: Policy Polarization in the 1972 Election," Paper presented before the American Political Science Association Convention, New Orleans, 1973. As a matter of fact, the debate is now raging in earnest; Kilpatric and Jones, "Issue Publics and the Electoral System," in Allen R. Wilcox, *Public Opinions and Political Attitudes* (New York: Wiley, 1974) and Pomper conclude in favor of "issue realignment." Burnham, *Critical*

Notes

Elections: The Mainspring of American Politics (New York: Norton, 1970) argues that conditions are such as to prevent a critical election and that party politics is therefore declining. Everett Ladd, in *American Political Parties* (New York: Norton, 1970), chaps. 5 and 6, argues that social conditions have changed but that at present they are not likely to produce a realignment of the parties. This question will undoubtedly replace "issue rationality" as the text for debate among survey researchers.

12. Compare Ernest S. Griffith, John Plamanatz, and J. Roland Pennock, "Cultural Prerequisites to a Successfully Functioning Democracy: A Symposium," 50 *American Political Science Review* (March 1956), 101–137; Edward C. Banfield, *The Moral Basis of a Backward Society* (New York: Free Press, 1958); Carole Pateman, *Participation and Democratic Theory* (Cambridge: Cambridge University Press, 1970).

13. Almond and Verba, *The Civic Culture.*

14. Stanley Milgram, *Obedience to Authority: An Experimental View* (New York: Harper & Row, 1974).

15. Milgram says remarkably little about his original expectations for this research. However, it is clear that he had expected there to be vastly more disobedience to authority among Americans than he found. His initial desire was to discover what personality traits separated Americans from Germans in authority situations.

16. Milgram, *Obedience to Authority,* 20.

17. Ibid., 133.

18. Ibid., 134.

19. T. W. Adorno et al., *The Authoritarian Personality* (New York: Norton, 1969).

20. Harry Eckstein, *Division and Cohesion in Democracy: A Study of Norway* (Princeton, N.J.: Princeton University Press, 1966). See particularly Appendix B, "A Theory of Stable Democracy," 225–288.

21. V.O. Key, Jr., "Public Opinion and the Decay of Democracy," *Virginia Quarterly Review* 37 (1961): 481–494 (and more briefly in *Public Opinion and American Democracy* [New York: Knopf, 1961], final chapter); Herbert McClosky, "Consensus and Ideology in American Politics," *American Political Science Reivew* 58 (June 1964), 361–382; Seymour M. Lipset, *Political Man* (Garden City, N.Y.: Doubleday, 1960), chaps. 4 and 5.

22. Similarly, the emergence of the slavery issue and the ideological aspects of the Civil War can be seen as the intervention of an "opinion group" located on the moral dimension of democratic theory.

23. The development of the argument in this book has indicated that the failure to include the study of democratic values was not simply an "oversight," but rather the result of systematic assumptions that rapidly developed into theoretical orientations.

24. Ronald Inglehart, "The Silent Revolution in Europe: Integenerational Change in Post-Industrial Societies," *American Political Science Review* 65 (December 1971): 991–1017 (reprinted in Giuseppe Di Palma, ed., *Mass Politics in Industrial Societies* [Chicago: Markham Publishing, 1972], 280–333. See also Alan Marsh, "The 'Silent Revolution,' Value Priorties, and the Quality of Life in Britain," *American Political Science Review* 69 (March 1975):21–30.

25. Milton Rokeach, "Change and Stability in American Value Systems, 1968–1971," *Public Opinion Quarterly* 38 (Summer 1974): 222–238; also Don A. Dillman and James A. Christenson, "Toward the Assessment of Public Values," *Public Opinion Quarterly* 38 (Summer 1974): 206–221.

26. Lipset and Raab, *The Politics of Unreason;* Herbert McClosky, "Consensus and Ideology in American Politics;" and Samuel Stouffer, *Communism, Conformity and Civil Liberties.*

27. Paul Sniderman, *Personality and Democratic Politics* (Berkeley: University of California Press, 1975), 116ff.

28. Richard Rose and Harve Mossawir, "Voting and Elections: A Functional Analysis," *Political Studies* 15 (June 1967), 173–201, should be listed as an exception.

29. As cited in V. O. Key, Jr., *Public Opinion and American Democracy* (New York: Knopf, 1961), 7.

30. McGovern's candidacy in 1972 as well as Goldwater's in 1964 are examples of campaigns that can prevent voters from expressing grievances against incumbent administrations. See Peter B. Natchez, *Issues and Voters in 1972 Election* (Morristown, N.J.: General Learning Press, 1974).

31. Yet even in the Great Depression the capacity of both the electorate and the political elite to ignore and fragment the political coherence provided by necessity should not be understated.

32. Peter B. Natchez, "The Reasonable Voter," Ph.D. diss., Government Department, Harvard University, 1969, chap. 6. Also H. Douglas Price, "Micro- and Macro-politics: Notes on Research Strategy," in *Political Research and Political Theory,* ed. Oliver Garceau (Cambridge, Mass., Harvard University Press, 1968) (New York: Knopf, 1971) 122–123.

33. See David B. Truman, *The Governmental Process,* esp. 213–261.

34. Philip Converse, "The Nature of Belief Systems in Mass Publics," 245. Individual self-interest in politics has appeared under a number of designations, each label adding something to the description. "Issue publics," for example, stresses the idiosyncratic and bounded character of such opinions. "Position issues" —used by Berelson, Lazarsfeld and McPhee and by Butler and Stokes—emphasizes the sharply divided nature of such opinions, that they represent fixed positions. See Berelson, Lazarsfeld, and McPhee, *Voting* (Chicago: University of Chicago Press, 1954), 184–185; David Butler and Donald Stokes, *Political Change in Britain,* 189, 361–362; and Donald Stokes, "Spatial Models of Party Competition," *American Political Science Review* 52 (June 1963): 368–377. "Opinion group" is a useful designation in that it stresses the links between this type of opinion and group theory. See Gabriel Almond, "Public Opinion and National Security Policy," *Public Opinion Quarterly* 20 (1965), 371–378.

35. V. O. Key, Jr., *The Responsible Electorate* (Cambridge, Mass.: Howard University Press, 1966), 61.

36. Kramer, "Short-term Fluctuations in U.S. Voting Behavior," 131–143; Albert Rees, et al., "The Effect of Economic Conditions on Congressional Elections 1946–1958," 44 *Review of Economics and Statistics* (November 1962), 458–465.

37. A remarkable quality of contemporary politics is that a large proportion of the population does feel this way, however. To be sure, it is a feeling that many political leaders have had a vested interest in promoting, but still one is struck by the capacity of the electorate to blame "the government" for decisions which they themselves have made.

38. Sidney Blumenthal, *The Permanent Campaign* (Boston: Beacon Press, 1980), 124. This particular piece of political advertising was created by Tony Schwartz, who has a very articulate understanding of television and its uses. See his book, *The Responsive Cord* (Garden City: Doubleday, 1973).

39. These remarks should not be taken to mean that candidate issues are an

unmixed benefit for systems of electoral competition. Obviously these issues can make the electoral system less accountable to voters in terms of policy and performance.

40. Again there is a downside risk to party issues in that a political system can become frozen in a political conflict that has lost its current relevance as, for example, the United States did in the Gilded Age.

41. Samuel H. Beer, *British Politics in the Collectivist Age* (New York: Knopf, 1965).

42. Key, *The Responsible Electorate,* 40.

Index

Index

Kaplan, Justin, 250*n*33
Katz, Elihu, 59
Kelley, Stanley, 179
Kemp, Betty, 149, 245*n*14
Keniston, Kenneth, 259*n*17
Kessel, John, 273*n*40
Key, V. O., Jr., 13–14, 43, 46, 99, 163, 182–209, 212, 215, 255*n*38, 256*n*46, 266*n*5, 270*n*8, 271*n*9, *n*13, *n*15, 272*n*23, *n*25, *n*29, *n*31, *n*33; and anticommunist prejudices, 142; *Authoritarian Personality* criticized by, 109; BASR voting studies criticized by, 74, 79–80, 85, 90, 270*n*3; on "critical elections," 268*n*23; on elites, 188–90, 222; on issues as retrospective judgments, 196–202, 229, 230; party identification indicator formulated by, 167–68; on public opinion, 186–88, 271*n*12, *n*19; review of *The American Voter* by, 13; Survey Research Center versus, 202–9, 211; on voter rationality, 190–95, 239–40
Kim, Jae-on, 136
Knowland, William, 141
Kornhauser, Arthur, 48
Kornhauser, William, 256*n*44
Kramer, Gerald, 212, 213, 274*n*4
Kramnick, Isaac, 148–49, 245*n*14

Ladd, Everett, 275*n*11
Lane, Robert E., 259*n*20
Language of Social Research, The (Lazarsfeld), 10
LaPiere, Richard T., 260*n*26
Laslett, Peter, 244*n*7, 245*n*15
Latham, Earl, 92
"Law and order" issues, 205, 206
Lazarsfeld, Paul, 5, 9–10, 74, 80, 83, 98, 103, 145, 171, 177–78; background of, 65–66; classical democratic theory and, 9, 15, 67–72, 264*n*33; and Elmira County study, 53, 62; and Erie County study, 47, 52; group theory and, 92, 96, 252*n*13, 255*n*39; and index of political predisposition, 65, 82, 249*n*27, 251*n*11; on individual voting decisions, 54–55, 57–59, 63, 66–67, 79, 86, 249*n*21; market research orientation of, 47–50, 247*n*2;

on position issues, 276*n*34; on voter rationality, 153
Leadership, political, 59–60
Leiserson, Avery, 99
Lepper, Susan, 274*n*4
Levin, Murray B., 261*n*39
Levinson, Daniel, 257*n*5
Lewin, Kurt, 266*n*2
Liberal Tradition in America, The (Hartz), 141
Life magazine, 248*n*6
Limited government, concept of, 31–32
Lippmann, Walter, 20, 243*n*1
Lipset, Seymour Martin, 37, 38, 79, 98, 120, 121, 132, 245*n*16, 246*n*20, 248*n*9
Locke, John, 33, 34, 148, 244*n*8, 245*n*15
Lowell, A. Lawrence, 20, 101, 243*n*1

Maass, Arthur, 203, 272*n*31
McCarthy, Eugene, 205, 206
McCarthy, Joseph, 141
McCarthyism, 10, 113, 142, 198
McClosky, Herbert, 83, 84, 86, 114, 117, 222, 252*n*13, 261*n*33
McGovern, George, 200, 216, 276*n*30
Machiavelli, Niccolo, 28
McKean, Dayton D., 255*n*38
McPhee, William, 71, 74, 145, 153, 171, 249*n*11, *n*17, 264*n*33, 276*n*34
MacPherson, C. B., 245*n*8
Madison, James, 259*n*20
Majority party, 199
Marketplace: feudal, 29; industrial revolution and, 29; inequalities in, 30; organization of, 28; voting and, 47–53
Marshall, T. H., 31, 38
Marsilius of Padua, 28
Marvick, Dwaine, 82
Marx, Karl, 148
Mass media, 47, 49, 50, 177, 179
Mass participation, 18, 158; belief systems and, 174; changes in theoretical approach to, 135; civic culture and, 125–31; constitutionalist opposition to, 69; and evaluation of public policy, 198; group theory on, 93–96, 100; industrialization and, 132–34; party politics and, 37; political stratifica-

283

Index

Political stratification, 186
Politics, Parties and Pressure Groups
(Key), 184, 270*n*6
Pollsters, 178
Pomper, Gerald, 274*n*11
Popular control of government, 225, 226
Position issues, 227, 276*n*34
Potential groups, 95
Potter, David, 79
Powell, G. Bingham, Jr., 132, 133
Power: in constitutionalism, 235; distribution of, 156–58
Preface to Politics, A (Lippmann), 243*n*1
Prejudice, 102–11, 222, 223; anticommunist, 141–42; elites and, 119–20
Presidential elections, 6; candidate images in, 176, 177; economic issues in, 212; Elmira study of, 53; Erie County study of, 50–52; hydraulic model of issue effects and, 216; individual voting decisions in, 54–60; influence of social characteristics on voting decisions in, 90, 91; index of political predisposition correlations in, 81; issues in, 196–97; party identification and, 167, 168, 170; political information levels and, 175; voter rationality and, 192, 193, 204–7
Pressure groups, 93
Prewitt, Kenneth, 132, 133, 252*n*18
Price, H. Douglas, 212, 213, 270*n*9, 273*n*4
Primary elections, 205
Primary group influences, 54, 83–86; social stratification and, 87
Process of Government, The (Bentley), 254*n*37
Progressivism, 68, 69, 246*n*20, 250*n*33, 263*n*18, *n*19
Prothro, James, 113
Psychological theory, 5
Psychology: of authoritarian personality, 102–9; *see also* Social psychology
Public good: constitutionalism and, 69, 156; notion of, 17, 32–33, 41; party issues and, 233–34; self-interests and, 227–28
Public opinion, 158, 239, 248*n*4; in group theory, 93, 95; Key's definition

of, 271*n*12; meaning and consequence of, 188
Public Opinion (Lippmann), 243*n*1
Public Opinion and American Democracy (Key), 43, 186–90, 195
Public Opinion and Popular Government (Lowell), 243*n*1
Public Opinion in War and Peace (Lowell), 101, 243*n*1
Public policy: hydraulic model and, 216; ignorance of, 175, 183; issues of, 229–31; Lazarsfeld's failure to consider, 66–67; linkage of popular preference and, 215; party identification and, 172; shared beliefs and, 236; voter rationality and, 195–98
Public relations techniques, 17, 179

Quantitative methods, *see* Survey research

Racial discrimination, 170; *see also* Civil rights movement
Raine, Alden, 161
Rationality, *see* Voter rationality
"Rationality-activist" model of participation, 127
Ratner, Sidney, 254*n*34
Reasonable voters, 239–41
Records of the Federal Convention of 1787, The, 259*n*20
Religious differences, 87
RePass, David, 213
Republican party, 6, 7, 193, 194, 202, 239, 262*n*8, 267*n*17, 274*n*10; and enfranchisement of blacks, 36–37
Research orientation, 25
Responsible Electorate, The (Key), 13, 191, 196, 202–3, 206, 229, 272*n*31
Retrospective voting, 13–14
Roazen, Paul, 256*n*2
Rokkan, Stein, 37, 38, 245*n*16, 246*n*20
Roosevelt, Franklin D., 51
Roper, Elmo, 47, 247*n*3
Roper Center, 190
Rorer, Leonard G., 259*n*17
Rosenberg, Morris, 261*n*39

Index

Twain, Mark, 251n3
Twin City area (Minnesota) survey, 83

Unconscious, notion of, 102, 108
Unions, 120
Utilitarianism, 68, 69, 263n19
United Press, 247n3

Voting decisions, 54–60; analysis of, 191; components of, 160; content of, 240; individual perceptions and, 162–64; issues in, 213; Lazarsfeld's model of sources of, 62, 63, 66–67, 79; party identification and, 164, 168, 170, 171, 180, 182; prejudice and, 223; primary group influences on, 83–85

"Value-free" research, 244n4
Values: authority relationships and, 219–21; civic culture and, 139–40; and critical perspective, 241; and democratic theory, 116–17, 157; distribution in mass public of, 135; electoral process and, 225; issues and, 234–37; levels of participation and, 132, 133; reluctance of political scientists to discuss, 184; shared, 144; undemocratic, 109–15, 141–43
Verba, Sidney, 88, 123, 125–35, 138–40, 142–45, 150, 174, 217, 219, 220, 252n18, 256n44, 262n3, n8, n9, 268n18, 273n40
Vietnam war, 222; as issue in 1968 election, 205, 206, 239; protests against, 140, 170, 205
Vile, M. J. C., 245n14
Voter rationality, 24, 183, 190–210, 238; issues and, 190, 193, 195–202, 213; Lazarsfeld on, 70; party competition and, 192–95, 199–202; self-interest and, 225; and stability of electorate, 180–82
Voting (Berelson, Lazarsfeld, and McPhee), 150

Wage labor, 29, 30
Wallace, George, 205–7
Wasserspring, Lois A., 262n3
Weber, Max, 244n4
Weimar Republic, 128
Weiseberg, Herbert, 161
West Germany, political participation in, 125, 127–29
Weston, Carinne C., 245n14
Whigs, 33
White, Robert S., 82, 251n11
Wilkie, Wendell, 51
Wolfe, Arthur, 161
Wolin, Sheldon S., 148, 244n8
Women, Status of, 30
Working-class values, 120–21
Wright, Benjamin, 173, 244n1

Yale University, 217
Yugoslavia, political behavior in, 136, 137, 263n22

Zeller, Belle, 255n38